1992 – The Big Market

The Future of the European Community

John Grahl & Paul Teague

Lawrence & Wishart
London

Lawrence & Wishart Ltd
144a Old South Lambeth Road
London SW8 1XX

This edition first published 1990

Photoset in North Wales by
Derek Doyle & Associates, Mold, Clwyd
Printed and bound in Great Britain by
Dotesios Printers, Trowbridge

Contents

Acknowledgements

We would like to thank all those who have helped us in the course of writing this book, especially Sue Eldred; Keith and Lucette Dixon; Jacques Fontanel, head of the Economics Department and Louis Reboud, of the CUREI Unit, at the University of Grenoble; John Kelly and Paul Taylor at the London School of Economics; Dick Allard, head of the Economics Department and June Nielson, Eilis Rafferty and Jules Winterton of the Library, at Queen Mary Westfield College, London; Clyde Barrow and his colleagues at Southeastern University, Massachusetts; Sarah Applebury and Jean Loughlin at Cranfield School of Management, and Tracy Bass, for help in preparation of the typescript.

List of Common Abbreviations

BICEP – US Cereal Export Programme
CAP – Common Agricultural Policy
COST – European Scientific and Technological Research Co-operation Programme
ECSC – European Coal and Steel Community
ECU – European Currency Unit
EDC – European Defence Community
EFTA – European Free Trade Association
EMS – European Monetary System
EPC – European Political Co-operation
ERDF – European Regional Development Fund
ERM – Exchange Rate Mechanism
ESC – Economic and Social Committee
ESPRIT – EC Programme for Research in Information Technology
ETUC – European Trade Union Congress
EUREKA – European Programme for Co-operation in Applied Research
GATT – General Agreement on Trade and Tariffs
GDP – Gross Domestic Product
GSP – Generalised System of Preferences
IT – Information Technology
ITTC – Information Technology Training Centres
LDC – Less Developed Countries
MCA – Monetary Compensation Amounts
MFA – Multi-Fibre Agreement
NATO – North Atlantic Treaty Organisation
OECD – Organisation of Economic Co-operation and Development

OEEC	– Organisation of European Economic Co-operation
R&D	– Research and Development
RDP	– Regional Development Programme
SDI	– Strategic Defense Initiative
SDP	– Social Democratic Party
SEA	– Single European Act
SPRINT	– EC Technology Transfer Programme
VAT	– Value Added Tax
UNICE	– European Employers' Confederation

List of Tables and Diagrams

Introduction

The 1992 programme of the European Community aims to remove all remaining barriers to the free movement and free exchange of goods, services and resources among member countries. The programme arose from the conjunction of the movement for European integration, which the EC has increasingly come to embody, with a resurgence of free-market forces in most West European countries. Because of this coincidence of aims and forces, the programme pursues integration exclusively through the reinforcement of competition and market relations. The context of this new, and perhaps temporary, political alliance was a persistent slowdown in European economic development (reflected in very high levels of unemployment) and a continuing globalisation of economic relations with the growth of international trade, investment and finance (both within the Community and in the Community's relations with outside countries).

In this context then, the prevailing neo-liberal, free-market explanation for economic malaise was summed up in the term 'Eurosclerosis': slow growth and rising unemployment were attributed to the gradual impairment of market mechanisms by government regulation, high taxation and centralised collective bargaining. According to the neo-liberal view, the rapid growth rates and increasing employment in President Reagan's USA demonstrated the success of market-oriented economic policies. The imitation of US models, even to the extent of attempting to 'Americanise' European society, was an important theme in neo-liberal discourse: it may have provided an additional point of contact with the European integration movement which had always regarded the USA as a model of successful political federation.

This kind of assessment essentially represents a misreading of both the strengths and weaknesses of the USA. On the one hand, industrial decay and declining competitiveness – in spite of the Reagan boom – tend to indicate the inadequacy of largely unconstrained markets to effect major economic adaptations, and the inability of US political structures to produce coherent reform. On the other hand, the unquestionable strengths of many US companies and industries cannot simply be ascribed to market forces, but owe a great deal to the cohesion of US society and the effective economic engagement of many states, cities and local communities.

The view taken of the 1992 programme in this book starts from a different perspective on contemporary economic difficulties. We abandon 'Eurosclerosis' as a sufficient explanation of the current instability in economic life, the high levels of unemployment and inadequate rates of investment. Instead those problems are interpreted as signs that market agents alone cannot determine major adaptations in technology, patterns of output and investment, or forms of productive organisation. As the long boom of the 1950s and 1960s in Western Europe faded, such major adaptations became imperative: the previous sources of growth – industrialisation, urbanisation and the manufacture of mass consumer durables – were becoming exhausted; new and more complex patterns of development were requisite, necessitating a new framework of institutions and new types of public control.

Although it is true that most forms of economic intervention and control performed badly in the 1970s and 1980s – resulting in rising unemployment and inflation – this was not due to excessive state interference in the private sector. The changing forms of economic development required a recasting of economic institutions, where this is taken to include not only state agencies and public economic policy, but also the norms and conventions produced by other economic agents in, for example, collective bargaining.

One key aspect of the necessary institutional and regulatory response to economic change is the development of effective forms of public control over international economic transactions. The rapid growth of international economic relations has tended to undermine essentially national systems of control. The increasing difficulty which governments have in stimulating employment when countries are very heavily engaged in foreign trade is one example; the pressures exerted on national labour agreements by increasing international competition is another. The main significance of European integration is that it has the potential to enable a renewal of regulatory mechanisms (including legal, administrative and conventional, as well as market, forms of control) within this new context of growing international interdependence.

In its present mould the 1992 programme removes barriers to private transactions and puts new constraints on national governments, but it does not promote the emergence of new Europe-wide institutions in economic life. At most it can only play a 'negative' role in the necessary process of reform. If it is not accompanied by other measures, its effects could even be damaging: competition will become more intense, but no constraining framework will direct competition towards development and away from pressure simply to reduce costs and rationalise employment in the weakest regions, industries and enterprises. Uncertainties will inhibit investment but encourage a preoccupation with short-term profit maximisation. The cohesion of the Community will be placed under severe stress by the fact that the losers from the intensified competition and erosion of (national) social controls will tend to be concentrated in low-income regions and countries.

1992 can only contribute to economic recovery and political unity in the Community if it becomes the starting-point of a new phase of institutional construction which rebuilds and renews social control over economic life. The plan of *1992 – The Big Market* is to pursue this theme through the main areas of Community policy. Our response is that, despite neo-liberal claims, market exchange is not an adequate principle on which to base either the process of European integration or the reconstruction of economic life within the integrated Community. We aim to give the historical context of each area of substantive Community policy currently under development in the 1992 programme;

to give a reasonable account of the strengths and weaknesses of those policies; and to make a fair assessment of the policy alternatives and options available to the EC, beyond the limits of the neo-liberal agenda.

With the end of the Cold War in Europe and the imminent reunification of Germany, the need for a coherent social and political identity has become all the more pressing, since the influence of West European developments on the whole continent will now be immense. The political and social models which Western Europe can develop, combining individual freedom with an active democracy, able to include all citizens in economic and political life, will not always necessarily be the direct concern of the EC; national, local and regional initiatives permit very wide experimentation and can be much more fully adapted to specific historical and geographic conditions. But a strong Community is nevertheless necessary to the health and strength of European political life at all levels, since without it, national governments (especially in Britain) as well as local authorities and associations within civil society will be increasingly constrained by global economic forces.

If it centralises the key instruments of overall economic policy, and deploys them effectively, the Community will be able to protect European society against the most damaging effects of global industrial and financial competition. In establishing the necessary forms of social control it will liberate, much more than it obstructs, the forces for democratic progress at local and national levels. The basic argument of this book is that this kind of social control is both necessary and possible.

1 Neo-Liberal Europe

In the history of economic policy, the 1980s will doubtless be the decade of the market. Calling into question the trend towards state intervention which had prevailed in most countries for a hundred years, the advocates of reinforced market relations, of privatisation, deregulation, tax reductions and trade liberalisation have dominated policy debate around the world. Neo-liberal doctrines, reviving the economic traditions of nineteenth-century liberalism rather than its optimistic view of unrestricted political and civil liberty, have been presented as universally valid – applicable to advanced Western economies and developing countries alike. Although policies virtually everywhere have been more market-oriented, the most dramatic display of the restored prestige of market mechanisms has been a vast wave of reform in the Soviet Union, China and Eastern Europe where the solution to economic stagnation has been sought in the attenuation of centralised economic control, or even the complete dismantlement of central planning and its replacement by decentralised commodity production and exchange. As disillusionment with existing state socialism has become universal, the clearest and most coherent projects for economic reconstruction which have emerged are based on one model or other of the market economy.

It may be hard to deny the claim of Eastern reformers that the market is historically necessary in their societies. In the West, however, the claim of neo-liberals has rather been that the market is *sufficient* as a principle of economic organisation and this much more extreme assertion has seemed increasingly implausible. At the end of the 1970s neo-liberals confidently attributed economic slow-down and rising unemployment in North America and Western Europe to an excess of state interference and prescribed a reinforcement of market mechanisms as the way to restored dynamism. By the end of the 1980s, the two most thoroughgoing experiments in neo-liberal policy, those of President Reagan in the USA and Mrs Thatcher in Britain, had failed to transform economic life in the way that was promised: in both countries growth had been rapid in the middle of the decade but it had become increasingly clear that this growth was due to cyclical booms and had been obtained at the cost of severe and unsustainable imbalances in external trade and payments. The prestige and plausibility of neo-liberalism definitely seemed on the wane as a result.

Nevertheless, in the absence of a coherent and convincing alternative strategy, market-oriented policies continued to be central to economic debate, even though they were now justified in more pragmatic terms. In many respects, permanent shifts had been accomplished in the revised assumptions and concerns of economic policy: for example, business enterprises were regarded much more favourably than in the past, with enormous emphasis placed on 'enterprise' as a source of employment and as a productive unit (while the question of the enterprise as a form of private wealth concentrated in the hands of a minority was raised very infrequently).

In the European Community, the same shift towards market-oriented policy has occurred. Indeed, the 1992 programme for 'completing the internal market', which has become the centre-piece of Community policy, is one of the most ambitious and far-reaching examples of neo-liberal policy. The programme has led to a redefinition of the project of European integration: rather than the construction of political institutions, or the emergence of a common cultural identity, overcoming nationalist antagonisms of the past, the thrust of integration is now towards the greatest conceivable freedom of market exchange, for goods and services, for factors of production, for currencies and financial assets. Other aspects of European unification, whether social, economic or political, may not have disappeared but they have certainly been reduced to a subordinate status – regarded either as 'accompanying' measures to support the process of market unification or as possibly unnecessary departures from the main direction.

The 1992 programme is neo-liberal both in its objectives and its methods. The aim of the programme is conceived in terms of the scope for private economic transactions within the Community, especially transactions across national frontiers: a frequent analogy is with the unified economic space of the USA. But the methods themselves conform to neo-liberal doctrine, since the unified economic space will not depend on new Community political institutions; rather, it will be achieved by the abolition of 'frontiers' between the member states. Administrative, legal or regulatory procedures which inhibit transactions across frontiers will be denied to national governments without any new powers being accorded to the central bodies of the Community. The full unification of national markets, with competition among enterprises on a Community scale, seems logically to require a major increase in the powers of EC institutions. However, beyond a very limited increase in the Commission's competence in the sphere of mergers and takeovers, no such reforms are envisaged. In other words, there is a strong deregulatory bias in the structure of the 1992 programme: even if extensive deregulation may not occur in practice the design of the programme tends to raise problems for the national regulation of economic activity without asserting the need for corresponding EC-wide regulation.

The 1992 programme is intended to be far-reaching and irreversible, wide in scope and profound in its effects. Although none of the individual measures which make up the programme is of overwhelming importance, and although loopholes will remain for the protection of national markets within the EC, the spirit of the programme and its political influence suggest ambitious interpretations. The scale of 1992 is vast because of the economic forces involved: the twelve member countries, with a total population of 320 million, and a total output close to or perhaps even a little above that of the USA form potentially the world's biggest economic unit. The market completion programme, intended to bring that huge economy into existence, attempts to transform the economic environment of over a hundred million employees and of millions of enterprises, including many of the world's largest.

As a result, the programme is more than merely an economic strategy: it has become a central contemporary social project, aiming to shape the way Europeans perceive their future, the direction of change which they anticipate and the way in which they construct individual plans and projects.

Although specific and detailed economic arguments have been advanced to justify the 1992 programme ('the costs of non-Europe' discussed below) the broad neo-liberal view of the European Community rests on a general diagnosis of Western Europe's economic malaise, described by the term 'Eurosclerosis'. The notion is that slower growth, rising unemployment and stagnant productivity in advanced capitalist economies result from the impairment of market forces. The necessary adaptations and adjustments to changing tastes and technologies are seen as obstructed by rigidities in the price system or in the reallocation of productive resources, for which the main responsibility lies with government: intervention, regulation, taxation are seen as obscuring market signals or blunting the incentives to respond to them. Organised labour is also seen as contributing to economic rigidities, by imposing collective agreements which fix rigid wage rates and circumscribe the tasks which may be assigned to workers.

Europe, according to this neo-liberal view, suffers particularly from sclerotic rigidities because it is precisely in Western Europe that state intervention and trade-union organisation, both frequently inspired by anti-capitalist ideologies, have placed the most damaging constraints on the free play of market forces and on the response of business enterprise to changing conditions. The usual contrast is with the USA, where taxes and public expenditure are lower, state intervention is less pervasive, and the values of enterprise and competition more deeply embedded in popular consciousness. This kind of argument has provided a basis for the whole range of neo-liberal strategies: cuts in taxation and in public spending; reduced control of private business; the privatisation of state-owned industries; legal restrictions on trade-union activity. In many ways the 1992 programme represents a culmination of neo-liberalism in Europe.

In practice, national states tend to be blamed for the obstruction of market forces and the consequent decline in innovation and enterprise. 1992 tends to move economic life as a whole beyond the competence of national governments, and to promote a 'big market' to which national governments themselves will have to adapt. In concrete terms the reforms which 1992 promises may be limited, but the direction in which it points corresponds completely to the neo-liberal assessment of Europe's economic problems and to the type of economic reconstruction which is held to provide a long-term solution.

The 'Eurosclerosis' argument is open to several serious objections. Firstly, the neo-liberal assessment provides a purely supply-side account of economic malaise, which minimises the role of aggregate demand. Now it is difficult to deny the importance of aggregate demand and, in particular, public spending on the huge increases in unemployment which European economies experienced in the 1980s: although unemployment was certainly rising beforehand it was only when governments deliberately curtailed demand in order to fight inflation that unemployment rose to its present levels (well over ten per cent of the Community's workforce). Standard Keynesian explanations of the economic slow-down may be inadequate and the political forces guided by Keynesianism did appear to lose control over economic developments in the 1970s, but this does not mean that Keynesian analysis has no bearing on present problems.

A more political objection to the neo-liberal argument is that the economic strategies which are proposed have more relevance to the distribution of wealth than its production. The neo-liberal policy agenda has clear implications for the way wealth and income are distributed, even when its relevance to full employment and economic development is unclear. If the benefits of Ronald Reagan's and Margaret Thatcher's administrations in terms of growth and employment are contestable, it is beyond dispute that both of them produced sharp increases in social and economic inequality. There is nothing covert or duplicitous about neo-liberals: they believe that the inequalities which they promote serve a necessary economic function. Nevertheless, the interests of most of the more prosperous members of society have been advanced by neo-liberal policy which helps to account for the strong political support which it enjoys.

The third flaw in the neo-liberal notion of Western Europe as being particularly afflicted by rigidities, is the questionable nature of the standard comparison between Europe and North America. The relative economic success of the USA in contrast to European countries depends in the first instance on the historical period chosen for comparison. For most of the period since the Second World War the European economies have enjoyed faster economic growth. The USA has certainly had a faster expansion of employment than Western Europe over a relatively long period, but this observation should be qualified in two ways: the radically different demography of the two regions means that a simple comparison of employment growth rates is misleading – the US labour force has expanded much faster because of immigration and higher birth rates, and therefore more jobs have been needed; more recently, continued rapid job-creation in the USA has been at the expense of falling real wages and deteriorating working conditions. In other dimensions of economic performance, particularly productivity, comparison tends to favour the European economies. Indeed, stagnant levels of productivity have resulted in a serious crisis of US competitiveness in international trade. The examination of this relative decline of US industry frequently leads commentators to question the benefits of a complete reliance on free markets and the private sector: for example, the low educational standards of the average employee in the USA are cited as one factor in poor economic performance; another frequently discussed problem is the lack of finance for industrial development in spite of, or because of, the huge private financial sector of the USA; a third example is the lack of long-term investment by US enterprises and their excessive concern with short-term profits. Finally, it is, of course, as simplistic to identify the US economy with the market as to see those of Western Europe as examples of comprehensive state intervention. On the one hand, manufacturing industry, the dynamo of European growth from the 1940s to the 1970s, is essentially just as capitalistic as industry in the USA. The forms of industrial enterprise are very similar on both sides of the Atlantic and the high level of state intervention in Europe is mostly a question of social welfare rather than production. On the other hand, economic life in the USA can involve high levels of public intervention: some important contemporary examples are provided by the efforts of local and state governments to regenerate employment in the blighted industrial zones of New England and the Mid-West.

The Eurosclerosis argument, like other examples of neo-liberal concern with rigidities, inflexibilities and blocked market mechanisms, tends to sound more convincing in general than in particular. When one asks for concrete instances of the rigidities which are holding back economic development, very little is offered. There are, of course, the job demarcations defended by some trade unions, but these are usually reactions to persistent decline in sectors such as shipbuilding rather than obstacles to growth and expansion. Certain types of state regulation may be cited, such as minimum wage rates, but no convincing case has been made which would link such types of control, often quite minimal, to the economic slow-down of the 1970s and 1980s. In fact, the whole idea of modern economies being inflexible, whether private enterprises or public sectors are involved, seems very implausible when one begins to examine it more closely. Modern systems of transport and communication, higher levels of education, new technology, all tend to make resource allocation extremely adaptable in Western economies, if it can be established that a definite change in the pattern of resource use is required.

Certainly, where a sector of the economy does have the prospect of sustained expansion – finance provides a recent example, as does the application of computers – then it is most unlikely to be held back by a lack of resources. Labour, enterprise and finance move very rapidly and flexibly towards any such prospects. The basic problem would seem to be more the lack of opportunities for expansion than the refusal of economic agents to take these opportunities. What neo-liberalism takes for rigidities are usually something quite different – the resistance of employees, unions, enterprises and other agents to declines in their income or losses of wealth resulting from economic change. The way to overcome such resistance is for adequate compensation to be offered to those who lose out from industrial restructuring or economic reform. The doctrinal insistence by neo-liberals that the losers from the competitive process should not be compensated is thus a source of this kind of resistance, which is not the same thing at all as a rigidity or immobility in the allocation of resources.

A number of fundamental weaknesses therefore mark the prevalent notion of Eurosclerosis as the explanation for persistent unemployment and slower economic development. An alternative and more satisfactory explanation would probably start from the two hypotheses of structural imbalance and system-wide uncertainties. On the one hand the economic structure, in the sense of the balance between different activities, is no longer well adapted to economic development, and major structural adjustments are therefore required. On the other hand, these adjustments are obstructed, not by sclerosis or rigidities on the part of economic agents, but by the deep uncertainties which obscure the future of the economic system at the present time, making future patterns of production and consumption impossible to predict. Economic malaise, in terms of both unemployment and instability, results from the efforts of individuals and enterprises to cope with these heightened uncertainties, in both constructive and defensive ways.

With this kind of view, suggested by a number of heterodox analyses which challenge the dominance of neo-liberal thinking, it may be possible to arrive at a superior explanation of Europe's economic difficulties and a more effective strategy to deal with them. At present, however, such alternative arguments have not been made with sufficient coherence and comprehensiveness to challenge the general authority of neo-liberal views and the approach to economic policy which they inspire. In consequence, even as neo-liberal policies are modified in industrial European countries in response to the practical problems they have encountered, the 1992 programme, with its project of a huge extension of market relations, continues to determine the policy agenda of the European Community as a whole.

The White Paper and the Single European Act

The claim that the 1992 programme is essentially a neo-liberal strategy raises the question of how such a strategy was adopted by the Community, since the political leadership of the Community is, in general, quite removed from the free-market conservatism that espouses neo-liberal ideas (with which we in Britain are familiar). The political personnel of the Community have for the most part been drawn from the Christian Democratic and Social Democratic traditions – neither of which suggest a radical challenge to the role of the state and the public sector in economic life, although both would accept the necessity of a (more or less regulated) market economy. Of its own accord, the Commission of the EC would hardly have been tempted by neo-liberalism, and similar considerations apply to the European Parliament. Until the elections of 1989, when it tilted to the left, the Parliament was controlled by a broad, informal coalition between moderate socialists and moderate, usually Christian Democrat, conservatives. That the Community's agenda came to be dominated by the 1992 programme was the result of political forces at the level of national governments, where the radical right had made much more impact.

The clearest example is, of course, Britain where the market completion programme would be seen by Mrs Thatcher and her cabinet as exactly the kind of policy which the Community should adopt – liberalisation of market exchange without any new, supranational institutions or any increase in the powers of the Commission. But similar ideological positions to those of the British Government influenced virtually all the north European member governments in the mid-1980s: Germany, the Netherlands, Belgium and Denmark – the four richest countries in the EC – were all governed by right-wing administrations committed to reductions in the share of public spending in national output and to a renewal of private enterprise and the workings of market competition. Even governments of the left were influenced by the resurgence of free-market ideologies: the key example is France, where a highly interventionist, public-sector led, socialist experiment had gone badly wrong, pushing the socialist government towards much more reliance on market forces. In Spain too, the socialist government, partly reacting against the corporatist legacy of the Franco period and its cumbersome, ineffective controls on industry, was limiting state intervention and attempting to stabilise public finance.

Ideological changes were not working in isolation; changing economic circumstances also favoured the move towards market-oriented policies. Financial conditions, in particular, had completely changed: interest rates were now very high in real terms (that is, after allowing for inflation), and European currencies were very weak vis-à-vis the Dollar. As a result public sector deficits were extremely difficult to finance and balance of payments constraints on European economic expansion were very tight. This kind of financial climate encouraged retrenchment. At the same time, some of the interventionist economic strategies of the late 1970s had proved disappointing and Keynesian attempts to overcome unemployment by demand expansion had met with very limited success.

Among national governments then, there was a general readiness to accept market-oriented policies, while a strong group of northern countries shared an explicit commitment to neo-liberal positions. The Council of Ministers (or European Council when prime ministers are involved) remains the key decision-making body of the Community (see Appendix G) and it worked to shape EC strategy in a neo-liberal direction by endorsing only those proposals which were in accord with the political situation in national capitals. The rejection of alternative policies was as important as the enthusiastic acceptance of 1992 and the single market. The European Council at Fontainebleu in 1984 had closed many possible paths of future development for the Community by preventing any major increase in its budgetary resources. In contrast, the Cockfield White Paper on completing the market rapidly won support; indeed, it would have been politically difficult for governments committed to free markets to have refused to support it.

Although the White Paper was certainly a major initiative by the Commission, it was not originally designed as the centre-piece of European integration over the coming decade. On the one hand, the proposed attack on non-tariff barriers to Community trade represented an attempt to regain lost ground as much as to advance. During the 1970s, member states had resorted to a wide range of national policies which tended to fragment the Community markets – industrial subsidies, discriminatory tax concessions, refinance of loss-making enterprises through public ownership and otherwise, employment subsidies and so on. Consequently, the economic integration achieved by the removal of tariffs had been somewhat compromised. The White Paper proposed to restore the principle of free movement for goods and resources by eliminating or controlling such interventions.

On the other hand, much of the White Paper was not new but simply codified measures which had been on the EC agenda for a long time, presenting them in a new format: for example, a quarter of the proposals concerned agricultural regulations and derived simply from the routine of the Common Agricultural Policy (CAP) and the perennial attempt to maintain genuinely open markets for livestock and agricultural inputs; similarly, the recognition of professional qualifications throughout the Community was a long-standing concern of the Commission. To a significant extent the notion of completing the internal market provided a new vehicle for old policy proposals.

At the same time the White Paper did reflect changes in the climate of policy discussion. In particular it recognised a growing impatience with the complex process of harmonising economic regulations across an increasing number of member states. Instead of introducing uniform Community specifications for goods, services, commercial procedures and so on, it was suggested in the White Paper that there simply be mutual recognition of national regulations by the member states. National differences in specifications and required business procedures would continue, but would cease to obstruct trade and investment across national frontiers in the Community.

Since both proponents and opponents of the 1992 programme have made much of this approach, seeing it as a major step towards deregulation of economic activity in the EC countries, it is important to point out that the change in approach was less radical than is sometimes suggested. Firstly, old-fashioned harmonisation was by no means abandoned – rather it was only now to be applied where a single uniform regulatory practice for the whole Community seemed unavoidable; and secondly, the mutual recognition of national regulations did not mean that there would be no harmonisation at all – often mutual recognition was to be preceded by changes in national regulation aimed at producing substantial comparability in the effect of the various systems, even though they might still have very different legal forms. Thus the proposal was for a less centralised and bureaucratic approach to harmonisation rather than for thoroughgoing deregulation.

Although the White Paper therefore represented more of a change in the presentation of policy than in its substance, the deliberate appeal to prevailing views on economic policy won enormous success at a time when other Community initiatives were meeting with indifference or hostility. Quite contrary to the expectations of the Commission, the White Paper rapidly became the key programmatic document of the Community. Meanwhile the much more ambitious attempt to promote political unity which had emerged from the European Parliament was reduced almost to an adjunct of the market completion programme.

The Parliament had originally proposed a draft Treaty for Political Union among EC member states, but the reluctance of national governments to contemplate such a step limited the outcome to a set of revisions to the existing Treaty of Rome in the form of an Act to be passed in each national Parliament – the Single European Act. Although the Act extended the competence of Community institutions, it did very little to increase their powers. The main step towards supranationality was in the extension of majority voting within the Council of Ministers, limiting the ability of a single country to block (by veto) measures which it regarded as against its interests. The key area to which majority voting was extended was the implementation of the market completion programme. As market completion was virtually the only policy for integration which commanded general support it became, quite contrary to the intentions of its original proponents, the main theme of the Single Act. The White Paper was explicitly mentioned in the Act, thus transforming it from a mere statement of policy to a binding legal document. The commitment to majority decisions on its contents greatly increased the momentum of the programme, as governments which felt threatened by particular measures were unable, on their own, to block them but were compelled to seek compromises.

Within the EC, it is the Commission which tends to propose policy but national governments, represented in the Council of Ministers (or prime ministers), which have the main decision-making power. The result of this process, with national governments resisting the growth of EC institutions, committed to financial retrenchment and determined to widen the scope of market forces, was to alter completely the priorities of the Community and its policy agenda. Fontainebleau put paid to any ambitious plans for EC spending while the Single Act, originally intended to further *political* unification, concluded by enthroning a purely economic strategy of removing obstacles to free, private exchange.

Nevertheless, the fact that Community procedure gives the Commission the task of formulating policy allows it to maintain pressure towards integration even in the most unpromising political circumstances. The centrality of market completion has been accepted, at least temporarily, by the Commission, as also by the majority of Members of the European Parliament. The Commission has subsequently done everything in its power to drive the programme through, maintaining as much as possible the original timetable and its deadline of December 1992. The removal of market barriers has been the only kind of integration that conservative national governments would accept, but they have been driven by the Commission to accept a maximum of such market integration and in ways which will be hard to reverse. The Commission's aim has been to establish a high degree of market integration as the basis for future progress towards political and institutional unification.

In a sense, political union has always been the hidden agenda behind the development of Community-wide economic relations – the EC itself was a way of circumventing the obstacles to direct political integration. The calculation today, by the political forces for European unity, is that market completion *without* aspects of centralised economic control will prove untenable, so that new institutions and Community powers will be required to control the economic forces brought into play by the big market. It is already apparent that the Commission has been attempting to use the momentum of 1992 to advance other projects, such as a

European Central Bank or a European Social Charter. Meanwhile the political conjuncture which imposed neo-liberal economic policies throughout Europe is beginning to shift, and national governments themselves may be readier to consider other approaches to European construction. Neo-liberalism then, while it certainly has dominated policy-making in the Community, is now increasingly exposed to challenge.

The Content of the Programme

The proposals contained in the White Paper on completing the market are organised around the notion of 'barriers' to exchange within the Community. Although it is necessary to think in terms of non-tariff barriers to trade in order to understand the workings of the EC, it is not easy to put clear limits on the concept. So, while the White Paper is ambitious, it by no means covers all the barriers to exchange that could be found.

The White Paper's categories are 'physical', 'technical' and 'fiscal' barriers. The first, and most well-defined, category of 'physical' barriers refers to the continued existence of customs posts, passport controls and related formalities at the frontiers between member states. The objective is to eliminate these tangible signs of division completely. 'Technical' barriers refer to the divergent regulations and technical standards in different member countries, including the rules specifying the necessary qualifications for some professions. Here the aim is not to effect complete convergence but to minimise the impact of such differences on the flow of goods and resources. Many government aids to national industry and some patterns of government purchasing are also treated as a 'technical' barrier because of their operation as a form of protectionism. The White Paper itself did not produce detailed proposals for reform in these areas but marked them out for subsequent action by the Commission. The 'fiscal' barriers include in principle, all the distortions of exchange produced by divergent tax systems, but in practice (and not very logically) attention was focused on VAT.

Other areas could have been included – for instance, the workings of different social security systems or the differences in labour law in the member states, which certainly affect the costs of production across countries. In fact, almost every governmental function could be regarded as producing barriers to free exchange. Very detailed proposals were only developed in two cases – agriculture, where there was a determined effort to end the scandalous obstacles to the free movement of farm products in spite of the CAP, and transport, where the restrictions and market-sharing agreements covering cross-border traffic were to be curtailed. In both cases there was a previous history of EC involvement and a backlog of detailed proposals which could be included in the White Paper.

In many ways the White Paper seemed the product of brilliant improvisation, repackaging some old policies and staking a claim for the EC in new policy areas where this seemed feasible, rather than the expression of a coherent and mature strategy. Nevertheless, the White Paper has given rise to clearly defined policies in a number of areas, and although the 1992 programme is a long way short of a full integration strategy, it does push integration forward in each of these cases.

The area of technical standards and regulations is enormously complex, not least because of the overlapping of private and public responsibility. Many of the standards which are used to ensure compatibility and interchangeability of products are voluntary and result from concertation among private companies and in various industries. These voluntary standards may often be given public recognition either as a matter of safety and consumer protection or in the specification of products to be purchased by government. In technologically dynamic areas such as electronics the choice of a new standard and its date of introduction can have a significant impact on the process of competition by favouring one design and excluding another. The Community's efforts to harmonise officially required standards among the increasing number of member countries could be slow and laborious and the new approach outlined in the White Paper has already gained considerable support. Three types of action have resulted. Firstly, the role of the European Standards Institutes, CEN and CENELEC, has been extended in relation to the corresponding national institutes such as the

BSI. Efforts are being made to ensure more rapid communication between national and European levels and to inhibit the generation of new national standards without Europe-wide consultations. In the case of governmental specifications, a Community directive has placed new legal constraints on the introduction and communication of technical standards. Secondly, the pursuit of full harmonisation of government regulations within the EC has been abandoned in a large number of cases in favour of a simple 'approximation' – that is, minimum change to existing national specifications to bring about a practical equivalence of standards sufficient to permit the free circulation of products. Thirdly, and as a necessary complement to the use of 'approximation', the mutual recognition of official technical standards by national governments has been extended. The aim of EC legislation in this area is to create the presumption that the standards enforced in one country meet, in substance, the requirements of another and to place the burden of proof that this is not the case on the government of the importing country rather than on the private exporter or its customers.

The dry and detailed nature of most of the particular cases of technical regulation should not disguise the potential impact of these reforms. Their success will ultimately depend on bringing about changes in behaviour determining the production of new standards, rather than on the harmonisation of existing ones. Private industry will have to 'think European' in the sense that, when a new standard seems to be necessary, there should be effective consultation with the producers or users concerned on a Community-wide basis. National governments and legislatures will refrain from declaring new technical requirements before consulting the Commission and other member countries; an important transfer of competence will result across many areas of government, from national to Community level.

Standardisation takes place in a complex interaction with economic integration. On the one hand, attempts at West European standardisation will fail unless there is a significant degree of economic integration, because there will not be enough at stake to encourage the consultation processes which are needed. On the other hand, the development of

European standards can be a powerful lever for integration: where common standards for a product exist it is much more natural to consider sources of supply in a different country or to think of looking for new customers abroad. Very rapid changes are hardly possible in this area, where the deadline of 1992 is not very meaningful, but a successful challenge to these 'technical' barriers could in the long run, be an important step towards integration.

A second sphere of regulation dealt with in the programme concerns the qualifications of professional workers: services, such as medicine or law, are for obvious reasons more affected than the production of goods. Here again, a new approach has been taken to harmonisation. In an attempt to cut through the endless procedures of agreeing equivalence of qualifications, a 1988 directive created a presumption of equivalence for most professions requiring diplomas or degrees at university level. The practical consequences of this kind of reform are so far very limited, because most professional workers are employed in a national context, and because, as a result of language barriers, few highly qualified workers cross national boundaries in the Community (although the number is growing). At the same time national governments are still trying to prevent the civil service from being opened to all EC residents. This is a huge limitation because in some countries the civil service includes most public employees and because the public sector obviously employs enormous numbers of professionals.

A third major set of reforms in the 1992 programme concerns financial liberalisation. Here progress has been much more rapid, giving rise to the complaint that the Europe of capital is developing much faster than the Europe of labour. The integration of financial sectors is being promoted by two types of measure. The first is free movement of capital within the Community, which has already been agreed. The second is freedom of establishment for banks and other financial institutions in all EC countries. This requires some preliminary 'approximation' of basic public controls on financial activity but is going ahead fast and will permit a British-based bank, for example, to set up a branch in France without having to meet any new regulatory requirements. The consequence will be a rapid and complete deregulation of finance in countries such as France or Greece where there has until recently been comprehensive public supervision of borrowing and lending, since it will be easy to get round purely national restrictions by using the banks of another country. Financial liberalisation, however, is not matched by any development of Community supervision: so far not even a basic withholding tax on interest payments has been agreed, or elementary procedures to avoid fraud, while projects to establish EC monetary institutions – long in abeyance – are only beginning to re-emerge.

A fourth group of measures concerns public procurement. In most European countries around a tenth of national output is sold to the government rather than to households or businesses. These huge markets are hardly open to suppliers from other countries, partly because of the use of differing national specifications, partly because government orders are deliberately used to favour national suppliers – thus in British government offices there are British computers, in German offices German ones. Another example is the survival in different countries of separate locomotive companies supplying national rail systems, although the level of demand for locomotives is now so low that one might expect only one or two companies in the entire European industry. The 1992 programme attempts to open up public procurement to Community-wide competition: government contracts will have to be offered more widely and tenders from suppliers across the EC will have to be considered. The main problems will be in sectors where a competitive supply industry is inappropriate – because of the high risks of new technology or because national governments want to maintain skills and activities in their own countries. Governments favour their own computer companies because they have interests besides the mere cost of equipment – they will not want to sacrifice a national presence in this sector merely to respect EC competition rules and in any case the lowest cost equipment would often be US, not European. In such cases the formation of European consortia or mergers among European companies are probable in order to avoid enormous risks to previously sheltered national companies. The fact that military procurement is not included in the 1992 programme will also tend to mitigate its effects.

The key case of public procurement is telecommunications.[1] Commission documents point convincingly to the costs of a fragmented European telecommunications system. National telephone companies, usually in the public sector, have protected national suppliers of exchange equipment at the cost of extensive duplication in research and development (R&D) expenditures. At the same time the price of telecommunications services to users is much higher than in the USA, for example, and this slows down economic development as a whole because telecommunications are central to the full exploitation of information technology. There is thus a strong case for European integration, but there are enormous risks if integration is brought about by deregulation of the sector and competition among suppliers of equipment. Many suppliers would be unable to bear the risks of continued research on their own and would be eliminated; the ability of governmental agencies to sustain investment and research in the sector might be compromised. Non-European companies would almost certainly win a large share of an open and deregulated market. In the telecommunications sector in particular, where the Commission has tried to develop a specific policy, progress towards integration is likely to be slow and few concrete results will be seen by 1992. It is likely that a neo-liberal integration strategy of deregulation and competition will not be generally acceptable and that new institutions, such as a European telecommunications authority, will prove necessary, even inevitable.

The next main element of 1992 is fiscal reform. Tax harmonisation has been a continuing theme of EC policy, so it is not surprising that the 1992 programme attempts to accelerate progress. The resulting situation, however, is confused and disruptive of national fiscal systems without contributing much to integration. Attention in the 1992 programme is concentrated on VAT and on an attempt to harmonise rates of VAT. There are two reasons for this. One is that VAT is, in a sense, a 'Community' tax: the adoption of VAT as their common system of raising indirect taxation (that is, taxes on spending) by all member states is one of the achievements of the EC and was a first step in the long process of unifying the whole tax structure; equally, the Community is partly financed out of the proceeds of VAT. The second reason was that 1992 aims to abolish checks on goods crossing frontiers. The existing procedure is that exports are exempt from VAT in their country of origin but attract VAT in the country which receives them. This avoids any distortion of competition but necessitates a documentation system when goods are exported which the Commission aims to abolish. Exports will now be subject to VAT in their country of origin, but to avoid this distorting competition and leading to trade which simply takes advantage of lower VAT rates (as has been seen between Northern Ireland and the Republic of Ireland, for example) the rates of VAT are to be brought closer together.

A further complication arises because the Commission has proposed that VAT continue to be a tax on consumption rather than production in spite of the fact that it will now be raised where goods are produced, not where they are consumed. This would necessitate a complicated mechanism to return VAT receipts from countries which produce large quantities of consumer goods to countries which import them. France, however, with a surplus of trade in goods subject to VAT is resisting the introduction of such a mechanism.

The approximation of VAT rates raises the question of which countries will have to change their rates: in practice the countries with relatively low VAT rates are refusing to put them up and this puts enormous pressure on the other countries to bring theirs down in order to avoid their home products being undercut. The implications for some member countries could be serious. In general, the rich, northern countries rely on direct taxation (based on incomes) to finance public services; poorer countries, mostly in the south, rely more on expenditure taxation (VAT) because they have large numbers of very small, traditional enterprises – peasant farmers and artisan producers – which can avoid or evade direct taxation. It is these southern countries which are threatened with fiscal destabilisation by the 1992 programme. If the programme included some centralisation of tax revenues and redistribution from north to south this would be less damaging and might have been a step towards a rationalisation of tax systems throughout the EC, but since there are no such provisions, the programme imposes tax cuts in a somewhat arbitrary and dysfunctional way.

The final important theme in 1992 is the elimination of internal frontiers themselves. Ironically this is one of the areas where agreement on implementation has been slowest, although the disappearance of frontier controls would be an impressive symbol of integration and for that reason is a priority of the Commission. Frontier checks on goods will be more easily abolished than those on people which are seen as a necessary aspect of policing and immigration control, and are connected, more emotionally than logically, to notions of national sovereignty and national identity. Britain in particular may be slow to dismantle passport controls because of the absence of an official identity card system.

In theory the dismantling of internal frontiers would necessitate a uniform external policy on who is allowed into the Community, either as a visitor or, more seriously, as a refugee or immigrant – otherwise the rules of the most liberal country would tend to prevail, with that country becoming the port of entry for the Community as a whole. In practice, however, governments are likely to avoid deregulation in this area.

France, Germany and the 'Benelux' countries have already established closer police co-operation in anticipation of the final disappearance of frontier controls between them. The Shengen agreements will move identity checks away from the frontiers and permit the rapid transmission of information on residents of each country among the five police forces. Outside these five countries passport controls may well continue beyond 1992 so that the Community will have two tiers as regards the movement of persons. The five parties to the Shengen agreement will in practice accept the results of each other's policies on the admission of foreigners, but without any formal recognition of a common right of residence. The attempt is apparently being made to keep co-operation at the level of police procedure as a way of circumventing parliamentary supervision or political discussion. In the Community as a whole, no agreement has been reached on common rules of admission or even as yet on a right of residence in other EC countries for EC citizens who are not economically active. In practice the citizens of other

EC states are likely to be accepted but lack of agreement in this area makes the status of people with non-EC nationalities particularly precarious (there are some ten million such people resident in the Community).

Although some of the passport controls will disappear, no explicit right of freedom of movement is being introduced, despite the fact that the Single European Act requires freedom for 'goods, persons, services and capital' (in that order). There are some obvious obstacles to full freedom of movement and residence: countries like Denmark fear large demands on their welfare systems, while some Mediterranean areas would face very large influxes of north Europeans seeking retirement homes in the sun. Nevertheless, the will to overcome such problems by means of Community policies and to permit free mobility for people (equivalent to that for capital or commodities) seems not to exist. In the absence of explicit political agreements considerable scope is being given to the 'discretion' of police forces.

This summary of the 1992 programme has aimed to clarify how far the programme falls short of complete economic integration, or even of establishing Community-wide markets for most goods and resources. To consider only the most simple limitation – cultural, educational and especially language differences will continue to fragment EC labour markets along national frontiers, and there is no effective and strategic challenge to these differences in sight. The social welfare and social security systems of member states will also remain completely separate and discontinuous. Both direct wage costs and other labour costs will therefore continue to be determined on an essentially national basis. This alone will make for persistent differences in cost structures and, in consequence, price structures among member countries. Cross-frontier arbitrage and competition may make these price differences unsustainable for some products, but the 1992 programme does little to increase the scope for such arbitrage, which is difficult in sectors dominated by a few large producers or distributors, as well as in sectors where there is an advantage in local production.

The notorious differentials in the car market illustrate how different price structures persist: large producers avoid open price competition and tend to respect the cost-levels of domestic producers when they export into other EC countries. Britain, with an inefficient motor industry, has high prices; those in Germany are substantially lower; Denmark, which has no domestic car industry and imports freely from Japan has the lowest prices in the EC and other EC producers therefore reduce their prices when selling in Denmark. This situation is untenable in the long run if economic integration continues, but it is likely to persist well beyond 1992. The rapid elimination of higher-cost producers will not be permitted by national governments which can still resort to safeguard clauses allowing protection in emergencies; and the reorganisations and rationalisations which will permit the industry to operate common prices in different countries while absorbing major cost differences have a long way to go.

The measures in the 1992 programme are clearly inadequate for its stated aim of 'completing the market'. Nevertheless the programme does drive integration forward, most effectively in the spheres of finance and of technical standards and regulations. There is a clear neo-liberal bias in the practical implemention of the programme, beyond the fact that it is *in principle* centred on markets and on exchange. In practice the programme increases the facility with which business enterprises can operate across national frontiers, whether they are selling products and services, relocating production and employment, or dealing in financial assets. Although the deregulatory tendency of the programme has been exaggerated (largely because the coherence and efficiency of markets themselves has been over-estimated) it remains a neo-liberal programme both in theory and practice.

'The Costs of Non-Europe'

To provide a detailed economic justification of the 1992 programme the EC Commission organised a huge research effort. Sectoral studies of the benefit to particular industries from market unification were commissioned, mostly from commercial research agencies. The Commission's own economic staff then produced an overall synthesis, with estimates of the gains in output and employment which would be expected from a thorough implementation of the programme. The figures provided are certainly an exaggeration, if indeed they are correctly computed and turn out to be net gains rather than losses.

The concrete advantages of the programme take the form of cost and price reductions. This already creates grounds for a certain ambivalence in the interpretation of its overall effect, since these advantages can only be realised when and if the resources which are saved in one economic activity are redeployed in another. In a Community with some sixteen million unemployed workers, considerable unused industrial capacity, and increasing areas of abandoned farmland, such redeployment cannot be taken for granted. The Commission study recognises that an expansionist shift in macroeconomic policy is needed to achieve the full potential advantages of the programme over the medium term. The continuing difficulties in bringing about such a co-ordinated expansion in the member states are not discussed in the study.

Even making the most favourable suppositions about the reduction of costs and the reallocation of resources, the study can only offer limited, though already exaggerated, advantages. In order to present more spectacular gains the authors of the Commission report are led to postulate nebulous and speculative dynamic effects through which the 1992 programme would accelerate the processes of innovation and adaptation in the EC economies, thus permanently raising growth rates. It is certainly true that the influence of 1992 on the processes of economic development will be much more important than the direct cost reductions it brings, but it is by no means clear what this growth effect will be or even whether it will be positive rather than negative.

The starting point of the study is a group of clearly identifiable cost reductions: if customs posts are closed then it will no longer be necessary to employ so many customs officers in the public sector, nor so many clerical workers processing customs documents in private industry. Even these advantages can only be achieved when the workers concerned are effectively reemployed, but the potential savings here are relatively tangible, if very small. Beyond this, a series of other savings are postulated which all depend on some degree of reorganisation and restructuring of production in the Community. One element here is the possibility of increased economies of scale, but these are again relatively small. More generally the hypothetical savings depend on more intense competition in the Community and the elimination of less efficient productive processes. Higher-cost producers will either be forced to improve their methods or will lose out to low-cost rivals.

There are two major difficulties with this line of argument. In the first instance, it is difficult to see how 1992 will greatly intensify competition, except in specific sectors, where it is certainly possible to anticipate severe competitive pressure on some banks and financial institutions; and some suppliers of equipment to national governments may come under intense pressure to cut costs. But there is nothing in the 1992 programme to bring about a major change in competitive conditions throughout EC industry – more effective Community standardisation, tax harmonisation, the removal of customs formalities are all useful reforms but it is hard to see how they will *transform* industrial structures. On the one hand, many industries are already open to intense European or global competition; on the other, more localised, sheltered types of activity will continue as such.

It should be stressed that the impact of economic integration and free trade on competition is not being denied: the gradual opening of most Western economies in the period since the Second World War certainly tended to squeeze profit margins for manufactured goods, at least in less efficient countries. The question, rather, is to what extent 1992 represents a rapid increase in the level of integration of the internal market. The assessment here is that it can only have substantial effects on a few sectors, at least in the years immediately following its implementation. The 'Costs of Non-Europe' study can only arrive at large cost savings by assuming that all prices above the average levels for the Community will be brought down not just *to* those averages but well *below* them. The resulting reductions are hard to believe in themselves and even more so when it is remembered that the corresponding productive reorganisations would amount to the diffusion of German, Dutch and Danish production methods throughout the Spanish, Greek, Portuguese and Irish economies.

The second objection to the cost-cutting claims of the

Commission's economists is that not all variations in the money cost of production result from real differences in the use of resources. To a significant extent the variations may be due to differences in the price of resources, notably in the wages received by workers. Not all resources are purchased at competitive prices; rather, their owners are able to obtain a degree of what is called 'economic rent'. This is especially true for labour in that few workers are exposed to immediate competition for the jobs they hold and thus a variation in wage rates can emerge for the same task. To the extent that competition levels out money costs, it follows that this will occur not only by raising the efficiency of resource use, increasing labour productivity and so on, but that the levelling process will also involve squeezing the incomes of workers and of owners in less successful companies. The resulting cost reductions should not properly be regarded as an economic gain at all – they represent a redistribution from the enterprise which is forced to cut prices, or from its workers, either to consumers or to more successful enterprises. The Commission study acknowledges that some of the cost reductions it considers are of this nature, but makes no attempt to correct for the distortion involved.

More important than the mere bias to the Commission's estimates is the neglect of the social damage which can result from imposing wage reductions or work intensification through increased international competition. Within a relatively cohesive and homogeneous society prices to some extent perform a redistributive function which is accepted by social convention. Thus certain goods or services are paid above competitive levels in order to secure some increase in the incomes of their producers – artisans or small farmers for example. The destruction of this kind of informal redistribution by competition from another country where the same conventions do not apply is a major disadvantage of international economic integration. Within a national economy both convention and government intervention compel the winners from economic competition to offer some compensation to the losers. Within the EC under the 1992 programme such compensation is virtually absent.

The claims made by the Commission, that there will be enormous savings of economic resources from the 1992 programme, are simply not credible. An equally important objection follows that the resources which are released will not be rapidly, smoothly and advantageously reallocated to alternative uses. Since Western economies lost their momentum in the 1970s, there has been a clear tendency for lower levels of resource utilisation. Disturbed by major uncertainties and by the instability of the economic environment, companies have not seen such great opportunities for expansion and investment, and as a result they have not taken full advantage of available labour resources.

A change has taken place in the behaviour of enterprises and other economic agents: competition now centres more on reducing the costs of existing output rather than expanding output or developing new products; there is a bias towards cost-reducing investment in new processes and away from investment in new products or additional capacity; money is held in reserve rather than invested; labour is managed with a view to rapid reductions in the payroll if required rather than the building-up of skills and capabilities. This kind of malaise affects not only managements, but also individual workers, who are understandably more concerned with security and less prepared to take the risk of changing occupations or regions, and investors who are reluctant to finance new undertakings.

Business-oriented governments, influenced by neo-liberal doctrines, have responded to this heightened concern with costs by directly encouraging rationalisation and by seeking to reduce the fiscal and regulatory burdens on business enterprise. A decade of such policies, however, has not overcome the loss of economic dynamism. European companies now have healthier balance sheets and wider profit margins but in the absence of clear long-term opportunities for investment, the general malaise persists. Increased market competition may even have intensified the uncertainties facing business and obstructed the search for new market possibilities.

The suggestion is that the main economic requirement is not further rationalisation and cost-cutting, but a new model of economic development, a new line of advance to replace the previous expansion centred on increasing volumes of consumer durables. Given a clearer view of future consumer needs and future technical possibilities, business would be in a better position to develop constructive long-term strategies. If this kind of view is justified, then the 1992 programme reinforces an inappropriate trend in economic policy because it continues the pressure for rationalisation and cost-reduction which has failed, over more than a decade, to overcome the stagnation of the Western economies. The analysis offered by the Commission encourages this impression: everything concrete in the report concerns cost-cutting and intensified competition; when new possibilities for expansion or investment are involved the argument gives way to speculation and supposition.

The report does suggest that new scope for expansionist strategies will emerge from 1992. Lower costs and prices will reduce the threat of inflation; improved competitiveness with outside countries will relax balance of payments constraints; public spending will be reduced directly by the suppression of internal customs posts and more efficient public procurement (indirectly by the improved performance of the private sector). Hence governments will be better placed to pursue growth and fuller employment, and the most optimistic scenarios presented by the report assume such a change in macroeconomic policy.

There are several reasons for scepticism about these claims. Firstly, it is not denied that the 1992 programme may well lead to labour-shedding and higher unemployment at the start, and these effects could be much more persistent, and therefore costly, than the report assumes. If uncertainties are increased by more intense competition in Western Europe then enterprises may be very reluctant to expand recruitment or investment, so that the present economic problems will tend to continue. Finally, the costs and benefits of 1992 could be very unevenly distributed among the different countries of the EC: countries whose industry is damaged by import penetration may face tighter balance of payments constraints and, as a result, be led to implement more restrictive policies. In principle other countries, with higher exports will be able to expand but they may not choose to do so. There is as yet no example of successful macroeconomic co-ordination in the Community, and the 1992 programme does not contain any measures to facilitate a collective economic expansion by member governments, although it may well make such an expansion all the more necessary.

During the 1980s the economic service of the Commission has considerably developed its expertise and the quality of its publications: it now makes closely argued and well presented interventions in the debates around European economic issues. In the set of publications which have portrayed the 'costs of non-Europe' and the benefits of 1992, Commission economists have successfully influenced professional and lay opinion in favour of the programme. More critical and sceptical assessments of market completion have not been so fully elaborated nor so widely disseminated. The exaggerated claims made for 1992 have thus been given more credence than they deserve: no previous studies of trade liberalisation measures have ever come up with such enormous benefits and there is no real justification for regarding 1992 as a completely unprecedented and exceptional policy package in this respect.

The Limits of the Market

Recent developments in economic theory have tended to produce a much more complex view of the way market exchange and competition takes place. As a result some highly simplified views of market efficiency have been increasingly criticised, and some of the theoretical bases of neo-liberal doctrines and free-market economic strategies have been weakened or undermined. As yet, however, these theoretical developments have had little impact on the economics of integration, where more classical concepts continue to be applied. Consequently, there is a tendency for integration policies to be interpreted in a simplistic way.

The key to the theoretical changes in question is the notion of information. Many classical accounts of exchange assume, in effect, that information is abundant and freely available to every market agent, so that the buyer of a commodity knows all the suppliers and the prices at which they are prepared to sell. Under such circumstances ('full information') only the most advantageous transactions will take place since no one will sell for less than can be obtained or buy for more than is necessary. At the same time, every transaction which is mutually advantageous to buyer and seller will be undertaken

– transaction costs, at least the costs of information about transactions, do not exist in the classical accounts. Economic theory increasingly emphasises that full information is a very unrealistic assumption to make about most markets.

There is a link between information costs and the degree of centralisation in a market. In the case of a highly centralised commodity exchange, dealing in a standardised product such as wheat or tin, contact between all buyers and all sellers is established by specialised dealers and prices quickly reflect changes in supply and demand. The centralised exchange itself is costly but given that it is in operation, a seller prepared to quote an acceptable price will always find a buyer, and vice versa. Occasional breakdowns or panics in organised markets with specialised traders show that the assumption of full information and rational choice is not always valid even in this case, but at least it is a reasonable approximation to reality.

Most market situations, on the other hand, are characterised by the very limited information available to agents about the transactions possibilities which are open to them. Labour markets, markets for consumer goods and services, for most producer goods such as buildings, factory equipment and so on, and markets for most business services are decentralised – there is no established institution guaranteeing that all buyers and sellers can reach each other. Generally, the lack of homogeneity in the goods or services exchanged would make such a central institution impractical. In decentralised markets transactions costs are high, because of the difficulty of identifying possible transactions partners, and there will often be different prices for the same commodity because the parties to one transaction are not in contact with the parties to the other. In decentralised markets it is costly for potential sellers and buyers to find each other. As a result suppliers and customers will try to establish long-term relationships, in which a given exchange is repeated many times. Long term relations between particular workers and their employers are a key example.

Decentralised markets do have the advantage of plasticity – there is no established central institution which needs to be reformed every time the economic structure changes. But decentralised markets do not rapidly balance supply and demand in the way that happens for major commodities like coffee or gold on the international exchanges. There can be a persistent excess of supply, for example, because suppliers are not in automatic contact with all buyers and many agents are committed to long-term relationships.

This kind of reasoning has an important bearing on free-market economic policies and the neo-liberal arguments by which they are justified. In the important case of the labour market, many free-market analyses implicitly assume a full-information structure with minimum transactions costs. If workers are unable to find employment it is concluded that there must be some rigidity, some external obstacle preventing the wage rate from equilibrating supply and demand. In a limited information context this approach is crude and inappropriate. It is costly and difficult for unemployed workers to identify potential employers and vice versa; simple wage reductions will not automatically stimulate the demand for labour because most employers, quite rationally, are involved in long-term relations with their employees and it is again costly to disturb such relations. Whereas flexibility is built into full-information markets, decentralised exchange requires a degree of inertia and internal rigidity to make it possible.

Nothing in the transactions costs approach rehabilitates obsolete projects for a centrally planned economy – the reverse is the case since the approach emphasises the difficulty of providing central agencies with sufficient information to match the supplies of complex goods, services and resources to the needs of their users. Nevertheless, a consideration of information problems also tends to undermine the neo-liberal view of markets as 'automatically' and efficiently allocating resources. Indeed, one implication of transaction cost theory is that the efficiency of market exchange cannot be assured by the market itself – some external social support is needed to make an exchange system work. In the case of centralised markets this support is provided by a clearly visible institution: an 'exchange', a clearing house or a financial centre with its rules of procedure and specialist intermediaries. But decentralised, limited information markets also depend on external elements: networks of associated producers which can distribute information on prices and costs; regulatory bodies, private and public, which can reduce uncertainty about the nature of the product to be sold and the quality which should be expected.

Particularly important are relationships inherited from the past – 'customer' relations which have become literally customary so that the buyers and sellers in a transaction have a good knowledge of each other's requirements and a strong interest in avoiding big fluctuations in price or interruptions of supply which could jeopardise the established relationship. But to emphasise that inherited relationships are of great importance in decentralised exchange is to assert that efficient relationships between market agents cannot be set up instantaneously and costlessly as much neo-liberal argument supposes. An example of the implications of this kind of thinking concerns the liquidation of loss-making companies: in an idealised, full-information context the resources released from the failed enterprise can be rapidly transferred to more successful companies which will make better use of them; but transactions costs considerations point to a set of established economic links with customers, suppliers and employees which cannot be rapidly or easily replaced.

This kind of economic theory, however, has as yet had little impact on models of economic integration where standard assumptions of full information continue to be applied. As a consequence there tends to be an exaggerated stress on tariffs and equivalent governmental measures as obstacles to international exchange, to the neglect of the social divergences which sustain separate national economies quite independently of protectionist policies. The models which are used imply that each national market is completely centralised: all French buyers of a given product enjoy full and free access to all French suppliers but a specific obstacle – a tax, a regulation, or a difference in standards – imposes a cost on the use of British supplies. In this centralised case the removal of the obstacle will at once put all suppliers and all customers, French and British, on an equal footing in a unified market.

Where such a model corresponds closely to reality the 1992 programme should indeed promote rapid and complete economic integration: the obvious case is finance – certain large-scale financial and banking operations are already highly centralised and institutionalised within each member country. If good communications are established between national centres then effective market unification can be brought about, so that finance and banking form one sphere in which rapid results can be expected from 1992. In many cases where there is a high degree of centralisation, more or less full integration already exists in the Community – for example, all European traders in standardised raw materials use the same commodity exchanges in London. Even in finance, many of the official barriers to Community-wide integration had already disappeared, at least in northern Europe, so that mainly Mediterranean countries will now be affected.

Beyond these cases of centralised exchange, there is the world of more or less decentralised market relations which includes the vast majority of transactions – for labour, for most goods and especially most consumer and business services, for land, buildings and many other resources. Effective exchange depends here on the existence of established social relations which mitigate the uncertainty and lack of information which would otherwise paralyse economic life. The social links involved are of many kinds – formal and informal associations, ties of common culture or affiliation – but they are all influenced by history and tradition, usually in a national or local context. Such markets cannot be simply integrated on an international scale because they are by their nature fragmented and incomplete even within a single country. It is not even clear what 'integration' would mean in this case: to define integration as the law of a single price throughout the market is very abstract, because there will be a wide range of prices within each single country. It might be useful to consider full international integration, say between France and Germany, as a state of affairs where exchange relations are as frequent between French customers and German suppliers as they would be with French suppliers – that is, the nationality of a market agent would have no effect on the probability of a given exchange.

Clearly this level of integration cannot be established by administrative measures; it would require a social and cultural shift of considerable significance to bring it about. Even if Germany and France were part of the same political unit and had the same legal system and public institutions, Germany would not automatically become a 'home market' for French products. To appreciate the weight of the social and cultural factors involved it is informative to consider trade between East and West Germany. Here, prior to reunification, the official and regulatory barriers to exchange were still enormous – the two states belonged to different trading blocs and had different, opposed political and economic systems. Nevertheless, East German-West German trade was and is extensive, forming a large part of all exchange between former Comecon and current EC countries, and this was made possible by the common language and background of traders and managers in the two German states. Social and linguistic integration proves to be as important as political and administrative unification.

The transactions cost approach to economics also suggests the importance of history in analysing economic relations: even if new economic links could be as easily introduced across national boundaries as within them, old established market relations would enjoy an advantage simply because they already existed and therefore did not require the same amount of investment in the search for appropriate buyers or suppliers. Where one of the parties to an exchange is a national government, the 1992 programme may force it to neglect the advantage of established market relations and put new and old suppliers on an equal footing. But the same constraints can hardly be imposed on private economic agents and there will therefore be considerable inertia behind existing, largely national networks of exchange relations.

The importance of transactions costs varies enormously depending on the commodity in question. For relatively standardised products produced by large companies, especially if EC-wide distribution systems already exist, a unified European market may be an immediate possibility in the sense that the national origin of a product will hardly affect its sales prospects. (In such cases, it should still be noted, considerable integration existed before the 1992 programme.) However, where there are large numbers of small, localised producers, as for many services and in labour markets which depend on the relations between employees and companies, social, cultural and historical factors will tend to perpetuate market divisions in spite of 1992.

Much discussion of economic integration has used a stylised distinction first suggested by the Dutch economist Jan Tinbergen:[2] on the one hand, there is 'positive' integration – the development of common institutions and co-ordinated policies in the public sphere; on the other hand, there is also 'negative' integration – the removal of barriers to free exchange in the private sector. The present discussion indicates that these categories are inadequate because full integration in the market sphere itself will require 'positive' action – that is, the construction of links and information flows which would not otherwise come about. Some EC policies have been designed to do this, by encouraging, for example, research co-operation between companies in different countries. The 1992 programme, however, offers only 'negative' integration in the standard sense – the removal of administrative barriers – in the expectation that the logic of market competition will then bring about a complete system of transnational economic exchange. This kind of thinking exaggerates the coherence of market relations and the autonomy of market processes, which in practice are unable on their own to bring about the organisational changes involved in economic integration.

Neo-liberal doctrine claims that the pursuit of individual advantage in the context of unrestricted exchange is an essentially adequate basis for social organisation as a whole. Both the failure of neo-liberal economic strategies, in Britain and elsewhere, and the evolution of contemporary economic thinking tend to undermine this claimed supremacy of market relations by pointing to the dependence of effective market systems on appropriate social structures. It is necessary to consider European integration in this context, as a complex social transformation, before the contribution of particular economic reforms to the integration project can be assessed in a realistic way.

In the economics of limited information, the passage of time is critical to the analysis of adaptation by market agents. The longer the period concerned the more likely it is that a given agent will obtain information about a given technical or marketing opportunity. Programmes such as 1992 actually seem more convincing when viewed as long-term strategies for integration, since many of the opportunities for economic gain which they bring about will only be perceived and acted upon by enterprises over relatively long periods of time. Of course, the state of technology and market demand is always changing so that individual agents never acquire a comprehensive knowledge of existing economic possibilities. In a dynamic context, integration depends more on a shift in the search strategies of economic agents – so that companies, for instance, systematically explore markets in other countries; individuals consider their careers and job opportunities in a European context; financial companies as a matter of routine try to link borrowers and lenders across national frontiers and so on.

The final significance of 1992 will probably depend on the extent to which it promotes this kind of shift in the strategic behaviour of enterprises, households, individuals and public institutions, rather than on the limited degree to which it will intensify international competition within Europe. Once again, these long-term shifts cannot be easily understood in purely economic terms, as simple changes in the strategies of market agents. They involve just as much the social reconstruction of agents, shifts in motivation and objectives as well as in strategies, and the emergence (or non-emergence) of a European dimension to the identities of individuals and organisations.

The European Merger Boom

As with most international economic relationships today, a very large fraction of economic interactions across national boundaries in the Community are not direct market exchanges at all, but are transfers of goods and resources within transnational companies. The sectors concerned already exhibit a relatively high degree of economic integration based on the intensive cross-frontier activity which is organised by multinationals within Europe. It is within these same highly concentrated sectors that the first tangible results of 1992 can be detected in a wave of mergers, takeovers and joint ventures which have a clear European dimension and are obviously influenced by the prospect of further integration.[3]

The interpretation of this merger boom is difficult: the

search for economies of scale in production and R&D may be one motive; in practice, many of the combinations may be defensive, aimed at stabilising the market share of large enterprises for which integration would otherwise involve serious risks. This kind of defensive consideration is probably important where national enterprises have been protected by public procurement, such as computers or telecommunications equipment. Some of the combinations, in the food and drink sectors and in civil aviation for example, seem to be influenced more by anticipated deregulation, but may again be essentially a matter of responding to the threat of more intense competition by regroupings and reorganisations. The existence of a clear European dimension to the merger boom should not be taken to imply that it is purely a European phenomenon. Mergers and takeovers continue as a global phenomenon and there are still large numbers of such operations between European and other enterprises, especially US giants. The rationale for these concentrations is the general internationalisation of economic life, and European market completion is only one aspect of that process.

Policy-makers in the Community are ambivalent and contradictory in their approach to rising levels of economic concentration in EC industry. On the one hand, these developments clearly weaken the standard interpretation of the 1992 programme as a move towards a much more competitive economic structure: the Commission thus proposed a reinforcement of its powers to control monopoly and a transfer of competence over large-scale mergers to Brussels. This is clearly logical to the extent that the sectors concerned are unified within the EC so that purely national monopolies or the abuse of dominant positions within isolated national markets ceases to be a problem or an issue. On the other hand, the European mergers and takeovers tend to be welcome to the Commission simply because they are a form of integration – even if this form is not particularly compatible with the neo-liberal interpretation of integration as an extension of the competitive process. In practice, the sectors concerned will probably be those which are most affected by 1992: where there is insufficient connection between national markets to stimulate the emergence of transnationals, there will also be relatively little effect from dismantling the administrative barriers between them as these were not serious obstacles to trade.

So despite the neo-liberal design, the process of integration which is in fact stimulated by 1992 will not have the purely market character suggested by the analyses of the EC Commission. Much of the integration process will be internal to large enterprises. It follows that some of the predictions of the Commission are implausible, particularly as far as prices are concerned. Transnational companies will not necessarily charge the same price in different countries – price discrimination will be the rule. Similarly, government purchasing will not necessarily be cheaper if governments now face a few giant European suppliers rather than a small number of national companies. Since pressure on prices and costs is at the centre of the Commission's assessment of the benefits of 1992, the merger boom and the trend towards giant European enterprises provides another reason to be sceptical of that whole assessment, even if it does accelerate economic integration within industry itself.

'Fortress Europe' and the European Identity

In principle, 1992 concerns the internal functioning of the EC economies and does not commit the Community to a given policy on external economic relations – trade and investment flows to and from outside countries. Again in principle, it is conceivable that the more unified European economy could be protected from outside competition by high tariffs or other trade restrictions on imports from non-Community countries and by barriers to inward investment by non-EC enterprises. This kind of inward-looking strategy is what US policy-makers had in mind when they referred to the threat of 'fortress Europe' – that is, a European Community favouring a strategy of economic isolation. Since the inception of the 1992 programme, US and Japanese representatives in Europe have lobbied continuously to prevent any such developments.

Within the EC itself, the big market has sometimes been presented in a mercantilist manner, as a collective response to the challenge of Japanese and US competition. Although Commission economists have never recommended extending direct protection beyond the sectors, such as agriculture, where it already exists, they have frequently given a general impression that European companies could enjoy some advantages over outsiders within the unified market, which has often been referred to, especially on the continent, as the *internal* market or *home* market of the Community. Alongside the usual free-market rationale for 1992 there is a somewhat different justification for the programme in terms of giving European companies a big home market, comparable to that of US or Japanese companies, and in this way strengthening the position of European industry in global competition.

This interpretation of 1992 has, however, become less and less plausible as the programme has developed and been ratified. To have some meaning as a 'home market', the European market would have to offer some advantage to insider companies over outsiders. For example, it would have to be easier for German companies to operate in France or Italy than it is for US companies; British exporters would have to find it easier to sell into Spanish markets than Japanese exporters do. Now there is no measure in the programme which confers such an advantage on insiders (except the abolition of internal customs procedures which will give a very slight benefit to EC companies compared to companies producing *outside* the Community, although not against US companies, for example, producing *inside* it). As each item in the programme has come up for discussion and decision, the Council of Ministers has rejected any hint of discrimination against non-EC producers.

This has been, firstly, because of the balance of political forces among member states. While the French government has sometimes been attracted by protectionist strategies, or at least, by the wish to exact compensating concessions from the outside countries which will have greater access to EC markets, Britain, Germany and the Netherlands have insisted on a free-trade interpretation of the single market and rejected any new obstacles to imports or investment from outside. The implication is that the EC is becoming more open, not more closed, to trade and investment flows: it will be easier for companies producing outside to sell into the EC because they will only need to gain access to a single member country – products acceptable in that country can then be circulated freely to all the others, at least in principle. The US and Japanese transnationals which produce inside the EC will benefit, step by step, from 1992 liberalisation in exactly the same way as European companies. Indeed, since US companies are very active in moving products and capital between member countries, they stand to be big winners from the programme.

The implementation of the 1992 programme coincided with the Uruguay round of trade negotiations within the General Agreement on Trade and Tariffs (GATT), the world trade organisation. The French government had wanted to establish a strategic link between these two processes, so that access to the European market would be made conditional on reciprocal concessions from other countries, especially Japan. However, this has not happened because other member governments rejected this kind of conditionality. As a result the application of the programme will itself meet many long-standing claims by the USA for greater access to Community markets. If public procurement is opened up to competition, US enterprises will be able to win a share of the government orders which at present go to national champions. In the sphere of banking and finance also, the new scope for establishing subsidiaries in other countries and for movements of capital will benefit Japanese and US banks operating inside the Community. French attempts to make this access conditional on a reciprocal opening of the US and Japanese financial systems to EC banks were successfully fought off by the British government determined to reinforce the role of the City of London by removing restrictions on international financial activity within Europe.

The rejection of a protectionist strategy by the Community is not basically a question of policy choice and even the French government recognised this, since it never attempted to close off sectors of the EC economy, only to manage the process of opening up the single market. In practice, the 1992 programme necessarily implies that the EC's economic space would be very open to global trade and investment flows, because nearly all member countries are already very open and because they are tied into the world economy in very different ways. Each member has specific links with outside countries and is dependent on different types of activity.

Since these connections are usually too important to sacrifice, each member state will insist on maintaining them. In the context of market integration, however, the only way for the connections to be maintained is for the Community as a whole to adopt an open-door policy for the sectors or countries concerned.

Britain, therefore, insists on an open policy for banking, and on an open policy in general towards the Japanese companies which are being invited to invest in Britain. Germany, which relies on cheap imports to reduce costs in the high-income export-oriented economy, could not tolerate protection against manufactured consumer goods; nor would Germany allow its close economic relations with East Germany to be put at risk. France has historic ties with North Africa, the Middle East and other regions and would not accept that its imports from these countries be blocked by EC-wide protection. The only real possibility for the EC economy as a whole was to adopt a very open position on external trade and investment as a condition of integration. 'Fortress Europe' was never a practical option.

This opening-up of European markets may indeed be one of the main effects of the 1992 programme, even though this was originally supposed to concern internal economic relations. As a result very serious problems will arise for the regulation and control of economic life in the Community. This is sometimes discussed in terms of the 'European identity' of the economic space which the programme is trying to establish: will there be anything specifically European about the economy which eventually emerges, beyond its geographical location, or will it simply be an enormous enterprise zone for the free play of global economic forces? How can European social and political priorities be enforced in an economic system which is so closely tied to those of other countries around the world?

The case of television gives a good example of the difficulties which arise. The EC as a whole has an enormous deficit in the exchange of television programmes and most of the programmes shown in the EC are US imports. The result is cultural and economic damage: Europeans are not sufficiently involved in the key creative activity of making television programmes while much of the imported material is very poor quality. The 1992 programme threatened to aggravate the situation by permitting Europe-wide commercial TV channels which would broadcast little apart from North American material, and by allowing broadcasts from one country to another. The French response, which was to propose the imposition of quotas on non-EC imports, was unacceptable to other EC countries; certainly it seems crude to control the nationality of programmes when what really matters is their quality. Some EC member states doubted their ability to meet such quotas, while Britain – with strong TV producers who make programmes in English – is a successful exporter and therefore most reluctant to introduce restrictions on international exchange. Meanwhile, US producers and the US government fought hard against any controls and threatened retaliation. In the end the French essentially abandoned their proposal.

The question of European identity, in the context of a very open EC economy, involves important policy issues: a serious attenuation of social control is threatened if effective answers are not found. Some commentators see the solution in terms of big European companies, whose strategies might be aligned with internal social objectives, but this seems most implausible. It will be very difficult for public policy to discriminate in favour of one set of enterprises, and in any case most big European companies increasingly formulate their strategies in global terms and are unlikely to recognise a specific obligation to the Community. It seems impossible to replace the national champions of the past by European champions.

If this is so, then the European identity in economic life will have to be assured by strong and effective public regulation of all the big enterprises in Europe, regardless of their origin, together with well-financed public intervention – in favour of, for instance, TV producers operating in Europe. This approach can avoid discriminating against one set of enterprises and in favour of another, while still strongly asserting European political objectives on such issues as industrial democracy or consumer protection. It is, of course, a precondition of this type of control that the public institutions of the Community be given greater powers and more money, otherwise the 1992 programme will have, in the end, little relation to the project of European construction. It will simply be one step in the continuing process of economic internationalisation, rather than offering a *coherent response* to that process.

Notes

1 H. Ungerer, *Telecommunications in Europe*, EC Commission, Brussels 1988.
2 J. Tinbergen, *International Economic Integration*, Amsterdam 1954.
3 A. Jacquemin, P. Burgess and F. Izkovitz, 'Horizontal Mergers and Competition Policy in the EC', in *European Economy*, no.40, 1989.

Further Reading

The original programme for 1992 is in the European Commission's *White Paper: Completing the Internal Market*, Brussels 1985. The most useful summary of the Commission's case is in 'The Economics of 1992', in *European Economy*, no.35, 1988. A shorter account is the Cecchini Report, *The European Challenge 1992*, Aldershot, 1988. For comment see 'Europe 1992', in *Economic Policy*, no.9, October 1989; *Oxford Review of Economic Policy*, vol.5 no.2, Summer 1989; and *1992 Myths and Realities*, Centre for Business Strategy, London Business School, 1989.

2 Agriculture and the Community Budget

The long-standing and intractable problem of the Community's budget has to be solved if the neo-liberal vision which inspires the supporters of the 1992 programme – creating a free-market zone completely open to global trade and investment flows – is to give way to a more constructive view of European integration. On the revenue side, money to support public action at Community level is kept to a minimum by conservative north European governments, suspicious of every aspect of European co-operation with a public dimension and anxious to retain national control over tax resources. On the expenditure side, the EC's budgetary problems essentially coincide with the problems of the Common Agricultural Policy (CAP).

Spending on agricultural subsidies is out of control and continues to absorb two-thirds or more of the Community's budgetary resources. CAP spending squeezes out other projects and programmes, often of greater value, but this is only part of the damage it causes. More importantly, uncontrolled farm expenditures provide the strongest possible case against any increase in Community revenues. It is argued, in particular by the British government, that more money for Brussels will only mean larger and more expensive surpluses of agricultural products – higher butter mountains, deeper milk lakes. The failure to limit the costs of the CAP traps the Community in a vicious circle: lack of resources means that most of what is available goes on farm support; but the unbalanced concentration of spending on agriculture which results blocks any increase in resources. An increase in these resources, that is, an expansion of the Community's budget – not by some small percentage but by an order of magnitude – is nevertheless a necessary condition for meaningful political and social integration. Neo-liberals, who favour a minimal state, are happy for integration to be a purely private-sector process supervised by a tiny official apparatus: the Community, according to this view, would become merely a set of interconnected markets. For a supranational community to have any real social content, it must be able to influence the external economic environment of its member countries and to control, or compensate for, the increasing pressures which global economic forces exert on its citizens, rather than simply knock away the weakened and inadequate defences which exist at national level.

The argument for a larger and more effective EC budget is partly a question of solidarity as a principle, the need for a substantial response to the extreme inequalities of wealth, income and opportunity which exist in Western Europe and which are incompatible with any sense of real belonging to a community. At the same time there are narrowly economic arguments for much higher levels of spending by the EC, and, in particular, for substantial transfers of resources from high-income to low-income regions through the EC budgets.

Expanding the Budget

The first argument then for a bigger budget is the general imperative of solidarity. This does not imply the introduction of an European welfare state which would displace national systems of unemployment relief and income maintenance. On the one hand, the disparities of income among member states are too great to make such a development feasible – unemployment relief in Denmark and the Netherlands is well above average income in Greece and Portugal; and in the circumstances, no generally accepted standards of welfare exist on a European level which could form the basis of a welfare state. On the other hand, existing national systems of welfare provision are in many cases obsolete and in need of radical reform, since they tend only to alleviate the effects of economic disadvantage and social exclusion rather than to address their causes. The kinds of reform and developments needed in the field of welfare would be obstructed by the transfer of welfare functions to the central control of an EC apparatus which, at present, could only be even more remote and formalistic than national systems.

What can best be done at EC level, and in many cases is only possible at this level, is to counter the economic forces which hold down income and block economic development in specific localities and regions, excluding much of the population from full membership of national and European society. This territorial view of inequality and disadvantage – focusing on inner-city decay, rural isolation and depopulation, the depression of old industrial areas – is the most appropriate one for the EC, as a supra-national institution, to adopt. It is already at the centre of many EC programmes, although only token sums of money are involved. For the smaller countries of the EC and those with low levels of income, such territorial concentrations of disadvantage are beyond national capacities so that Community action is indispensable. At the same time, Community interventions do not interfere with national systems for the relief of poverty and income maintenance for individuals, although they could relieve the pressure on these systems by reducing the number of individuals who become their clients.

This kind of intervention, and the redistribution between countries that it requires, is necessary for integration itself, not just as one policy option among others. Without such solidaristic policies it will be impossible to produce the perceptions of common interest which are the basis for effective co-operation in other spheres. Within national states it can usually be assumed that some minimal alignment of individual interests and perception of common purpose exist, supported by a common language and culture. It is dangerous to make the same assumption in a wider transnational context where the coincidence of interests which stimulates economic interaction has still to be constructed.

The MacDougall Report, the most far-reaching study of the Community budget, showed that even in the USA the working of the Federal budget makes for a substantial equalisation of income and employment among various states by raising more tax in the rich states and spending more money in the poor ones, thus mitigating the disparities produced by market forces and helping to sustain a sense of national unity. As yet, no such transfer of resources is possible in the EC because of the tiny size of its budget. Meanwhile the accession of Greece, Spain and Portugal to the Community and the impact of recession have both widened the inequalities within the EC.

There is thus a general case for redistributive policies at Community level on these grounds of solidarity, but such policies also have a specific instrumental role to play in bringing about European economic recovery. In the short term, fiscal transfers from richer to poorer areas are a necessary condition for the expansion of output and employment. In the longer term such transfers are needed to change the geographical pattern of economic activity in order to sustain a continuing process of development.

Throughout the 1980s Western Europe has provided a text-book example of the way structural economic imbalances lead to poor macroeconomic performance. An economic system with serious structural problems will also tend to suffer from low overall levels of resource utilisation, because every attempt to expand the system as a whole will result in unsustainable financial outcomes. Instead of all units in the economy improving their financial position as demand increases, the stronger units will accumulate financial surpluses which are increasingly difficult to recyle to the weaker units, still incurring deficits. As a consequence, the whole process of expansion is soon blocked since the weaker units of the economy are unable to go on expanding their purchases.

In concrete terms, the structural imbalances in Western Europe mean that the West German economy nearly always enjoys a substantial surplus on its balance of payments, while most of the other countries, in varying degrees, suffer from balance of payments weaknesses which constrain their rates of economic growth. Any general acceleration of production and employment in Western Europe tends to increase the demand for German exports by other countries much faster than it increases German demand for imports from its European neighbours. Germany thus moves *further* into surplus and the other countries into deficit – a process which reaches a financial limit as it becomes more and more difficult to recycle German credit to the weaker economies.

The overall expansion could only be sustained if German expansion started before that of other countries and proceeded at a significantly faster rate. But German governments have consistently and justifiably declined this locomotive role for their economy because it would widen the already broad gap between German wage levels and those of other European countries, which would result in the medium term, in serious pressure on Germany's costs and therefore on industrial employment. This locomotive pattern of expansion is, in any case, undesirable from an overall European point of view as it intensifies existing disparities in income and concentrates growth in the richest areas.

The standard responses to this economic impasse are for the weaker economies to devalue their currencies and/or raise tariffs on their imports from the stronger ones. The very process of economic integration, however, makes the use of such measures very difficult. Protectionism by the weaker countries would compromise the free movement of goods and services within the Community, which is a basic premise of integration. Repeated devaluations of the weaker currencies – besides being a very crude method, often ineffective in the short term, of coping with balance of payments problems – would again threaten the integration process, in particular undermining the European Monetary System. EC law, in fact, does not completely exclude this kind of policy: a range of derogations from the rules of unrestricted trade continues to exist and member states continue to make use of them. These are essentially emergency provisions, invoked for short periods of time by countries faced with currency crises for example, and are in any case subject to close supervision by the Commission. The use of protection for long periods or repeated resort to currency devaluation would be a different matter: such measures would hardly be compatible with political unity in the Community and would be bound to put the whole movement towards economic integration in doubt.

The immediate macroeconomic advantage of a bigger Community budget would be to ease the balance of payments constraints on the weaker EC economies, particularly those of southern Europe, and thus compensate for the structural imbalance which inhibits general expansion. Such an outcome obviously requires that the fiscal transfers within the

Community are commensurate with the existing imbalances on trade. Transfer of two to three per cent of Community Gross Domestic Product (GDP) would seem to be a minimum order of magnitude if significant results were to be achieved. The overall budget would have to be considerably larger than this because Community activities could not be confined simply to promoting transfers, nor could EC expenditure be completely focused on the weakest economies, if genuinely Community-wide programmes are to continue.

With a longer perspective, a larger EC budget could do more than simply compensate for existing structural weaknesses; it could contribute to their correction by promoting structural change. In fact, it would actually need to do so in order to initiate a sustainable, long-term pattern of development which could decisively change expectations towards renewed confidence in the prospects for employment and activity. Nothing is as unlikely as a resumption of European economic development on the same pattern as the 1950s and 1960s, completely concentrated in the industrial North, with the Mediterranean regions acting essentially as a source of reserve labour power. The cumulative distortions produced by this kind of growth are so great as to block any attempt at renewal: there simply is not room, in the congested and overdeveloped North, for the high rates of quantitative growth which are still needed in the Mediterranean countries of the EC and in its African neighbours. The advantages of geographical concentration in general seem to be declining, as population moves from the big European cities and industrial occupations are replaced by service-sector ones.

This major shift in the geography of economic development cannot be effected by private investment flows alone, even though there is a strong tendency for large north European companies to locate labour-intensive production around the Mediterranean. Public resources on a large scale are needed to reinforce private investment decisions, by reducing the uncertainties of locational choice and by establishing clear territorial priorities in resource allocation. Fiscal redistribution also has an important advantage over private investment as a way of shifting resources, in that it does not require transfers of ownership. A Mediterranean country is likely to accept an expanding German and British stake in its industry if growth is so rapid that domestically owned assets are accumulating just as fast or even faster; but growth based on completely external ownership of industry, or on escalating indebtedness to foreign banks, is both economically and politically destabilising.

Previous discussion of macroeconomic problems in Western Europe has produced the idea of 'development deficits' for the weaker economies, as well as invoking the notion of a 'Marshall Plan', between northern and southern countries. The present argument has tried to relate this kind of idea to the construction of a new model of European economic development. The transfer of development resources within the public sector, on a principle of solidarity rather than private advantage, offers a much better prospect of a sustained and coherent geographical shift in economic activity, which is a key aspect of this model.

Thus the cohesion of the European Community as well as economic recovery and the renewal of economic development require a budget large enough to bring about a major transfer of resources among member states. Since the budget cannot be confined to such transfers but has to bring them about in the context of a set of priorities within Community-wide spending programmes, the overall size of the budget would have to be significantly larger than the north-south redistribution which is envisaged. Although all conservative governments in the EC have been resisting a big expansion of the budget, the most determined opposition has certainly come from Britain, and it is well worth examining the British case.

Britain Against the Budget

In the deliberations of the Council of Ministers and the European Council, the two strongest and most consistent opponents of a bigger budget are Britain and West Germany. German reluctance is relatively easy to understand: as the most populous and the most economically powerful member of the Community, Germany is already its main paymaster; any expansion of the budget would be to a large extent at Germany's expense, and equally Germany would lose from any reform of the budget to transfer resources to low-income countries. Within Germany there have been signs recently of a growing impatience with the Community, and in particular, of a lack of interest in the new Mediterranean members, remote geographically from Germany and distant also from its chief external concern with the rapidly changing scene in Eastern Europe. Under a conservative government since 1982 the Germans have tended to see EC expenditures as an unproductive drain on their own economy.

Understandable as this position is, it may represent a narrow view even of Germany's own interests. The sustained success of the West German economy since 1948 has resulted as much from an exceptional degree of social and economic cohesion as from the frequently evoked merits of the 'social-market economy'. Today Germany is being compelled to internationalise its productive systems very rapidly, and the lack of comparable cohesion and perceptions of common interest between Germany and its neighbours could become a serious obstacle to its own economic adaptation.

In more concrete terms, West Germany has an export-oriented economy with a persistent tendency to generate balance of payments surpluses. If Germany were required to reduce or eliminate that surplus in a precipitate way (by reining back its exports), major structural problems would arise in German industry. There is therefore a real German interest in financial arrangements which permit the German surplus to be recycled in a consistent and constructive way – even if such recycling involves some redistribution to other countries. Signs of stagnation occur in Germany whenever the international economy slows down and the demand for its exports falls. Developmental transfers towards the South could therefore help to secure a more stable and favourable climate for German adjustment.

However, the main obstacle to a major expansion of the EC budget has been Britain, where there has been a cynical change of position since the Mediterranean enlargements of the 1980s. When Britain joined the Community in 1973 its representatives argued for a big increase in spending. This was seen as a way of correcting the concentration of expenditure on agriculture which was not to Britain's advantage. The British at that time saw the solution in an expansion of the EC's other activities, which would, for example, benefit declining industrial areas. The establishment of the European Regional Development Fund was a response to this British advocacy.

In a Community of nine, redistribution from high-income to low-income countries would have favoured Britain, Italy and Ireland; but in the present Community of twelve the main beneficiaries of effective redistribution are bound to be Ireland, Spain, Portugal and Greece (plus, at a regional level, southern Italy). One reason for the switch in Britain's position on the budget was simply that it would no longer gain, and might even lose, from an increase in spending.

The other main reason for the switch was, of course, the political disposition of the Conservative government which took office in 1979 and has held it since. Opposed to much public spending on ideological grounds as well as hostile to the supranational aspects of the Community, Mrs Thatcher and her ministers have fought long and hard against any major expansion of the EC's budgetary resources. The only acceptable correction for an imbalance between other spending and spending on agriculture has now been to cut the latter. At the same time, British ministers have successfully defended the special refunds which Britain receives as compensation for the perceived injustice of existing budgetary arrangements, rather than advocate a general reform of Community funding to make such special treatment unnecessary. The British government has also contested the power of the EC Commission to determine how it will spend money in the UK even on agreed programmes. Pressure is exerted to establish national control over EC regional or social projects in Britain and subordinate them to the expenditure priorities of Whitehall.

In the 1980s recession and very high interest rates put enormous strains on public spending throughout Western Europe, intensified by the resurgence of economic liberalism and a growing scepticism towards state expenditure. Right-wing governments (with more or less monetarist programmes) were in office for most of the decade in all the north European member states except France. Similar policies – reductions in public expenditure and the maintenance of high interest rates – have been forced on left-wing governments in the South by sheer financial pressure. In this climate British opposition to Community spending focused a general hostility towards the ambitions of the Brussels Commission.

The turning point in this battle of the budget was the meeting of the European Council at Fontainebleau in 1984. The immediate budgetary crisis was contained – but largely along the lines proposed by Britain. An increase in revenues was agreed, but on a grudging scale, hardly sufficient to finance existing programmes. No structural reform of revenues was accepted and the ad hoc arrangements giving Britain a refund to compensate for the illogicality of Community taxation was perpetuated. The Fontainebleau Council meeting was even seen, by the (Conservative) British Commissioner Christopher Tugenhadt, as marking the end of the movement towards a federal Europe. Certainly Fontainebleau was a lasting setback for the process of European unification as it was understood at the time, and this helps to explain why the next major initiative for integration took the form of a thoroughgoing liberalisation of markets in the 1992 programme.

The additional resources granted to the Community at Fontainebleau only postponed crisis for a few years – the European Council meeting at Brussels in 1988 was forced to return to the question of the budget. On this occasion, the balance of forces was less favourable for Mrs Thatcher – a consensus now existed, within a Community expanded to include low-income Spain and Portugal, for increases in spending on regional development and industrial technology. The British failed to secure deep cuts in farm support as the price of higher support for other programmes, and there was even a minor reform of revenues. However, the existing ramshackle system complete with Britain's anomalous 'rebates', was not much changed and was extended for a further five years.

It should be noted that British opposition to EC spending is not only due to Thatcherism. The Labour opposition has been almost equally hostile, frequently castigating the government for making too many concessions to the Brussels bureaucracy. (Mrs Thatcher's convincing reply – that she has indeed done as much as possible to squeeze the EC budget – tends to make this a rather unrewarding theme for Labour representatives.) In a sense this is a surprising position for an avowedly socialist party since it involves root-and-branch opposition to public spending, so vehemently defended at national and local level. It can only be explained by Labour's deep attachment to national, parliamentary sovereignty and its complete lack of knowledge of, and sympathy with, the history and workings of continental agriculture. This is, nevertheless, a damaging position of immobility for Labour, as it prevents the development of concrete policies to reform the structure of Community revenues and expenditures. Without such policies Labour's call for economic expansion in Europe will remain at the level of general propaganda.

Structural Reform of the EC Budget

In recent years widespread agreement has emerged on the type of reform that is needed to the structure of EC revenues. The obstacle to reform is simply the refusal of member states to increase their contributions by a significant amount. On the expenditure side, however, structural reform is essentially a matter of the CAP and there is as yet no agreed direction of reform.

Community revenues have not been linked to the ability of the different member countries to pay and have been tied to sources which have tended to decline relative to the growing incomes of member states' economies. Not only have the funds been insufficient, but they have therefore also been raised in a way which goes against principles of equitable distribution of burdens.

One main source of Community revenue is the proceeds of the common external tariff, which is levied on goods imported from non-member countries. Although the EC's external trade has grown rapidly, tariff revenues have not kept pace because of repeated reductions in tariff rates. Successive rounds of negotiations within the General Agreement on Trade and Tariffs (GATT), the world trade organisation, have brought tariffs between the main industrialised countries down to very low levels, typically five or six per cent on the value of manufactured goods. At these levels there is no serious obstacle to international trade flows and future reductions seem likely only to deprive governments of useful revenue. It seems rational to maintain some customs duties on world trade, both to sustain public revenues and to give some support to individual countries or trading blocs with problems of competitiveness – tariff revenues grow with a country's import bill and therefore tend to increase when there is a balance of trade deficit. Tariffs require the winners in international competition to compensate the losers, at least in a small way.

Nevertheless the power of free-trade ideology and the momentum behind free-trade lobbyists is such that further tariff reductions are the most likely outcome of the present 'Uruguay' round of GATT negotiations, and in any case there is no prospect of increases. Trade with developing countries has seen even larger reductions in tariffs. The global Generalised System of Preferences (GSP) agreement, as well as successive Lomé agreements between the EC and developing countries in Africa, the Pacific and the Caribbean, have virtually abolished tariffs on most imports from developing countries. Of course this does not mean that they enjoy free access to European markets: very damaging quantitative restrictions – on steel, textiles and clothing, and many farm products, for example – continue to block LDC sales both in the EC and elsewhere. But these restrictions are not a source of revenue for the EC.

One set of tariffs has not been reduced – the 'variable levies' on agricultural imports, so called because they are not a constant proportion of the value of these imports, but are levied at whatever rate is necessary to prevent them undercutting EC supplies. Such farm imports have not grown in general because there are usually surpluses inside the Community, and the only agricultural imports to expand fast are those not subject to the levy. Here again, therefore, the EC is without a growing source of revenue.

The stagnation of tariffs and levies has made the EC increasingly dependent on its third main 'resource' – its share of VAT revenues. The Community is entitled to a small part of the money raised by this consumer tax, currently equivalent to a 1.6 per cent rate of VAT. As might be expected, this is a more reliable source of funds, but there is still the general problem that the VAT paid by a household is not even in proportion to the household's income; still less does it take a progressively rising share of income as consumers get richer. VAT is a tax on consumers' expenditure, not on their income: as income rises the proportion of income that is saved rather than consumed tends to rise and thus escapes VAT. This is particularly important in the case of Germany, whose prosperous and relatively old population has a huge propensity to save. Nor does VAT even cover all consumption: as people get richer the line between consumption and investment tends to be blurred – housing expenditures, exempt from VAT, are one example, as is the consumption financed by companies and enjoyed, usually, by the best paid employees.

VAT is barely therefore a proportional tax on income and this has the double effect of making it unfair (lower incomes tend to be taxed at a higher rate) and inadequate as a source of revenue (as incomes rise in the Community, VAT revenues fail to keep up). The rate of VAT going to the EC has been raised several times to prevent budget deficits but this does not tackle the intrinsic weakness of VAT itself as a source of revenue.

Beside these quantitative restrictions on EC revenues there are also serious political constraints on the use of revenues, which interfere with the finance of such expenditures as the Community might choose. This is most obvious in the case of the British budget rebates, but in fact national governments have repeatedly used the power of the purse to fragment and distort the EC budget by making agreement on resources conditional on their being spent in certain ways in certain countries. As a result there is often no clear demarcation between genuine EC spending, in accordance with Community priorities, and the finance, via the EC, of nationally determined programmes. The struggle by the British government to control the EC's social fund expenditure in Britain is a very clear example. To the extent that Brussels simply provides cash for activities (training, investment support, rural diversification) – which national governments would carry out in any case – then the nominal size of the EC budget exaggerates its real impact on the economies of member states. Without budgetary reform, however, such distortions are hard to avoid since the Commission will always be trying to extract a little more revenue from national governments and will thus be predisposed to damaging compromises.

Budgetary 'crisis' has become institutionalised in recent years – with the whole apparatus of the Community more used to working *without* an agreed budget than *with* one. The regime of 'provisional twelfths', which permits each month for each programme one twelfth of the annual spending in the previous budget, allows the Community to function without an agreed budget but at the cost of some delay in adapting expenditure to current policies. In the end the Council of Ministers finds some more cash – often by simple transfer from national budgets – but the situation is the opposite of what was intended when the EC was endowed, at the end of the 1960s, with its 'own resources', that is, with what was meant to be an automatic and stable supply of revenue, not subject to debate or delay by member governments.

The necessary line of reform is relatively clear. At present a 'federal income tax' for the Community, making citizens pay according to their income is not feasible, both politically and because the national systems which assess income and raise income tax are so disparate and incompatible. The alternative is to raise revenue according to the aggregate income of each member state, leaving it to national parliaments to decide how this aggregate burden should be allocated among individuals. A simple rule is needed that each member government must transfer a given proportion of national output (GDP) to the Community. Established notions of equity in all member countries would require the rule to be 'progressive' – that is, the fraction of GDP paid to the EC would rise with the level of output per head of population in each country. Some measurement problems might arise – GDP is a statistical construct, not something which can be physically measured, and there is always room for discussion about its definition and estimation. In general, however, the procedures for measuring GDP are long established and well understood, and there would be much less difficulty than with most forms of tax assessment because only twelve contributions would need to be raised. Such a progressive tax on GDP would permanently resolve the Community's shortage of funds while being much fairer than existing procedures (and seen to be so by the citizens of the Community).

The European Council in Brussels at the start of 1988 did in fact begin the move towards a GDP-based system, but in a hesitant and confused way. The EC was given a new 'resource' based on GDP, but instead of this *replacing* the existing VAT system it merely *supplemented* it, thus perpetuating the unfairness of that system. No progressive element was introduced, the new contibutions being simply proportional to each country's output, and the increase in resources was small – holding total revenues from all sources, to a maximum of 1.3 per cent of Community GDP. The mechanism to compensate Britain for overpayments was continued because the overpayments themselves were continued. Thus the reform did not resolve the budgetary problem but merely provided sufficient funds for a few more years.

The deep obstacles to a full reform of Community revenues are a lack of political will and the jealous defence of national sovereignty. But opposition to a stable expanding tax base for the EC has a very clear pretext – agriculture. How can one justify giving more resources to an institution which wastes most of its present resources on unwanted farm produce? Thus, for the Community, tax reform and reform of the CAP are very closely interlinked.

The Agricultural Surpluses

British 'common sense' has rarely been so consistently and disastrously misapplied as in the case of the problems of European agriculture and the CAP. The economic analysis involved is regarded as so simple that it has become a standard exercise for beginners: problem – supply exceeds demand; solution – cut the price. This reasoning is understandably favoured by a Conservative government inspired by free-market ideology, although Conservative Ministers of Agriculture have never been enthusiastic about cutting the prices received by British farmers. More surprisingly, deep price cuts are also the preferred approach of the socialist opposition. In this case, where the social aspects of the problem do not affect Britain directly and where the failure of existing policies provides a good stick with which to beat the hated apparatus in Brussels, Labour representatives stress the logic of competitive market pricing and the irrationality of public intervention. They would not dream however, of adopting the same approach in other cases of overproduction or excess capacity – shipbuilding, for example, or car manufacture – where all the painful social consequences of adjustment by competitive market forces alone are well understood. To counter the usual emotional reaction of the British labour movement to mountains of butter and beef, it is probably best to make a comparison with surpluses of other products – say, stocks of coal.

Behind the 'common sense' analysis favoured in Britain there lies an unconscious assumption that the historical development of British agriculture is in some way natural and superior. It is in fact quite anomalous in European terms, and indeed in global terms. Robert Peel's abolition of the Corn Laws, triggered by the Irish famine and representing the decisive triumph of industrial over agricultural interests, is taught to British schoolchildren as just another heroic Victorian step along the path of social progress, like the introduction of secret ballots or the abolition of debtors' prisons. In fact, it was a measure without either precedent or imitator: in no other industrial country has the role of agriculture in the national economy been left to the play of world market forces. Virtually everywhere else agricultural and industrial interests have been accommodated within a *social compromise*, effected by various forms of state intervention. In continental Europe and in Japan, industrialisation was from the start accompanied by the protection of agriculture which continues to this day. Even in the USA – always an exporter of farm products and so having no need for protection of agriculture – the relative price of farm and non-farm goods has been a key political issue for almost a century. Britain's reliance on purely market outcomes is absolutely the exception.

Nor does the historical record demonstrate the superiority of this British path. On the one hand, agricultural protection has not in the long run inhibited the industrial growth of other European countries, though it has been practised in all of them – notably Germany. Similarly, the high price of protected rice hardly seems to have impaired the competitiveness of Japanese industry. On the other hand, Britain's abandonment of agricultural protection – in the unique circumstances of the 1840s, when famine hit Ireland and when Britain had more or less a global monopoly of manufactured goods – has not been without costs. In particular, it contributed to the exceptionally rapid and brutal character of urbanisation in Britain, with consequences for both the urban and rural environment with which we are still grappling today.

Assessment of the CAP should begin with the historical fact that the CAP by no means *introduced* a system of protection for European farmers: they were all protected already and had been for a century. (Even Britain's farmers had been protected in the depression of the 1930s and continuously subsidised after the Second World War.) The problems of the CAP also have very little to do with protectionism as such. Historically the CAP was an attempt to *unify* existing systems of agricultural support in the six original member states of the EC. Its problems stem from *integration*, not from *protectionism*.

Within each nation, the status and income of the farm population were governed by a complex social compromise conditioned by the country's economic circumstances. Among disparate nations only crude versions of such adjustment were possible. Agricultural markets could be integrated relatively easily, since most of the products concerned were homogeneous or readily comparable. But the social context of farming in the different countries remained heterogeneous and defied easy assimilation. This explains why the CAP has never completely displaced national systems of state intervention in agriculture but has had to co-exist with them.

The CAP provides a text-book example of the dangers of market-led economic integration carried out in a social vacuum. The factors which distorted the initial formulation of the policy, and which are still at work today, concerned the negotiating positions of France and Germany – both, in the mid-1960s, with substantial and highly organised farm populations. France's key interest, given the relative strength of its agricultural sector, was to secure free access for its farm output to the markets of the other members. In particular, the French saw bigger agricultural exports to Germany as compensation for Germany's strength in industrial markets.

French negotiators therefore insisted on complete integration of agricultural markets, with (as a result) common prices throughout the Community. Germany, on the other hand, already enjoying huge success as an industrial exporter, was not concerned to obtain commercial advantages for its agriculture but to maintain an adequate level of income for its relatively uncompetitive farmers. (German standards of 'adequate income' were of course already very high, because of the country's industrial success.) So German negotiators did not have a particular interest in unified markets or common prices, but they did insist that farm prices in Germany be at a high level. The two positions, French and German, together determined that the common prices of the CAP would, from the start, be at a level which encouraged excess production of the main products concerned: cereals, beef, milk and butter.

The basic interests behind these initial French and German positions have changed little in the two decades since the inauguration of the CAP, although the rapid decline of the farming population in both countries has made the issue less central to economic policy. The compromise, clumsy in itself, was of course doubly inappropriate for new members of the Community. In Britain, with a small farming sector and a long-standing reliance on imported food, consumers suffered. (Assertions that this would not happen, on the part of enthusiasts for British entry, were naïve or dishonest.) British farmers, however, soon learned to play the game of overproduction and Britain's trade deficit in food products has narrowed since it joined the Community.

The farmers of the new Mediterranean members, like those of southern Italy, are the poor relations of the system – most of their products do not receive levels of support comparable to those accorded to temperate products, although these are the farmers with the lowest incomes. The accession of Spain and Portgual in 1985 nevertheless threatens to put more pressure on the CAP – the EC's agricultural population was nearly doubled by the enlargement and its arable land increased by 50 per cent (with a consequent trend for even bigger surpluses in the future). Only Ireland, of the countries which joined after the CAP was set up, drew major benefits from the existing system.

The Franco-German compromise remains stable because of the continuing centrality of the Paris-Bonn axis to the Community, and reform proposals, such as those advanced by Britain, which run counter to French and German interests have no prospect of implementation. Despite this, reform of some kind has become inevitable because of the escalating costs of the present system and the uncontrolled growth of excess production. What was not predicted by anyone at the beginning of the CAP was the *dynamic* response of supply to the guarantee of high prices.

The situation is somewhat analogous to the booms that capitalist economies go through in time of war. In both cases, capitalist production continues to benefit from all the advantages of flexible organisation and decentralised decision-making, while escaping the chronic uncertainty which is a principal weakness of capitalist system. Just as the state in wartime guarantees an unlimited demand for war materials, so the administered prices of the CAP have removed any risk of loss from an expansion of farm output. The profits made by successful farming units are confidently re-invested in the expansion of production facilities and the introduction of new technologies. The result has been an explosive growth of productivity which has dramatically increased production of the main surplus products, even as the number of people active in north European agriculture has continued to drop.

The process has increasingly involved the displacement of traditional family farms by highly rationalised 'agribusiness' enterprises, whose forms of organisation are essentially the same as those of capitalist industry. This transformation has been very uneven – there are huge disparities in the size, technical level and yield of European agricultural units, which do still include millions of more traditional family concerns, using much less intensive methods than the leading enterprises. As a result, it is *increasingly* expensive to use high prices to underpin rural incomes: an ever larger share of the agricultural subsidies is captured by the expanding output of agribusiness rather than supporting the lower-income farmers.

Once again, this is more a problem of integration than of intervention as such. The range and diversity of farm producers is much wider and harder to manage in the

Community as a whole than it would be within a single country. In any case the colossal growth of output has both reduced the effectiveness of the CAP, as a social policy in favour of small farmers, and made it impossible to contain the costs of price support. It has also shifted farm policy from an internal European problem to a major issue in world trade and one of the main questions in dispute between the Community and the USA.

Cereals – the Global Crisis

In text-book accounts of the CAP, the diagrams display, as an indispensable reference point, the level of 'world prices' – that is, the prices of organised farm produce markets outside the EC. Those external prices are taken as a measure of the 'distortions' produced by Community intervention – the implication being that, if EC price support were ended European prices would fall to 'world' levels. The difference is dramatic – particularly when there is a good harvest in North America: in 1985 the same wheat which cost over $200 per tonne in Rotterdam could be bought for less than $100 in New Orleans. It is wrong, however, to regard world prices as reflecting accurately the balance between global supply and demand – external prices, as much as those in the EC, result from large-scale public intervention, especially by the US government which massively supports the exports of its farm sector.

What the low prices certainly do represent is the financial cost to the EC of its own export subsidies. The main outlet for the surpluses induced by high internal prices is to export them outside the EC, at a loss measured by the gap between these internal prices and the much lower external ones. These exports completely justify the term 'dumping', since they involve selling a product abroad at less than its cost of production. The growth of EC production has necessitated a rapid growth of such exports, so that, in the key case of cereals, the EC is now the world's second largest exporter behind the USA. In fact, in the 1980s, the EC and the USA have become locked into a damaging subsidy race, seeking to undercut each other to secure larger shares of stagnant world markets.

The situation cannot be understood as the result of interference with an otherwise stable and efficient 'free market'. What has happened is rather the consequence of a breakdown in public control. As in other spheres, the USA was able single-handedly to regulate world agricultural trade for much of the period following the Second World War. The USA itself was the dominant source of supply, which it controlled through various forms of intervention such as acreage limits. At the same time the US government was able to exert great influence over international demand through its foreign aid programmes which, up to the 1960s, accounted for a large part of international trade. Officially financed stocks, nominally for 'strategic', but in fact purely economic purposes, were used to limit price fluctuations.

Again as in other spheres, the growth of the world economy and of international trade tended itself to erode US hegemony. The 'green revolution' and an explosive increase in yield per acre made limits on acreage an ineffective means of restricting output. The growth of trade led to international markets so big that even the USA was unable to control them.

In the 1970s the increasing lack of effective control did not seem to matter. Government support and a declining dollar maintained the competitive strength of US farm exports, while international demand was expanding fast. Economic performance in the developing world was relatively good, credit was cheap and many third-world countries, such as Nigeria, imported more and more cereals. At the same time China and the USSR were driven to compensate for the failure of their own agricultural policies by large imports from the West. Demand was so strong that the US government even tried on some occasions to use grain supplies as a political lever on the Soviet Union – notably when Jimmy Carter declared an embargo after the Soviet intervention in Afghanistan – but without much success because even then there were many other sources of supply.

In the 1980s, however, the economic climate changed and the absence of control over international trade started to exact a heavy toll from US agriculture. International recession, the crisis of third world debt and very high interest rates compelled the developing countries and the socialist world to rein back their imports. A massively overvalued dollar undermined the competitivess of US farm exports and many rural areas of the USA entered a crisis which continued throughout the years of the Reagan boom, with thousands of farmers and sometimes even whole farming communities going bankrupt. West European exports, sustained by continuing intervention through the CAP, took an increasing share of world markets.

It is symptomatic of the change in the standing of the USA that its response to crisis in its agricultural sector was not to seek a return to the regulated global order of the 1960s. Effective international regulation would today require agreement between the USA and other major agricultural exporters. Rather than pay the price of such an agreement the USA tried to make use of its strength to assert its own interests within the existing anarchic and deregulated situation. Farm support programmes and export subsidies multiplied (including the aggressive BICEP programme which financed a US assault on traditionally European outlets for farm produce in the Near East and North Africa). In the mid-1980s, total government support for farming in the USA considerably exceeded the EC's spending on farm support, (although European propaganda on this point ignores the fact that, because prices are kept at a very high level in the Community, most of the effective subsidies to EC agriculture are paid directly by European consumers without passing through the Community budget). Given the much smaller farm population in the USA, subsidies for each producer were substantially higher than in the EC.

In spite of this pressure, the EC has steadily refused to change its own policies in response since these are supported by the two key member states, France and Germany. The outcome has been an escalating export subsidy war, with each side squandering huge sums of money simply to neutralise the effect of the other side doing the same thing. Anything further from a 'free' world market would be hard to imagine.

The USA has also applied political pressure, as when trade was threatened to avoid Spanish markets being closed to US exports after Spain's accession to the EC. In general, however, such pressure has had limited success since France and Germany have a basically common position. The USA has managed to prevent the erection of new European barriers against its exports and has begun to intensify its export efforts in Europe on those commodities which enjoy relatively free access. The result has been to increase the disorganisation of European agriculture. US cereal substitutes such as soya, are a very competitive source of animal fodder, particularly in countries like Germany where exchange rate fluctuations have raised the effective price of wheat. The EC can subsidise European farmers in response to this challenge but is politically unable to use direct trade barriers and so the costs of the CAP rise even more. Meanwhile every tonne of cheap animal fodder which is imported displaces a tonne of European cereal-based fodder which has therefore to be exported at a loss – 'dumped' onto world markets. The CAP, a system once justified by the need for self-sufficiency, ends up reinforcing a weird pattern of specialisation in international trade.

Other transactions have been seriously damaged by this US-EC rivalry in cereal exports. Other exporters, such as Australia, Canada and Argentina, do not have the resources to match US and European subsidies – their farmers simply have to accept much lower prices. It can be argued that importing countries benefit from the cereal price war but the weight of opinion is that such benefits are transient and tend to delay and disrupt necessary structural reforms by the importers. Certainly both China and the USSR are striving to eliminate their import dependence, which everyone sees as a damaging economic weakness. Successful agricultural reform in these countries would, in fact, be expected to turn them into exporters of cereals, in view of their huge farm sectors. Similar considerations are generally held to apply to most grain importers in the third world. For economic advance in the long run they will have to modernise their agricultural sectors and establish a balance between home consumption and home production. Subsidised wheat imports certainly bring welcome relief to urban populations in the developing world but at the same time necessary rural reforms are discouraged and postponed.

In other words, there are many losers and few winners in the cereals price war. But the origins of this conflict and the way it has developed make the frequent invocations of free trade completely unrealistic as a solution to the world's agricultural problems. During the 'Uruguay round' of multilateral trade negotiations within GATT, the USA has claimed that EC cereal exports, being subsidised, are simply 'illegal', but this seems to be an unsuccessful attempt to avoid the political processes which alone could resolve the conflict. There is now such a close interdependence between European and US farming that effective reform requires negotiated agreement between the two trading blocs. A good analogy is often made with the disarmament process between East and West – what is needed are 'mutual' and 'balanced' reductions in farm subsidies by both sides. Limits on output and control of stocks will have to be agreed by the main exporters, otherwise most of the benefit of reforms in one of them will accrue to the others: if the EC unilaterally reduced its exports it would simply be easier for the USA to continue its own farm support policies.

These negotiations are all the more essential because the *quantities* of farm output are no longer the only subject to discuss. The droughts and harvest failures of the late 1980s in North America testify dramatically to the ecological limits of contemporary agribusiness. It is not just a question of making room in the market for the output of today's giant farm units, but of setting new targets for agricultural development which include reducing the input of dangerous chemicals and countering soil erosion. The current surpluses of cereal production actually provide a good opportunity for beginning this kind of reorientation.

In both respects – ecological and commercial – the CAP now has an important external dimension. This undoubtedly makes reform more complex, but it also increases the benefits of maintaining political unity within the Community during the reform process. If political compromise fails to produce workable reforms and the CAP simply disintegrates, then the Community as a whole will lose out in the global process of agricultural restructuring, with the result of both monetary and environmental costs. The dogmatic and ahistorical view of the CAP taken by most British commentators is therefore a serious obstacle in the search for effective solutions to the problem of overproduction.

What Kind of Reform?

In the first instance, it is necessary to consider the 'obvious' and 'natural' reform so favoured in Britain – price reductions. The logic of text-book supply and demand diagrams requires the following 'solution': as prices fall supply will be inhibited and demand encouraged; there must exist a price level at which the market will restore the necessary equilibrium.

Quantification of this argument starts to expose some of its weaknesses. By how much must prices fall? Prices have in fact been steadily reduced in real terms in the 1980s, with the annual increases usually below the rate of inflation. (Germany has mitigated the effect of these reductions by manipulating the 'green Mark' (see Appendix B), but the prices guaranteed by the Community have nevertheless been falling relative to the general price level). In addition a number of administrative measures have been taken which are equivalent to price reductions: there are longer delays before farmers are paid for products sold into intervention; quality controls and other conditions for intervention buying have been tightened up; the gap between target prices and the prices at which surpluses are bought has widened, and so on.

The impact of these price cuts on excess production has been small because the most efficient producers already have costs well below market prices and are able also to reduce their costs at a rapid rate by obtaining higher productivity and higher yields per acre. The strength of the most efficient units, however, does not mean that the price squeeze is easily accommodated by the smaller, higher-cost producers who continue to be eliminated from farming.

In fact major price cuts – of the size needed to bring European and world prices into line – would produce a huge crisis in EC agriculture, even more severe than the crisis in North America in the early 1980s. No country with a large number of vulnerable farm units would contemplate such action – hence the controversy between British and German representatives whenever prices are on the agenda. These two most right-wing governments in the Community are unable to define a concerted reform strategy for agriculture, and this makes it difficult for them to reach any kind of agreement on a general right-wing strategy for the EC.

It should be emphasised that neither the agricultural support programmes of the EC nor those of national governments are preventing the elimination of the European peasantry – only making the process slower and less brutal than it would otherise be. The last 40 years have seen massive urbanisation of West European populations, with the proportion of economically active people in farming typically falling from nearly half to around a twentieth in continental countries. This is a huge demographic and cultural shift, the significance of which is not always grasped in Britain where the equivalent change took place more than a century ago. Nor is the process finished – even though the boom in European industry ended fifteen years ago, and in spite of very high urban unemployment, workers continue to leave the farms. One legacy of this population shift is that the farm population is now very *old* (see Appendix A). In the long run this must ease adjustment problems for what has become literally a dying industry. In the short run, however, it means that many of those working in agriculture are less mobile, less able to adjust than younger people.

Price reductions (relative to the prices of other products) should certainly continue, but this could only represent a solution to the surpluses in the very long term, and other policies will be needed. In any case it is unrealistic and unnecessary to make 'world prices' the goal. On the one hand, world prices, as we have seen, are kept artificially low by US government intervention – negotiating an increase in world prices is an essential part of any reform strategy. On the other hand, the real problem of West European agriculture is not the burden on the consumer but the burden on the EC budget. Here again the singular British tradition of unrestricted imports distorts our assessment of the issue. In practice, a solution to the problems of the CAP means not getting rid of protection – which does not cost the EC money – but getting rid of the surpluses – which does. The aim should, therefore, not be to have free imports but simply to have *some* net imports (that is, imports in excess of exports) by getting Community production down below its consumption. Indeed, from a financial point of view it would be desirable to maintain some protection provided there were significant net imports, as the levies would then generate revenue for the EC. Even the elimination of surpluses, however, cannot be brought about quickly by price reductions – unless these were on such a scale as to bankrupt hundreds of thousands of producers. This would be not so much a reform of the CAP as the abandonment of its social objectives.

The second, more plausible type of reform to be widely advocated also involves abandoning one of the aims of the CAP, this time not the support it gives to farmers but its existence as a supranational, community-wide policy. It is suggested that farm support be broken up and returned to the member states, each of which would be free to implement the policies which seemed politically or socially desirable at the national level, and to pay for such policies itself.

There are obvious attractions in this kind of strategy: the EC's budgetary problems would be resolved while farm support policies, in becoming nationally differentiated, would be better matched to the different environments in which they operate. Germany, for example, would be free to subsidise part-time Bavarian dairy farmers, but at its own expense, while Britain could return to its traditional, nationally appropriate, policy of free imports with limited compensation payments to domestic producers.

In fact, a substantial degree of national autonomy already exists in agricultural policy – it has been pointed out that there are still substantial farm support-programmes at national level. Currency fluctuations also result in considerable national control over farm prices because the price divergences which result from fluctuations are only eliminated at a rate which is negotiated among ministers of agriculture and which is therefore influenced by national policy (see Appendix B). Before one set of price differentials have been closed, new currency movements may well widen them again. In the case of Germany, where the effect of successive Deutschmark revaluations has been to raise farm prices well above the level elsewhere, there is even an agreement in practice to accept the divergences as permanent since it reduces German pressure for general, community-wide price increases. Since disintegration of the CAP has already gone so far, and seems to offer considerable advantages, why not complete the process?

As with price reductions, the involvement of national states in farm policy is too useful to be excluded from a reform strategy for the CAP. In particular, if some of the financial burdens of farm support can be returned to the member states then there is corresponding relief for the Community budget. There are two main reasons, however, why it is not possible simply to dismantle the CAP into twelve national policies. The first is that this would represent a huge retreat in the integration process, and would therefore be resisted by all the European forces with a political or economic stake in the integration project. Beyond a certain point, different national policies and different systems of support would be incompatible with the free movement of farm goods inside the EC. Already the makeshift system of MCAs only partially overcomes the barriers to free movement which arise from different price levels. A thoroughgoing 'nationalisation' of agricultural policy would abolish the common market for agricultural goods and reintroduce the customs barriers which have been abolished. This would be an impossible precedent to accept when the 1992 programme is pushing integration ahead in other sectors. It would also compromise the social dimension of the Community if it proved impossible to respond to the social problems of agriculture except at national level. Equally, this fragmentation of European agriculture would make impossible effective negotiations with the USA and other major agricultural exporters.

Secondly, at a more concrete level, this 'disintegrating' kind of reform would be a major blow at French interests. The promotion of exports of agricultural products and foods has been a consistent part of French economic strategy: France has huge net exports, especially to other EC countries; agribusiness and food processing form one of the few sectors in which there are world-leading French companies; and for France, the breaking-up of agricultural markets in Western Europe would be close to a destruction of the EC itself. Within these severe constraints then, some moves towards increased national responsibility for farm support are possible and could play an important part of a wider reform strategy.

The next type of reform to consider is the replacement of production subsidies by straightforward income maintenance. The logic behind this kind of proposal is that it would be a more direct and economical means of achieving the social objectives of the existing CAP. If the real aim is to maintain the incomes of small farmers, why not just give them the money, rather than disguise the transfer as a payment for output which is not really needed? Since such support would only go to low-income farmers, the Community would avoid the present misdirection of resources into the profits of large-scale agribusiness.

The objections of farmers themselves to such a policy deserve more respect than they are usually given in Britain. The industrial analogy would be to close more loss-making pits and shipyards, but with bigger redundancy payments and more dole for the workers who lose their jobs. Loss of dignity and the danger of social isolation apply as much in one case as in the other: farmers, like any other occupational group, value their collective identity and do not want to see large numbers of their colleagues reduced to the status of welfare claimants.

A more technical objection is that it would be impractical to introduce a Community-wide system of income support because the social conditions which determine the level of an 'acceptable income' are still too different from one country to another. The minimum level of income required in Germany would be absurdly high in Ireland or Italy. Without a convergence of incomes and standards of living in member countries, systems of direct income support for individuals at Community level would not be seen as fair.

In essence the 'income maintenance' proposal is a more civilised version of the proposal for drastic price reductions as it involves ending price support. Most of the objections to rapid price cuts continue to apply, in particular the fact that they would produce a huge social and economic crisis in agriculture. No doubt national systems of income maintenance would be used anyway as part of the response to such a crisis, but it would be difficult to co-ordinate such relief at Community level. Indeed the crisis would be a serious threat to the Community's existence. The value of the proposal is that it stresses the need for much more effective targeting of the Community's farm spending and a redirection of subsidies away from highly profitable agribusiness; but this redirection of resources cannot simply take the form of welfare relief payments to farmers.

Three reform proposals – price cuts, handing the problem back to the member states and replacing subsidies by income support – have been examined and found to be inadequate. A different reform strategy will now be outlined which is interventionist rather than relying on market forces, while avoiding a break-up of the existing CAP. The two main elements of this strategy are production controls and rural diversification. Since both these elements have been increasingly important aspects of actual policy, the strategy would develop existing initiatives rather than make a complete break with them. In that sense it is certainly less 'radical' than drastic price cuts, but it does, nevertheless, have the merit of avoiding a rural crisis while facilitating a progressive escape from the problem of surpluses.

To begin with production controls, it is ironic that even with the resurgence of neo-liberal economic doctrines and even with a Council of Ministers dominated in the 1980s by market-oriented governments, the sheer practical problems of the CAP have been driving the Community towards an increasing reliance on production controls – surely one of the most heinous offences against free-market doctrines. Production ceilings were introduced for milk in 1983 as the only feasible way of controlling the CAP's biggest and most expensive surplus. The results were by no means perfect – the quotas were exceeded and expenditure was not completely contained. Nevertheless, 1988 saw the extension of ceilings to the second most expensive product, cereals, with an amusing debate between the representatives of free-market governments in Bonn and London as to what the output target should be. Similar measures are quite conceivable for beef and wine if money continues to be short.

At present such measures are stop-gaps, intended mainly to prevent the CAP from falling apart. It is likely, however, that production controls would be more effective and less disruptive if they were openly embraced as a continuing strategy for the reform of European agriculture. They should not be vague targets of indefinite duration, but specific goals themselves explicitly linked to a plan for the elimination of surplus production over ten or fifteen years. (This would not mean the elimination of agricultural support, which is hardly feasible over such a period, but it would bring the cost of public support under effective control.)

An objection in principle to administered production controls is that they are economically reactionary – they stop the growth of productivity by preventing the most efficient producers from expanding at the expense of the least efficient. This kind of argument loses most of its force in the case of a product which is already in vast surplus because of official intervention. A deterioration in productivity is exactly what is needed in the sense that output should be reduced without a corresponding collapse of employment (so that output per worker should fall). Continuing output expansion, induced by very high prices and profits for some producers, is not a form of progress in present circumstances. Quality improvements in the food already being produced and a reduction in its cost (including the heavy environmental costs of some farming techniques) would contribute to economic development in the Community whereas further output growth would not. Successful farming units would not be prevented by output controls from pursuing either product or process improvement. This change in objectives away from simple output maximisation would be itself a key target of agricultural reform.

Similarly there should not be any fundamental objection to a market in production quotas – so that farmers with high costs could sell their quotas to low-cost units. This kind of transaction tends to develop anyway when output controls are introduced and there are advantages in not making it illegal: smaller farmers are, of course, excluded from production if they sell their quotas, but this is a voluntary exclusion which is compensated for by the agri-businesses which take over their market share. Policing production controls will in any case be a difficult task, and it is important not to complicate it more than necessary by additional restrictions.

The actual record of production ceilings in the CAP has not been a brilliant success. Overall targets for the production of milk have been used to limit intervention buying since 1977 and output quotas for individual producers were adopted in 1984. But milk price support continues to absorb 30 per cent of CAP spending and it is not yet clear whether production has been brought under control. Still enough has been achieved for the system to be continued and for overall targets to be introduced for cereals. (Overall targets without limits for specific producers are, however, not a real control but rather a means of lowering prices – when the target is exceeded intervention prices are reduced.)

The case of milk, in fact, provides a useful illustration of the kinds of difficulty which production quotas meet in practice. There seem to be two kinds of problem – political and technical. It is doubtful if one can do more than contain the technical problems because they are inherent in any attempt to exercise centralised administrative control over a large number of competing producers: problems proliferate which make for Byzantine complexity in administration, so that new administrative distinctions generate new anomalies and vice versa. Anyone familiar with EC documentation will be aware of the already vast complexity of the CAP, where an endless flow of regulations has to deal with 'certain types of beetroot', 'certain varieties of lemon exported from Israel', and so on and on. The political problems, by way of contrast, arise from the reluctant and half-hearted way in which milk quotas were approached by the Community, so that the policy began with ineffective half-measures.

A typical technical difficulty arises from the fact that milk is not just milk: even in such an apparently homogeneous product there are important qualitative differences, so that production quotas were applied, for example, to the special types of milk used to make certain French cheeses, and since these types were not in surplus the result was to sabotage a perfectly useful productive activity. In fact, the EC does not support the price of milk directly because milk itself is too perishable – instead unwanted milk is processed into butter and skimmed milk powder which are bought, in 'mountains', into intervention stores (prior to being sold at knock-down prices, and amid general anguish to the USSR). Ideally then, the production controls should be applied not to milk but to the manufacturers of butter and milk powder, but there would inevitably be other policing problems in this practice; for example, it would be necessary to exclude certain types of butter which are not in surplus and have a ready market. Such are the tribulations of a command economy! It is important not to idealise administrative controls by ignoring such problems or believing that they can all be resolved by a sufficiently complex bureaucracy. On the other hand, as an alternative to the dislocation and social distress that would follow a price collapse a certain level of such difficulties may be the more acceptable option.

The limited success to date of milk quotas mostly stems from a political problem which should be quite resolvable: the quota system has been applied in a half-hearted way and with a desire to avoid giving offence to the dairy-farming industry. Between 1977 and 1984 a 'co-responsibility levy' was raised from dairy farmers' quotas for individual production units, but the levy was so small relative to the price of milk that it did not inhibit production. Even after the introduction of quotas in 1984 the penalties imposed for excess production were not an effective deterrent. Farmers were charged about one French Franc per litre for the excess output, which in the case of low-cost units was less than the profit margin. The slow-down in output was therefore minimal. Under both regimes butter and milk powder continued to be bought into intervention stocks even when the target output levels had been exceeded. Thus the policy in fact amounted to little more than mild price reduction, and had limited effects as a result.

There is no technical reason why production limits should not be much tougher than this. Penalties should be set at a level which imposes cumulative losses on producers who exceed their quotas. Policing the limits could be left to national governments which would undertake to indemnify the Community for breaches of discipline. Limits on production by individual farmers can be reinforced by clear 'quanta' – that is, limits on the total amount which the EC is prepared to buy, based on the difference between Community consumption and planned output. Under such circumstances there is a danger of an underground low-price market emerging in response to tight quotas, as the most efficient producers, who can sell at a profit well below official prices, seek to make use of their excess capacity. The danger should not be exaggerated: policing could once again be left to national governments and to official agencies which are well informed about their national industries (the British Milk Marketing Board, for example), with penalty payments to the

EC in case of infringement. Farmers themselves would be an important factor in policing, since underground sales would very likely be an attack on the majority by a few of the largest and most prosperous farming units.

Output limitation would not work permanently. Persistent over-supply would put growing pressure on administered prices. Structural changes might be used to evade official controls (for example, mergers might occur between cereal farms and companies in milling and baking). Eventually the confident expectation that the system was going to break down would become a self-fulfilling prophecy. Things would be different with a planned withdrawal if it is made clear that quotas are being used, not to maintain inefficient farmers in production but to allow for a more gradual and less violent transformation of agriculture, with the winners of the competitive struggle being compelled to compensate the losers. (Allowing the sale of quotas is one way of arranging such compensation, as well as reducing pressure on the control system.) To establish this context of adaptation rather than preserve existing structures, two complementary policies would be needed – steady downward pressure on prices and a positive commitment to structural change.

Steadily falling prices and production levels would have to be maintained to move from the present phase agricultural crisis management towards restored control. A transitional strategy of the kind outlined above would require a long-term commitment by member states to eliminate surpluses and this would reduce the scope for ad hoc price adjustment each year by the Council of Agricultural Ministers. Agreed procedures for price adjustment, related to the control strategy, would need a strong political commitment by the council, replacing the present annual squabble over sharing out the cake.

This does not mean that price setting can be depoliticised. It is impossible to tell how much pressure the strategy will exert on high-cost farmers in any given year. When the pressure is particularly intense, with accelerated departures from farming, political resistance is both inevitable and desirable. This is different from today's political context in which there is no agreed strategy, only a confrontation between farmer-oriented politicians, determined to sustain prices, and others determined to cut them. More internal coherence among member states would also be needed to achieve the most favourable results in external negotiations – essentially with the USA. Surpluses could be eliminated with less cost to the extent that there would also be a reduction in export pressure from the USA; if costs of adaptation were lower it should be possible to obtain a more rapid reduction of EC output. US agreement would also be useful in modifying the methods of agricultural output and the quality of products to meet health and ecological requirements. The EC-US conflict on hormones in meat shows that it is much more difficult to make progress in this direction without such agreement.

Quantitative restrictions, however, are only the negative side of a reform strategy for the CAP, permitting a controlled withdrawal of human and material resources from agricultural production. The full strategy also needs to include interventions to guide these resources towards more socially productive applications and this is particularly the case when there is so much urban unemployment that the absorption of displaced rural labour cannot be taken for granted.

Today the whole context of farm production is changing. For the first time since the Industrial Revolution the population of Europe's biggest urban agglomerations is falling. A complex of factors is behind this shift – changes in the structure of employment permit a wider dispersal of population while a growing need for space and a developing concern for the quality of the environment lead more and more people to leave the city. The decline in agricultural employment now needs to be balanced not by urbanisation but by the transformation of rural life itself.

This kind of development provides an additional argument against drastic price cuts which would eliminate existing rural communities and close down their transport and other services just at the point when a regeneration of the rural economy is becoming possible. A more gradual run-down of farm production would preserve the services and community organisation needed for that regeneration.

Besides its guarantee fund, the CAP has always had a small, structural ('guidance') fund which aimed at reallocating resources in agriculture rather than simply underpinning prices. Today the range of structural policy has to be much wider. The reallocation of labour and land within agriculture and improvements in the quality of farm output are still necessary, but the development of new rural activities is even more so. The CAP's guidance expenditures have mostly been in near token amounts, used to finance the departure of farmers from production. There are now more resources and the possibility of a more serious structural policy aimed at rural development to complement the defence of agriculture in a unified reform strategy. Leisure and sport activities, tourism, the redistribution of industrial and service production away from the cities, new rural services for both permanent and temporary residents – all the emerging activities now making claims on rural space – can offer a new basis for the redeployment of agricultural and rural resources. Constructive structural guidance would avoid the need to deliver the agricultural economy to the uncontrolled play of market forces, which would effectively abandon small-scale agriculture to its fate. However, without a clear strategy for public enterprise, public services and public intervention, private investment in rural areas will be inhibited by uncertainties while the shift of population out of the big cities will generate frightening new inequalities and exclusions.

Conclusion

The cost of the CAP has become the main justification, particularly in Britain, for a refusal to increase the EC budget. But such an increase is needed to finance the fiscal transfers from surplus to deficit regions of Europe without which it will be impossible to expand the European economies. The same fiscal transfers which should take the form of investment in human and material resources, are also necessary to reorient economic development in Europe towards the areas with the greatest need for, and possibility of, a rapid increase in incomes. The reorientation in turn is necessary to overcome the present impasse, where all but the most congested and costly regions face extreme financial constraints on their development. As the 1992 programme intensifies competition in the Community these constraints will tighten, making budgetary compensation all the more essential.

The CAP is a bad alibi which can only be presented as an absurd and irrational policy by ignoring the realities of European social history. The protection and subsidy of agriculture are an admirable expression of solidarity in the face of the colossal economic forces which have almost eliminated the West European peasantry within two generations. Nor is this refusal to abandon those who lose in the economic race as costly as monetary calculation might suggest – the unrestricted rule of market forces would be even more costly on a social scale. The excesses and inefficiencies of the CAP arise not from its protection of agriculture but from the fact that it has to act on an international scale, by intervention in markets which have been integrated without a corresponding integration of social systems.

Neither the protection of agriculture nor the Community-wide nature of the CAP can or should be simply abolished. The problematic surpluses of farm products can be handled by determined public intervention in the form of production controls rather than by the release of market forces. At the same time structural interventions should help to adapt agricultural areas to the newly emerging forms of rural development.

Further Reading

See G. Dimitriof et al., 'The Effect of the Common Agricultural Policy of the EC: a Survey of the Literature', in *Journal of Common Market Studies*, vol.27 no.2, December 1988. On agriculture, see the annual *Report on the Agricultural Situation in the Community* from the EC Commission. On the global agricultural crisis, see M. Franklin, *Rich Man's Farming*, Routledge/RIIA, London 1988. On rural diversification, see EC Commission, COM(88)501, *The Future of Rural Society*, 1988. A recent study of the budget is M. Shackleton, *Financing the European Community*, Pinter/RIIA, 1990. Economic disparities among member countries are discussed in 'Economic Convergence in the Community', *European Economy*, no.41, July 1989.

3 Money and Finance in the Big Market

The political forces behind the 1992 programme have been pushing Europe towards a new level of integration within the private sector, but at the same time attempting to block other aspects of European construction. The sphere of money and credit provides a key example of the problems caused by this imbalance. The market completion programme is removing the remaining obstacles to the emergence of private, Community-wide, credit and financial networks; but there is no agreement on any corresponding development of *public* monetary institutions. The European Monetary System (EMS) is working well as a method of stabilising exchange rates, but the institutions which were originally intended to accompany it have never emerged. The Delors Committee on monetary integration was an effort by the Commission to accelerate institutional advance towards monetary unification, but the conservative report which the Committee presented in 1989 leaves the main political questions of unification unresolved.

Meanwhile, the increased mobility of private capital between member countries, confirmed by the 1992 programme, is putting ever tighter constraints on monetary and credit policies in member states. In principle, coherent Community-wide policies could be produced by co-ordination among monetary authorities in the member countries, but in reality the differing political contexts and economic priorities in which national monetary policies are formulated prevent effective co-operation. In the absence of strong central institutions, fragmented decision-making results either in incoherence – with no consistent overall position – or in hegemony – where weaker countries are forced into line with the stronger. The present situation is precisely characterised by both these weaknesses: on the one hand, Britain's non-participation in the EMS creates a fundamental disorganisation and division in EC monetary policy in general; on the other hand, German financial strength is so great that the other countries participating in the EMS, without Britain, are basically dominated by Germany.

The outcome is a crucial weakness in the structure of the EC which is bound to obstruct any Community strategy for economic recovery, since monetary and financial disorders are a central feature of the present economic malaise and, at present, there is no adequate means of dealing with those disorders. A great deal is at stake, therefore, in the effort to break this impasse which is being made by the EC Commission and its President Jacques Delors, with the support of some national governments, especially France. On the basis of the report of the Delors Committee, the Commission is trying to put monetary integration back on the agenda, in particular through the construction of a System of Central Banks. If this initiative succeeds in relaunching the process of monetary integration, the range and power of Community economic strategy will be enormously increased. However, the method of monetary integration proposed in the Delors Report will tend to make progress slow and to find itself beset with political obstacles.

A comprehensible discussion of these policy issues requires some preliminary analysis of the general significance of monetary policy and of the role of monetary and financial factors in the present crisis of employment. Before considering the EMS and European monetary integration, this chapter will look at the background to their development, arguing that the most effective strategy for monetary unity is not to impose ever tighter discipline on member states but to build up the ECU, the monetary unit of the EC, as an international reserve asset.

Money and Credit

In much economic theory money is treated as being 'neutral', as having no real effects on the economy (except, perhaps, in the very short term). The insight behind such formulations is that, since money is a symbol of wealth and not wealth itself, the form it takes is fundamentally arbitrary. It cannot really matter, for example, what the monetary unit is called – the terms, 'Pound' and 'Dollar', are purely conventional. Nor can the size of the monetary unit be of any basic importance – when France replaced 100 old Francs by one new one in 1959 the arithmetic of buying and selling became a little easier but real economic relations were unchanged.

It does not follow, however, from the conventional nature of monetary signs, that monetary systems are in any sense neutral or that they have no important effects on the production and distribution of real wealth. The absolute quantity of money, in abstract, may be purely conventional, but the processes through which money is created or destroyed have profound consequences.

In modern capitalist economies, money is produced as private credit – through the lending activities of banks. It is a continuous process – money being eliminated when borrowers pay back their bank loans and recreated when they receive new advances. It would be hard to imagine anything less neutral, since the way in which banks and similar financial intermediaries extend credit is a determining influence on all economic activity. Which companies, households and institutions will be financed, and for what production or consumption activities? What conditions will be attached to the finance – what will be the interest rate, what security will be required, how long before payment is due? Such questions are always important, but they become even more urgent when an economy is subject to large disturbances and acute uncertainties because at such times an exceptional number of companies and other economic units will record deficits and therefore require refinance. The monetary system to a large extent determines which units will be refinanced, to what extent, and on what terms. The activities of governments themselves may be financially constrained by the monetary system, in different ways depending on the degree of control over the system exercised by government.

Obviously the implications of such financing decisions are more than narrowly economic – they have enormous social significance because of the way in which financial pressures circumscribe the possibilities open to negotiators. Which bargains between economic agents can be financed? To give one example, the monetary system helps to determine the time period over which a bargain is struck – the longer the length of time available the easier it is to arrange a compromise; the shorter the time available the more likely it becomes that conflict will occur. Of course, this is not a one-way relationship: the social environment, the degree of social cohesion, in turn affect the range of strategic options open to banks and financial agents. However, the workings of the monetary system can have a decisive effect on all bargaining processes in society, including the key bargains between employers and employees.

Although money today is predominantly created by the lending of private banks, and although most money consists of deposits in private banks, the social and economic importance of the monetary system makes public supervision and control unavoidable, and only an extreme minority of free-marketeers deny the necessity of such control. Historically there has been some degree of state control over monetary institutions throughout the development of modern industrial economies; the closest approach to complete monetary laissez-faire was perhaps in the USA in the early nineteenth century – a period of chronic monetary instability and recurrent banking crises. Today, public regulation is universal. Systems of control vary greatly, but the most important regulatory institutions are public 'central banks' which developed to co-ordinate the lending of banks and to refinance those in difficulty. The central banks usually issue money themselves but their key present-day role is to oversee the issue of money by private banks, so that monetary systems have evolved as combinations of private and public control over bank credit. Monetarist theories, which advocate reducing the element of public control to a bare minimum, have encouraged the recent deregulation of banking in many countries, but consequent problems of instability have tended to limit further moves towards the dismantling of public control.

Commerce between economic agents in different countries gives rise to international monetary relations and, here again, an overall regulatory instance has proved to be necessary to prevent chronic instability. In the absence of supra-national monetary institutions with sufficient authority, overall control has been provided through the hegemony of a single nation state whose monetary institutions regulate international payments and delimit the field of activity of the subordinate states. The domestic money of the hegemonic power has become the key currency in international economic relations, being the most widely used to denominate prices, to make payments, and as an investment medium. Until the First World War Britain fulfilled this hegemonic role; at the end of the Second World War the international monetary order was reshaped under the leadership of the USA, with the Dollar becoming the key currency.

Europe and the Dollar

The rise and decadence of an international monetary system centred on the US Dollar, and regulated under US hegemony, is the context in which European monetary co-operation has evolved. In the first place, the context was one of a robust and stable international system: the strength of the Dollar was beyond question and public, intergovernmental, borrowing and lending dominated private financial activity which was subject to close and effective supervision. This initially stable system was gradually transformed, in the 1960s, by a massive growth of private financial activity, both in the USA and internationally, posing increasing problems of control. Finally, as the postwar boom ended, effective control over the system was undermined because the USA was no longer able to reconcile its role as international monetary regulator with the need to manage its domestic economic problems.

The first consequence of this loss of control has been continuing instability (wide fluctuations in all financial markets – culminating in the world-wide stock market crash of October 1987, and very volatile exchange rates between different currencies since fixed parities were abandoned in the early 1970s). Such instability makes economic calculation more complex and investment more hazardous. The second consequence has been higher interest rates and more costly credit, especially in the 1980s. Raising interest rates has been the only method available to public authorities to try to control a dislocated and unstable financial environment. Lack of co-ordination among different countries has led to the interest rate weapon being used in an unorganised way, with central banks bidding up rates against each other; private lenders have been increasingly deterred by uncertainties, without public authorities being able to compensate for the higher credit costs which result. These high interest rates have also tended to discourage investment, particularly the long-term investment needed to establish new patterns of economic development.

It was only during this third phase, when US monetary hegemony became increasingly problematic, that the question of specifically European monetary integration arose. Before the late 1960s, monetary relations in Europe were secured by the coherence of the global system centred on the USA: for instance, fixed parities between European currencies resulted from the fact that each of them was fixed *in terms of the Dollar*. The dislocation of this global system at the same time disorganised the internal monetary arrangements of Western Europe.

US hegemony in its first, effective phase is exemplified by the European Payments Union (EPU). The EPU, which was the first institution for internal European monetary co-operation in the postwar period, was essentially the result of a US initiative. While pursuing the Marshall Plan for West European economic recovery after World War II, the USA recognised that it was impossible for European countries to make their currencies immediately convertible into Dollars. Their economies were so weak that unmanageable balance of payments deficits would have resulted if unrestricted access to US currency had been allowed. The USA therefore accepted the strict rationing of Dollars by European central banks with the exchange of local currency for Dollars only permitted for import priorities such as factory equipment. At the same time, however, the USA sponsored – through the EPU – a much fuller measure of convertibility of West European currencies with each other, so that Sterling, Francs, Deutschmarks and so on were freely available for trade between Britain, France, Germany and so on.

Effectively a major move towards European monetary

integration was imposed by the USA itself, since the EPU was made a condition of Marshall Aid. It was a mark of strong US leadership that the USA accepted and even organised the non-convertibility of currencies into Dollars throughout such an important region. The EPU in fact furthered long-term US objectives since the internal convertibility of European currencies was seen as a transitional phase towards their external convertibility. And this strategic objective was actually achieved in 1959 when convertibility of West European currencies into Dollars was restored. The long time-horizon of the EPU initiative, the concessions that were made to immediate European interests, the way in which internal European monetary relations were organised, the pursuit of a long-term strategy were all signs of confident and effective international leadership by the USA.

During the period of secure and stable US monetary leadership the question of monetary unification within Europe hardly arose. The Bretton Woods System gave a leading role to the Dollar as an international reserve asset, used to settle debts between governments and to finance balance of payments deficits. Each country undertook to maintain a fixed exchange rate between its own currency and the Dollar, within narrow margins; and, in fact, the rule of fixed exchange rates was generally observed with only few and infrequent devaluations or revaluations. In this context the stability of internal exchange rates among European currencies followed from the stability of each of them in relation to the Dollar. The original text of the Treaty of Rome only contains the briefest references to monetary co-ordination because, in 1957, monetary problems seemed obviously secondary to the real issues of trade and industry. It was symbolic of the situation that the first monetary unit adopted by the European Community was 1/35 of an ounce of gold – coinciding with the gold content of the US Dollar. It was natural to use the Dollar as a unit of account within the EC because of its unquestioned supremacy as an international currency.

In the 1960s there was both a huge extension of the dominant US system of money and finance and a rapid transformation of that system. Following the rapid growth of trade and the worldwide expansion of US multinationals, private international credit in Dollars developed, channelled through the Euro-Dollar market which brought together borrowers and lenders of Dollars outside the USA. US bankers also became more and more engaged in external activities, so that the whole private sector of American finance was increasingly extended into a global system. This reversed the pattern of the late 1940s and 1950s when the public sector had been clearly predominant in international finance and most borrowing and lending had been between governments.

A parallel shift was taking place within the USA. From the New Deal reforms of the 1930s there had emerged a highly regulated financial system, dominated by government borrowing and lending. Again, through the 1960s, the very rapid growth of private credit for both firms and households reversed this situation, calling into question the previous regulatory structure by multiplying the channels through which credit could be extended from one private agent to another. At the same time as the US financial system expanded – at home and abroad – it was also becoming much more a private system, increasingly difficult to control and more susceptible to disturbances.

The West European countries no longer enjoyed such a stable international monetary environment, and in the late 1960s there were signs of dissatisfaction with the Bretton Woods regime. France under de Gaulle changed its official reserves from Dollars to gold, a public gesture of distrust in American leadership.

When serious internal economic problems developed in the USA in the late 1960s and early 1970s, the whole system was dislocated because the policies, often inflationary, which were used to stave off recession in the USA, were incompatible with global stability. President Nixon, for example, rather than raise US interest rates, temporarily prevented US banks from lending abroad – a completely illegitimate move for the central financial power which should always be ready to accommodate other countries. The gold backing of the Dollar was gradually eroded, then abandoned; and a series of reductions in the value of the Dollar failed to stabilise exchange rates. Stabilisation exercises had become much more difficult during the 1960s because of the growth of private international credit flows, which rapidly changed direction in response to possible exchange rate variations. By 1973 the last attempts to fix exchange rates had been abandoned and currencies were allowed to fluctuate on foreign exchange markets. It was the change in the real balance of economic forces and the decline in US competitiveness which first disrupted the international payments system, but this disruption in turn, through the volatility of exchange rates, exacerbated the uncertainty and instability of productive systems.

The Island of Stability

In this context of worldwide disruption the members of the EC began to reconsider the question of their internal monetary arrangements. At the beginning of the period, the six original members adopted the Werner Report of 1970 which proposed a very ambitious programme for full economic and monetary union. Undoubtedly the programme underestimated the scale and complexity of the difficulties to be overcome: 1980 was chosen as the target date for full monetary union – essentially the adoption of a common currency – but this soon turned out to be unrealistic as economic disturbances and rising inflation produced divergences in the monetary policies of member states.

At the same time, unstable exchange rates began to compromise even the economic integration which had already been achieved. Supposedly 'common' prices in agriculture, in particular, were driven apart by currency fluctuations. More generally the huge volumes of trade and investment among EC countries were themselves now disturbed by the uncertainty and instability which resulted from changes in exchange rates. A foreign investment decision, or the decision to import a foreign product, which might be clearly advantageous at one exchange rate became unprofitable at another. It is possible, at a certain cost, to insure against some 'exchange rate risks' but by no means against all of them. Currency fluctuation threatened to cause serious disintegration of trade and investment activity in Europe.

From the beginning of this period a particular pattern emerged in European currency markets which persists to this day, determined by the strength of the German economy and the consistently low level of inflation in Germany. This performance has made the Deutschmark an object of international speculation to a much greater extent than other European currencies (although Swiss Francs are a similar case). When there is a loss of confidence in the Dollar, wealth-holders around the world – big companies, banks and wealthy individuals – tend to sell Dollars and buy Deutschmarks to insure themselves against the declining value of the Dollar and to profit from any strengthening of the Deutschmark. In this way the German currency acts as an alternative store of value when the Dollar is distrusted; gold is another such alternative monetary asset, and indeed gold and Deutschmarks both tend to rise and fall against the Dollar at the same time. As a result the Dollar and the Deutschmark tend to fluctuate in opposite directions: when the value of Dollars falls there is a rush into Deutschmarks which drives their value up. Other European currencies, more susceptible to inflation, less well known and trusted internationally, do not exhibit the same kind of movement.

This difference in the behaviour of European currencies means that the weakness and volatility of the Dollar has tended to be massively disruptive of internal European economic relations. A decline in the Dollar drives up the value of the Deutschmark relative to the Franc, for example, without there having been any change in the real economic forces which affect trade between France and Germany. Exports from Germany to France can suddenly become unprofitable because of this exchange rate movement which has nothing to do with real costs or productivity in the two countries, but simply reflects the purchase of Deutschmarks by companies and banks around the world, many of which have no connection whatsoever with Germany. Since trade between Germany and other member countries is a large fraction of the total internal trade of the Community, the instability of the Dollar does not just affect trade between the USA and the EC but has produced disruption within the EC itself.

The first limited steps towards effective monetary co-operation in the EC were in the attempt to defend the Community's internal trade against this kind of disruption. In 1972 member countries – including Britain, Ireland and

Denmark which were about to enter – agreed to stabilise exchange rates among their own currencies, an arrangement known as the 'snake' from the thin wriggling shape traced by EC currencies as they all moved up and down together against the Dollar. The disproportionate strength of Germany in international trade and finance meant that the 'snake' in practice was little more than a Deutschmark zone: the fundamental external relationship of EC currencies to the Dollar could only really be influenced by Germany as it tried to control the Dollar-value of the Deutschmark; other countries simple tried to keep their own currencies stable in terms of the German currency and had to accept whatever Dollar-value for their currencies this implied.

The way the 'snake' worked during the 1970s placed enormous stress on EC economies. As the Dollar fell sporadically against the Deutschmark, the Dollar-price of EC exports rose, threatening their competitiveness in world trade. West Germany itself managed to meet this challenge through a vast process of industrial restructuring: rapid technical innovation held down costs and maintained German competitiveness for complex products, particularly factory equipment and other investment goods; meanwhile German companies used the strong Deutschmark to carry out enormous foreign investments, moving labour-intensive production processes to countries with lower wage-costs, which now even included the USA itself.

Most of Germany's neighbours, however, were unable to respond in the same way to the pressure of rising exchange rates. Many of them repeatedly suspended their participation in the 'snake', devaluing their currencies against the Deutschmark in order to maintain the Dollar-competitiveness of their exports. France, for example, entered and left the 'snake' three times between 1972 and 1978, torn between the need to stabilise its trade with Germany and contain inflation on the one hand, and the need to improve its competitiveness and relax external constraints on economic growth on the other. Only the Netherlands and Denmark, whose trade with their German neighbour is all-important stayed in the 'snake' throughout its period of existence (even then with devaluations). To conclude, the first minimal response of the EC to the dislocation of US monetary leadership was basically a failure – centrifugal forces predominated over the attempt at coherence.

The successful introduction of the EMS in such circumstances testified again to the ability of the EC to relaunch repeatedly the project of integration in spite of recurring periods of stagnation and of relapse into purely national policy formation. The idea of a new measure of monetary co-operation, expressed by Roy Jenkins, then President of the Commission, was promoted by the German Chancellor Helmut Schmidt and the French President Valery Giscard d'Estaing. From their initiative the European Monetary System was born in 1978, and came into operation in March 1979. The EMS continued the pursuit of exchange rate stability but within the framework of a formal agreement and specified procedures.

The very existence of this framework represented a concession by Germany and a move towards a less unequal allocation of the burdens of monetary co-operation. Under the 'snake' each country had the responsibility of maintaining its own currency in fixed parity with those of the other participants. In practice this meant that they had to adjust their own policies (interest rates, government expenditure and tax rates) in order to maintain parity with the Deutschmark, while Germany itself was so strong that no corresponding constraint was imposed on German policy. As we have seen, the imbalance was so marked that only relatively small countries with close economic links to Germany were prepared to accept the discipline of the 'snake' throughout its existence. In the EMS, on the other hand, the responsibility for maintaining or adjusting the set of exchange rate parities is held more in common by all the participating members. Beyond this, some of the procedures of the system were adopted specifically to prevent complete German domination over exchange rate policy. Despite these measures, the problem remains that the EMS has only moderated the exercise of German monetary hegemony to a minor extent, and that this is bound to continue in the absence of strong central institutions to supervise its functioning.

The core of the EMS, as of the 'snake', is a fixed exchange rate system. Participants try to hold the value of their currencies steady relative to each other, constructing Western

Europe as an 'island of stability' in a world of exchange rate turbulence. However, the way in which the parities are specified, the procedures for maintaining them and, when necessary, changing them are all much more elaborate than in the 'snake', placing obligations on the members as a whole.

Parities, firstly, are specified in terms of the European Currency Unit (ECU), a basket of member states' currencies which is used as the unit of account for the EC. This way of specifying parities makes a general concertation of participating countries formally necessary for parity changes. If, for example, the French Franc is devalued relative to the ECU, then some of the other currencies will have to be revalued because the ECU itself contains a fixed number of French Francs. Since this Franc content now makes up a smaller fraction of the ECU's value, then the other currencies in the basket must logically constitute a bigger fraction, implying the ECU-revaluation of at least one of them. A general realignment of parities is necessary, requiring preliminary discussion and agreement before it can be announced. (In practice the finance ministers of participating countries meet on a Sunday when the foreign exchange markets are closed.)

The margins of fluctuation which are permitted around the central parities are rather wide in comparison to those of the Bretton Woods System of the postwar period. Currencies can move within a range of plus or minus 2.25 per cent relative to each other, and in the case of Italy, with its well known tendencies to inflation, the margin was increased to six per cent up or down. Spain, participating from the summer of 1989, was also given this wider margin because of its economic weakness. These margins give a degree of slack which makes the set of parities more robust and easier to defend against speculative attack. Once again, defence of the parities involves a measure of collective responsibility: when two currencies reach their limit of permitted fluctuation there is an obligation on both central banks to defend the parity – thus in the strong currency country the central bank must lend to the central bank which is under pressure, to enable it to prop up its own currency on the foreign exchanges. These short-term loans are, in principle, unlimited in amount to avoid giving speculators the impression that the weaker central bank may be running out of ammunition.

Relative to previous international monetary systems – the gold standard of the late nineteenth century or the Bretton Woods system – these obligations on strong currency countries to assist the others represent a higher level of organisation: in previous systems it was basically the task of individual central banks to maintain sufficient foreign exchange reserves to defend their own currencies, and international assistance to them, although usual, was not obligatory or unconditional.

Besides these margins around the parity between each two currencies in the system (the 'cross-rate'), there is also a rule governing fluctuations between any one currency and the ECU – which is a collection of all the currencies. Clearly the margins around the cross-rates imply margins around each currency's parity with the ECU. Movements of a currency from its ECU-parity are known as its 'divergence' since they measure its average movement away from all the others. The rule creates a presumption that any country whose currency diverges beyond a certain limit (75 per cent of the maximum 2.25 per cent against all the others) will take corrective action – easing its monetary policies, if its currency is appreciating; tightening policy if its currency is depreciating against the ECU. This rule amounts to a significant concession by Germany, since it provides some safeguard against the typical pattern of events which occurred under the 'snake', when – as the Deutschmark rose against the Dollar – all the other currencies were forced also to appreciate willy-nilly. Under the EMS the Deutschmark would tend to approach its divergence limit in such circumstances and thus the Bundesbank would be obliged to take some corrective action. It could either try to reverse the movement of the Dollar or take steps to strengthen the other EMS currencies – for instance by reducing interest rates or by buying Francs, Lira and so on. The mechanism of the divergence indicator thus provides a kind of majority vote on the overall movements of the system, limiting the ability of Germany to impose a restrictive monetary policy on all the other participating countries.

There is general agreement among commentators that the EMS has successfully stabilised the exchange rates among European currencies, so that movements of the French Franc against the Deutschmark, for example, are much steadier and more gradual than they would be if left to market forces. One sign of this is the absence of sudden reversals in exchange rates – where a currency rises today and falls again tomorrow, demonstrating that the rise was speculative and unsustainable. The parity changes that take place within the EMS are usually quite small (revaluations and devaluations of three or five per cent) and respond to imbalances in trade and payments rather than speculative pressure. Parity adjustments, however, are relatively frequent and routine when clear disequilibria do occur, so that speculators are not offered the tempting target of prolonged and expensive resistance to an inevitable parity change. This relative stabilisation of exchange rates has been accompanied by the stability of short-term interest rates – in contrast to the experience of Britain, outside the system, which has been repeatedly forced to raise interest rates to defend Sterling.

Luck certainly played some part in the success of the EMS – for its first few years of operation the Deutschmark was unusually weak, making it easier for the other countries to keep their currencies in line. Nor have monetary conditions outside Europe set a high standard of performance – non-EMS currencies, in particular Sterling and the Dollar, have been exceptionally volatile. Nevertheless, the first, limited objective of the EMS does seem to have been achieved and Western Europe has become an island of exchange rate stability in a turbulent world. The result has been to give some insulation to the EC's internal trade and investment flows from the effects of a wildly unstable Dollar.

The Erosion of Financial Control

The short-term stabilisation of exchange rates by the EMS is definitely a useful achievement, but it is fundamentally insufficient when measured against the financial conditions needed for economic recovery. In fact, when one looks beyond exchange rates at other aspects of finance, the years since the EMS began to operate in 1979 have been among the worst in European experience. 'Real' interest rates (that is, corrected for inflation) have been unprecedentedly high, inhibiting in particular the long-term investments which are needed for renewed development and reinforcing the bias of investment towards cost-cutting rationalisations. The same high interest rates, although they have not discouraged consumption, have become a formidable mechanism of inequality among households, transferring huge levels of income from debtors (usually poorer) towards creditors (particularly those with substantial savings, usually richer).

Finance has not only been expensive, it has also been highly unstable, with huge, dislocative swings in the values of different assets, culminating in the worldwide stock exchange debacle of October 1987. On that occasion determined government responses prevented the crash itself from causing major damage but the episode added to growing concern about the performance of financial sectors in Western economies. Another worrying development is the wave of contested takeovers in American, British and more recently continental European industry. These have produced massive increases in the valuation of certain companies quite unrelated to changes in their productive performance; these swollen valuations then become the base on which big loans are floated to pay for the takeovers, making the credit structure more fragile and exposed to major defaults, especially if there is a recession in the USA. Correspondingly, a managerial climate is produced where profits are sought through mergers or other financial operations rather than from real investment.

The continuing role of the US Dollar is inseparable from these financial malfunctions. The Dollar remains the key currency in international trade and investment, and its role has become even more important, in spite of the declining competitiveness of US industry and the rise of powerful new industrial producers. A perverse chain of causation means that the very failure of the US authorities to stabilise the value of the Dollar or the system of Dollar credit can enhance the position of the Dollar as an investment medium. As turbulence mounts in international trade and capital flows, it becomes increasingly necessary for each agent concerned – whether government, bank or industrial company – to maintain larger reserves of internationally acceptable purchasing power (most obviously Dollars, or Dollar-denominated assets) as a buffer against the very disturbances produced by the Dollar itself.

The role of the Dollar as a reserve asset has therefore hardly been shaken by two decades of wild swings in US monetary policy, from inflation and Dollar depreciation in the 1970s through a violent disinflation and drastic rise in the Dollar in the early 1980s and back, via huge trade deficits, to renewed depreciation since 1985. The centrality of the Dollar sustains the worldwide expansion of a vast network of private financial institutions dealing primarily in Dollars – banks, finance houses, stock market dealers. This global network of private finance – made up of thousands of competing units – can, even in principle, only be controlled by the US monetary authorities who have some purchase on the cost and availability of Dollar credit. Increasingly, this network escapes effective control in practice by either the US authorities or those of other countries. In fact, the internationalisation of finance proved a major factor in the undermining of the previous regulatory system in the USA. New technology has furthered internationalisation by allowing rapid communication and transfers of funds among all the financial centres of the world.

The domestic financial sectors of European countries have been increasingly caught up in this internationalisation of Dollar-finance, which has eroded their previously powerful systems of national regulation and control. Traditionally, in Western Europe, banking and financial intermediation have been highly concentrated: a few large institutions have absorbed most liquid savings and assigned credit to various types of activity – industry, housing, agriculture, etc – while managing switches of funds between sectors. Competition has been oligopolistic – a question of rivalry for shares of the market, rather than direct pressure on the margins of the institutions involved. This type of structure has generally proved to be both stable – because disturbances did not spread rapidly across the whole system – and easily controlled – because a few large banks or other intermediaries at the top of the hierarchy could be co-ordinated directly and in turn exercised control over given sectors, regions or groups of customers.

The US financial system, with many more banks, had a much more competitive structure. It was controlled not through the concertation of a few large institutions but, on the one hand, by the short-term interest rates set by the central bank, on the other hand, by formal regulations embodied in law and enforced by inspection and supervision. As the US system expanded internationally this framework of regulation was becoming increasingly ineffective and the strongest political influences were pressing, not for a modernised regulatory structure but for a maximal deregulation. The result was an international financial environment, conditioned by unrestricted competition, which tended to undermine traditional European patterns of control. When more and more borrowers and lenders have access to international credit markets, the strength of national intermediaries is reduced because they can be bypassed. Where deregulation permits all credit institutions to operate in all financial markets, the partitions which separated particular types of finance are broken down. This is illustrated in British high streets by the intense rivalry between deposit banks and building societies both for deposits and mortgage business. In the past these institutions were functionally separate, but the separation depended on limits to the competition between them.

The broad trend in Europe is moving away from highly structured and closely regulated national credit systems, towards increasingly deregulated and competitive financial sectors closely interlinked through international credit markets. The changes have gone further in Britain, where governments have encouraged them, than in Germany, for example, where governments have put up more resistance, but the basic pattern can be seen everywhere.

The consequence has been to place heavier burdens on European industry and to obstruct the search for new forms of economic development. In periods of major structural change, money and finance take on a heightened significance and malfunctions in financial sectors are particularly damaging. When economies are growing rapidly, without the need for sudden structural change, a large number of activities will typically be self-financing: companies will finance much of their new investment out of retained profits. Economic upheavals and major structural adaptations tend to reverse the relative status of industry and finance: access to money and credit becomes the key to security and flexibility, while the value of productive assets – such as industrial plant – is insecure and difficult to assess. Thus periods of structural transition may be characterised by financial tensions – high interest rates and increased difficulty in securing adequate investment finance.

A strong financial system, almost by definition, is one which is able to lower such tensions and to sustain an adequate level of investment activity in periods of structural adaptation. A classic example is the steady flow of long-term industrial finance typically provided by the big German banks. Savers are reassured and encouraged to continue lending by the strength of the banks as an intermediary with industry, while industrial companies are shielded against a sudden collapse of their share prices and drying-up of credit. Similar strong financial institutions are regarded as having made a significant contribution to the industrial success of Japan.

Fragmented and uncontrolled financial systems are unable to ensure a continuing flow of investment finance, because individual agents have to respond to each switch in market conditions without being able to calculate the overall effect of their decisions. Bandwagon effects tend to predominate in the assessment of risks – any borrower denied accommodation by one lender tends to find it impossible to obtain finance; costs of credit rise because of the effort that goes into the search for financial security, rather than for advantageous investments. The financial sector, when faced with major uncertainties, absorbs an ever-bigger share of resources in disorganised, fragmented, intermediary activity which imposes heavy costs on the economy as a whole.

Recent economic history has given many examples of the instability and irresponsibility of disorganised private finance but the central example is obviously the crisis of international debt. In the 1970s, Western banks competed to lend, on very easy terms, to Latin American countries, whose creditworthiness to each lender was enhanced by their ability to borrow from all the others. With the drastic rise in interest rates at the beginning of the 1980s full repayment became impossible for the debtor countries. Private finance then threatened to dry up completely as each lender joined a scramble for individual safety, regardless of the fact that the overall consequence of such action would be to intensify pressure on the borrowers and make default inevitable, while crippling the trade of the debtor countries and thus blocking even partial repayment. Only continuous official intervention by central banks and international monetary institutions have contained the crisis through the 1980s, without beginning to resolve it. Meanwhile a decade of development has been sacrificed.

It should be emphasised that the argument here is not based on a demagogic condemnation of finance as such, or on a superstitious distrust of economic intermediaries. Merchants, bankers, brokers, in fact intermediaries of all kinds, including advertisers and sales representatives, play a necessary and therefore productive role in all modern economies and as the complexity of economic life increases the need for intermediation – for communication between interdependent production and consumption units – increases relative to the size of the economy. What are being criticised are primitive and ineffective structures of financial intermediation, which precisely do not ensure the continuity of economic interactions, as for example, when the debt crisis threatened to exclude Latin American countries from world trade.

The highly organised intermediaries which channel funds to German or Japanese industry perform the same functions more consistently and at lower cost than the competitive financial structures of the USA. German and Japanese industrial companies therefore borrow far more than their British and American counterparts (and also invest more). They are able to do so because the banks have a close and continuing relationship with their industrial clients, and are not simply competing to borrow and lend anonymously on financial markets. Industrial companies in Japan, unlike the USA, do not have to restrict their borrowing to avoid a sudden loss of credit-worthiness, or to provide against the possibility of financial crisis in which they would be unable to roll over their debt. Similarly Japanese banks have not had to restrict their lending through fear that their depositors might be enticed away to other institutions. Close, long-term relationships between banks and industry are an important advantage in industrial development; but such long-term relationships are not compatible with atomistic competition in the financial sector.

The global extension of US finance has tended to erode the more organised and effective national financial systems of Western Europe. Competitive pressures for short-term profitability have been increasing on European financial institutions. Their sources of funds have become more precarious as depositors have gained wider access to internationalised credit markets; their loans to industry or holdings of industrial equity have become more circumscribed by competitive forces and can no longer be so easily adapted to specific industrial circumstances.

The terms and conditions of international finance are today linked to the predominance of the Dollar. This is true, first of all, for interest rates: because the Dollar is the key medium for international investment and because other countries have to maintain the convertibility of their currencies into Dollars, US interest rates largely determine rates in other countries. The very easy US credit of the 1970s tended to generate inflation throughout the world, just as the astronomic US interest rates of 1980-2 precipitated a worldwide recession. But US influence is pervasive in all aspects of international finance: the world credit system is essentially the global projection of the US system and therefore, the only real control is the policy of the US monetary authorities who influence directly the conditions under which banks or other credit institutions dealing in Dollars have to operate. What, for example, will be considered an adequate ratio of reserves to liabilities for a bank? What procedures have to be observed in lending and borrowing? What are the rules for payment of tax on interest received by lenders? The predominance of the Dollar in world finance means that US financial practice tends to determine the norms which prevail worldwide. The US central bank, the Federal Reserve, is the only institution always able to refinance (in Dollars), banks which are short of funds: this power, of 'lender of last resort', gives it a central regulatory role in world finance. Increasingly, however, this has meant minimal and ineffective control: the old, Rooseveltian system of financial regulation in the USA has, partly because of internationalisation, lost its purchase on credit activity; powerful interests, sustained by the resurgence of free-market ideologies, have prevented its renewal.

Finance throughout the world has been increasingly deregulated, increasingly unstable, increasingly expensive and inefficient. The EMS has insulated one key area from the effects of this instability – namely the exchange rates between European currencies. This makes an important contribution to the stability of trade between the participating countries; at the same time, short-term interest rates have been more stable, and perhaps lower, than they would have been without the EMS. Despite that, the EMS still leaves European economies exposed to the kinds of disturbance illustrated by the stock market crash in 1987 or the continuing wave of speculative takeovers which disorient industrial activity on both sides of the Atlantic.

The Double Hegemony

The limitations which restrict the EMS to a purely defensive role can be discussed in terms of the ECU, the embryonic European monetary unit. Potentially the ECU could be the pivot of a European system of finance, displacing the Dollar over a wide area and challenging the anarchic credit markets which are associated with the Dollar's supremacy.

At present the ECU is primarily a unit of account, used to denominate the Community's revenues and expenditure although these are actually effected in national currencies. Within the EMS, ECUs are used to finance short-term loans for exchange market intervention, but only the intergovernmental transfers are made in ECUs – the intervention itself is usually in national currencies. ECUs also have a transaction role in the EC's borrowing and lending activity. Encouraged by this, and by the relative stability of the ECU compared with the Dollar, there has been growth in the private use of ECUs in international credit operations. Recently, however, the very success of the EMS has tended to limit the private use of ECUs – when the value of national currencies is stable, there is less advantage in using ECUs to guard against exchange rate fluctuations.

The undeveloped nature of the ECU as a monetary unit is illustrated by the complete separation between official and private circuits within which it is used. The ECUs officially issued to EMS governments, as foreign exchange reserves, by the monetary co-operation committee, FECOM, could not be subsequently used in a private credit transaction, since there is no market intervention in ECUs. Those which are used privately have to be assembled, by private agents, from the national currencies included in the ECU basket. The consequence of the separation is to deprive FECOM of any control over these private transactions and at the same time to deprive banks which deal in ECUs of the guarantees against instability which a national central bank provides for users of its domestic currency.

A more ironic indication of the present limits of the ECU is the way in which its market value vis-à-vis other currencies is calculated. To determine each day the exchange rates of the ECU the officials of FECOM telephone each capital city to obtain the value of the currencies in the ECU basket. The information they actually gather is the exchange rate of each currency against the US Dollar, because this is the most important exchange rate in most countries, and the one for which data is easiest to hand. So, even as a simple unit of account the ECU remains a shadow of its US rival.

The potential role that can be envisaged for the ECU would make it, by contrast, the exclusive international reserve asset held by all EC central banks, and the main reserve asset also for the central banks of countries whose trade is predominantly with the EC. Every full member of the strengthened EMS would maintain a fixed parity against the ECU and, as at present, it would be a collective decision which determined when a balance of payments deficit would be financed (by the issue of ECUs) and when it required adjustment by devaluation or otherwise. The objective would be to maintain steady pressure towards the adjustment of disequilibria, both deficits and surpluses, without either the unrestricted and ultimately inflationary finance of growing imbalances or the sudden, brutal refusal of accommodation which have marked the international payment system in recent years.

Associated with the official use of ECUs as foreign exchange reserves and for international settlements, extensive private use would be encouraged to finance international trade and investment within an ECU zone made up of the EC and closely associated countries. Growing private and public use of the

ECU would sustain each other – private agents would have confidence in a currency to which central banks pegged their national currencies and which was widely used and accepted by European governments. At the same time, the private use of ECUs and the existence of private ECU balances would give European authorities an important lever over financial conditions – by altering the terms on which banks could borrow and lend ECUs or refinance their existing ECU loans. As private dealing in ECUs widened the market, intervention by central banks to influence exchange rates would take place increasingly in ECUs, making it possible to restructure and stabilise the functioning of foreign exchange markets.

Just as with the existing Dollar-based system the public use and private acceptance of the ECU would be mutually supporting, but the balance between private and public control would swing back towards the latter. The basic strategy would be a sharp delineation of those financial operations which were guaranteed within the ECU system, and were clearly subject to effective regulation, from operations which carried no such public endorsement and therefore involved much higher degrees of risk for the private agents concerned. Whereas the gradual deregulation of Dollar-based finance has eroded public control by forcing European authorities to accept an ever wider range of financial practices and to allow a proliferating number of agents to participate in them, the ECU-based structure could promote the re-regulation of international finance. The existing, highly structured financial systems of West European countries, with small numbers of powerful banks in close contact with the authorities, would be the core of the private ECU-using network. Other financial institutions would be given public recognition, and allowed access to the central banks which issued ECUs, only if they accepted the same constraints on their methods of working.

One simple example of the kind of control needed is fiscal responsibility. Today competition among European and other financial centres has eroded the possibility of taxing returns on capital in a large number of cases. Whereas small savers, depositing their money within their own country, usually have their interest receipts taxed at source, large international loans usually escape such taxation: payment of interest on bonds or bank deposits without deducting tax is seen as necessary for the competitivity of each financial centre, in a deregulated environment where 'off-shore' financial centres, inside or outside Europe, can undermine those of the major countries. It is difficult to challenge this state of affairs while the dominant, Dollar-using, financial agents can operate freely through the Cayman Islands and so on. Even the German government has limited powers to enforce responsible practices: in response to French concern on the impact of financial liberalisation, the German government imposed a 'withholding' tax on international loans in 1989, but the impact on its financial sector was so negative, (with rapid outflows of capital) and the response of major German banks was so emphatic that the tax was removed within six months. The German banks, of course, were competing with banks in Britain and elsewhere which are not subject to any similar constraints. Concerted action within an ECU-based system could impose uniform and stringent fiscal obligations on financial intermediaries and undermine the use of tax-paradises for credit operations by depriving any such operation of legal recognition and public guarantee.

Private financial systems always do require public supervision – most obviously in crises such as the non-payment of Latin American debt, or the stock-market panic, where a public lender of last resort is called upon to prevent collapse. This type of public guarantee can be made the basis of effective public control over a strong financial system. In the USA such public control has been prevented, in recent years, by atomistic competition in the banking system, by the concern to avoid recession in the uncompetitive US economy and by the paralysis of public decision-making where political power is manipulated by private interests. The abuse of weakened monetary control has become flagrant in the USA – for example, private savings banks which are demonstrably insolvent have been able to continue borrowing funds for unrestricted speculation, because public bail-outs of failing banks can be taken for granted. The only effective lever of public control left is for the Federal Reserve to raise interest rates, but since any major increase in rates could trigger financial distress and widespread defaults in the fragile financial structure, it has become increasingly dangerous to use this instrument. Destabilising, inflationary credit expansion has therefore continued, accompanied by speculation of various kinds. And, given the primacy of US finance, the same situation tends to prevail everywhere, as there is a virtual power vacuum at the centre of international financial relations – an absence of any regulatory body and public control.

An ECU-based European financial structure, putting the giant banks of EC countries at the top of a hierarchy of credit institutions and giving them privileged access to central banks in return for taking on responsibility for stabilisation in specific sectors, could re-establish public control over a wide field. Fiscal responsibility – forcing big wealth-holders to pay tax on the interest they receive – is only one example. Other dimensions of public control would be to limit speculation against weak currencies, to stabilise stockmarket behaviour, to permit effective intervention in such situations as the house price explosion in Britain. In the early years of US economic hegemony, these types of control existed in the USA itself, but globalisation of US finance alongside US economic decline has made the restoration of social control incompatible with the continuing predominance of the Dollar.

A challenge to the Dollar is therefore necessary for the EMS to develop from a purely defensive arrangement towards a new, stable international framework for credit relations. This does not mean that the Dollar should be displaced as a world currency by the ECU: the objective of social control rather requires that ECUs circulate essentially within the EC and between the EC and its most closely associated trading partners. The intention is not to subject the USA to the same kind of domination as it has itself exercised in the past, but to ensure that US influence on international finance should cease to be unilateral. In this, as in other spheres, the advantage of European unity is to make possible a more equal dialogue with the USA, as a step towards a more pluralistic control over international relations, not to rival the USA as a superpower.

The unilateral exercise of financial power by the USA was demonstrated by the way in which other central banks automatically came to the aid of the Dollar in 1987. Between

1982 and 1985, very high US interest rates, imposed without consulting other countries, encouraged a worldwide wave of speculation in the Dollar, carrying its exchange rate to unprecedented and unsustainable levels against other currencies. Governments and central banks around the world struggled to limit the depreciation of their own currencies by increasing interest rates and holding back growth in their economies. As the wave broke and private wealth-holders fled from the Dollar, the same central banks came to the rescue, absorbing over 100 billion unwanted and depreciating Dollars into their foreign exchange reserves in 1987 alone. In the most direct way, the tax-payers of Germany, Japan and Britain limited the losses which would otherwise have faced private holders of Dollars by assuming some of these losses themselves. This action by other countries eased the pressure on the Federal Reserve System of the USA when it was trying to cope with the aftermath of the Wall Street Crash.

It was the status of the Dollar as the major international reserve currency which permitted, even required, such a response to US difficulties. In fact, it is almost an automatic rule of sound central banking to buy Dollars in this way when their price falls simply because Dollars are the key medium of international investment. The extent of the privilege involved can be measured against the treatment which other countries could expect in such a situation – the treatment of third-world debtors, for example, who could expect drastic austerity measures to be imposed by the International Monetary Fund, in return for very limited accommodation. And, indeed, the USA recognises no reciprocal obligation to defend other currencies in an emergency.

The move towards more reciprocity in international money and credit could be effectively promoted by the development of the EMS as described, transforming the ECU into a major reserve asset. Opposition to closer monetary co-operation has come from Britain, but it has been West Germany which has most consistently blocked the development of the ECU because it would necessarily mean some loss of its existing monetary power. The original agreement establishing the EMS provided for an 'institutional phase' to follow the introduction of the exchange rate mechanism. A European Monetary Fund (EMF) was to take over a substantial part of the gold and Dollar reserves of member central banks, issuing ECUs in return. A hierarchy of responsibilities would then emerge: the supranational EMF would conduct the external policy of the system, deciding for example when to buy or sell Dollars against the ECU. National central banks would manage the relation between their own currencies and the ECU, by constraining domestic monetary policies in order to preserve the given parities. The EMF would finance national balance of payments disequilibria in ECUs when the central bank concerned was unable to do so, or would signal the need for a collective adjustment of parities if devaluation seemed necessary. In external negotiations the EMF would represent Western Europe in the reconstruction of the world payments system. (Such a united representation could, for example, give real force to the demand for a cancellation of third-world debt, at present expressed by France.) The detailed content of such a reform is not relevant here but its general aim would be a reassertion of social control over international credit relations. The Dollar would no doubt have a major role in any reformed system, but the power of the US monetary authorities – at present unilateral – would be balanced by explicit responsibilities towards other countries. Reciprocal constraints would be placed on the EMF itself and on other participants.

Of course the Europeans only have an effective negotiating position for a change in rules if they are not prepared to accept the existing rules indefinitely. For example, European interest rates would not be increased to follow a rise in US rates, unless the tightening of US policy were considered internationally responsible; similarly, the EMF would not unconditionally absorb the excess Dollars produced by US inflation. This declaration of European monetary autonomy might, initially, involve wider swings of the European currencies against the Dollar, but the new constraints on US freedom of action would tend to limit such swings. The pressures arising from fluctuations of the Dollar would be distributed in a different way. Provided the European system acted together there would be as much danger to private agents in finding themselves short of ECUs as of Dollars, in contrast to the existing state of affairs where wealth denominated in Dollars is regarded as more secure. The institutional phase – the move to a EMF – involves not only a further internal consolidation of the EMS; for the first time it would also give the system an effective *external* policy, able to constrain US policy and thus to negotiate a reform of international payments.

The repeated refusals of the West German government have been responsible for blocking advance to the institutional phase of the EMS. Since the fall of the Social Democrats in 1982 Germany has had a conservative government which takes a somewhat sceptical view of European construction and puts a very high priority on fighting inflation. A transfer of monetary powers to Community institutions is seen as a sacrifice by Germany for which there would be no concrete return, and which might well put price stability at risk if the political forces controlling the issue of ECUs were tempted to expand credit. However, without a strong central institution, the EMS is left in the absurd position of being a purely internal agreement. Full consultation and general agreement is required to change the values of participating currencies relative to each other and to the ECU, but neither individually nor collectively do the member states have any influence over the value of the ECU in terms of Dollars. There has been no centralisation of gold and Dollar reserves such as would be necessary for a supranational European monetary authority.

The FECOM, which manages the present arrangements, holds twenty per cent of members' reserves and issues ECUs against them, but this does not give it any effective control as it holds the reserves only as a short-term loan. In fact, the FECOM only acts as a channel of communication among national central banks. In principle each of these central banks is free to pursue whatever policy it sees fit against the Dollar, with the consequent value of the ECU being the sum of all the independent actions. In practice, the vacuum in external monetary policy is filled by Germany hegemony. The Bundesbank is the only European central bank with enough power to move the whole set of EMS currencies vis-à-vis the Dollar. Other countries simply have to accept the Dollar exchange rates for their own currencies which are implied by, on the one hand, the internationally agreed rates against the ECU and on the other hand, the Deutschmark rate against the

Dollar, over which they do not even have a right of consultation. Technically, the divergence indicator should prevent Germany from following a completely idiosyncratic policy, but in practice it is not an effective constraint on the enormously powerful German monetary institutions.

The incomplete construction of the EMS has left it as, essentially, a Deutschmark zone, with minor modifications. Conservatively managed and preoccupied with internal equilibrium, the Bundesbank has blocked the emergence of EMS institutions which might impose real limits on its freedom of action. At the same time Germany has obstructed the private use of ECUs in its banking system by treating them as a foreign currency, effectively holding back European monetary co-operation in the private sector also.

The result of these narrow and conservative strategies in Germany is that the monetary policy of other countries participating in the EMS is subjected to a double hegemony. Directly, their foreign exchange policies are controlled by Germany, the only EMS member with real purchase on Dollar exchange rates; but the immobilism and minimalism of German policy itself, content with an island of exchange rate stability while otherwise accepting existing international arrangements, leaves Europe exposed at the same time to all the turbulence and disorientation produced by the ungovernable networks of US finance, whose global extension continues to erode social control over credit and, therefore, over investment.

British Sovereignty?

Germany policy, of course, is not the only obstacle to the further development of the European Monetary System. There are signs in the context of the 1992 programme and the impulse it has given to institutional change in the Community, that German immobilism is weakening and that the Bundesbank is now ready to contemplate a move forward in return for guarantees of substantial influence within the structure which would emerge. Certainly Germany would never agree to abdicate its monetary dominance in favour of an inflationary coalition of south European debtor countries – a real collective commitment to contain inflation will be a necessary condition for institutional progress. However, there may be growing German impatience with the international status quo which assigns it the thankless task of compensating for a series of US policy adventures – putting it under pressure to inflate or deflate its national economy in order to preserve the freedom of manoeuvre enjoyed by the USA. Meanwhile, the election of George Bush suggests that there is as yet no political commitment to financial stabilisation in the USA: an obvious condition for stability is some correction of the Federal Government deficit, but conservative political forces, expressing the interests of privileged sections of US society, continue to resist the necessary increases in taxation. Because of its leading role in relation to the Dollar, Germany therefore has good reasons to put the qualitative development of the EMS back on the agenda.

In this context, Britain, which has never participated in the EMS exchange rate system, is more than ever the major obstacle to European monetary co-operation. At one level the issue is national sovereignty and Mrs Thatcher's resistance to the supranational aspects of the EC, but the internationalisation of financial relations seems to have already deprived Britain of any real autonomy in monetary questions. Britain has certainly conducted an independent exchange rate policy, but at the cost of interest rates which are consistently higher in real terms than those of Western Europe, and it is still without any real ability to resist either appreciation or depreciation of Sterling on the international currency markets. In fact Britain's inflation rate has been rather higher than those in other West European countries, in spite of a more restrictive monetary policy. More seriously, the economic mismanagement of Conservative governments has resulted in an unprecedented balance of payments deficit. This cannot be financed indefinitely, even at extremely high interest rates: sooner rather than later a massive correction of our foreign trade will be required. It is difficult to see how such an adjustment can be accomplished without a substantial depreciation of Sterling and the inflation which that will involve. As so often in the past, the pursuit of a strong currency without measures to strengthen the economy has proved to be self-defeating.

Besides the mirage of sovereignty there is also an alarming conflict of interest which tends to oppose Britain to the whole project of European monetary union. As argued above, the central value of this project is the prospect it offers of countering the turbulence and inefficiency of the present, inadequately controlled structures of international finance. Britain in recent years has been increasingly committed to the pursuit of its national advantage within these same structures. Britain's historic specialisation in international finance and the traditional role of the City were substantially reinforced in the 1980s, even at the expense of other sectors of the national economy. Rapid financial deregulation, the abolition of exchange controls, the big bang which opened the London Stock Exchange to foreign dealers, were all aimed at making London a competitive location for international financial transactions, even when this has meant inappropriate financial conditions for British industry – very high interest rates, or an over-valued exchange rate. Banking, insurance and finance were by far the most dynamic sectors of the British economy in the 1980s – enjoying the lion's share of economic growth and being easily the most important source of new employment.

Britain in fact has adopted a pattern of international specialisation which gives it an interest in the perpetuation of existing financial conditions in the world economy – in the multiplication of transactions and forms of credit to protect against, or to take advantage of, financial instability; in high interest rates and other credit costs which divert resources to the financial sector; in the increasing mobility of funds which undermines stable long-term relationships between financial institutions and industrial companies. These may all be malfunctions from the point of view of the economy as a whole, but banks and other intermediaries can benefit enormously from such malfunctions and the financial sector of the British economy – deregulated and heavily involved in international transactions – has benefited more than most. Strong private interests in Britain will tend to oppose any development of the European monetary system which imposes new restrictions on financial activity, and in any conflict between the EC and the USA the same interests will be aligned with US positions assuming that these favour continuing deregulation and greater mobility of private wealth. The potential opposition between Britain's traditional Atlanticism and the whole European project is particularly clear in the field of finance where Britain's influence has already been used to promote financial liberalisation without any accompanying attempts at control.

Financial Liberalisation in the Community

The 1992 programme has posed a clear challenge to the existing monetary arrangements within the European Community. The big European market threatens the degree of monetary stabilisation which has already been achieved within the EMS through the release of private financial forces which could weaken or even destroy its exchange rate mechanism. Notably, the financial items in the 1992 agenda have been settled more quickly than any of the others: decisions already taken will rapidly establish full mobility of capital within the Community and allow banks and other intermediaries to operate freely in all member states. Agreement on liberalisation has run far ahead of any well-defined projects for control of the emerging, integrated, financial space. As a result economic policies within the Community may be even more tightly constrained.

Discussion of European monetary questions frequently refers to a well-known 'impossibility theorem'. The theorem demonstrates that the following three things are in principle incompatible: fixed exchange rates among a set of national currencies; independent monetary policies in the countries concerned; and full mobility of capital between one and another of the countries. The logic of the theorem is straightforward: with full mobility, capital will always flow from a country with lower interest rates to one with higher rates – unless there is a risk of exchange rate movements. Thus, with completely fixed exchange rates, a differential in interest rates will be unsustainable as the country with lower rates will undergo an unlimited outflow of funds. Eventually one of the three things will have to give way – the exchange rate, the difference in policy, or the freedom of capital movements.

The reasoning is not just an exercise in theory, but has

important practical applications. It offers, for example, one way of looking at the break-up of the Bretton Woods system which governed international payments for 25 years after the Second World War. In the 1950s only two of the three elements existed, namely fixed exchange rates and independent monetary policies. International capital movements were subject to strict control and dominated by intergovernmental flows. The emergence of huge international credit markets in the 1960s made the Bretton Woods system inconsistent by generating unmanageable flows of private capital between currencies.

The same logic can demonstrate the precarious nature of the existing EMS, which does combine the three incompatible characteristics but not in such a pure form as to make the logic of the theorem directly applicable. Exchange rates are only fixed within generous margins of fluctuation and only in the short run, with parities being adjusted every year or so. Consequently the corresponding restrictions on monetary policy are far from total. There are also many countries which still control movements of capital into other currencies.

In terms of the theorem the exchange rate situation in the Community could be characterised as follows. Britain and Germany have independent monetary policies and allow free entry and exit of capital, but they do not have a fixed exchange rate. A group of small, rich, north European countries have free capital movement and fixed exchange rates against the Deutschmark, but accept tight constraints on their monetary policy. This is most clearly the case for the Netherlands, which normally adopts the interest rates prevailing in Germany but it also applies to Denmark, Belgium and Luxembourg (although these last two have some residual capital movement restrictions). There are then a group of weaker, mainly southern economies which maintain some significant controls on capital flows and either do not participate in the EMS exchange rate mechanism (Greece, Portugal) or do so with wider margins of fluctuation (Spain, Italy), thus preserving scope for divergent monetary policies. France in recent years has changed its relationship to the system: a large number of its previously comprehensive restrictions on capital movements have been removed; correspondingly French monetary policy is now much more aligned with German performance. In the early 1980s the French could defend the Franc by very high interest rates for foreign depositors while trying to encourage economic expansion with low internal interest rates. This kind of option has disappeared and if the Franc-Deutschmark rate came under pressure today, interest rates would have to rise in France itself. The future of the EMS depends to a large extent on whether, in these circumstances, the French will seek to stabilise the Franc-Deutschmark rate over a long period of time or whether they will use repeated and frequent devaluations to make possible somewhat less constrained internal policies.

A key aspect of the market completion programme is the complete liberalisation of private capital movements within the Community. More or less complete freedom already existed for less liquid, longer-term investments, such as the freedom for short-term liquid placements in the form of bank deposits in other countries. Associated with this freedom to move money is the necessary removal of exchange controls by the same date, with the weaker, southern economies and Ireland permitted a derogation until the end of 1992. One result will be to extend the number of agents who will be able to move wealth easily across national frontiers in the Community. In the past there cannot have been too much difficulty for big companies or very rich individuals, but now small companies and the merely prosperous will enjoy the same facility.

Important safeguard clauses have existed since the foundation of the Community which permit countries with severe balance of payments difficulties or extremely disturbed capital markets to impose temporary restrictions on foreign exchange. This possibility will continue to exist, but the use of such controls will be subject to the agreement of the Council of Ministers. At the same time the EC has stronger powers to offer medium-term loans to countries suffering balance of payments problems in the new regime. These provisions suggest that determined efforts will be made to hold member countries to the discipline of free capital movements.

Financial liberalisation in the Community is being extended in two other ways. Banks will be free to set up subsidiaries in other member countries without having to obtain separate permission from their banking authorities or satisfy a second set of regulations, as is the case at present. Following the standard procedures of the 1992 programme, the EC is not requiring harmonisation of bank regulations before this measure takes effect: instead there will be mutual recognition of the various regulatory structures, together with an equalisation of some basic conditions imposed on banks, such as the reserves they have to hold against their liabilities. As in other spheres, this procedure amounts to a *deregulation* of banking: in particular, it will tend to require the dismantling of controls on the highly regulated and closely supervised French banking system. The increased freedom to move money between countries will be complemented by a new possibility for private financial institutions to operate throughout the EC. The practical restrictions involved in having to use a French bank for financial transactions in France, an Italian bank in Italy and so on, will be removed.

Finally, the 1992 programme will liberalise the supply of specialised financial services within the Community – insurance, brokerage, investment advice and so on will be subject to greater competition. The conditions under which specialists will be able to offer services in other countries, and will have access to particular financial markets, are still subject to debate, though as usual it is the British government which is pressing for maximum deregulation.

The 1992 programme therefore liberalises both capital movements *between* countries and the organisation of credit and banking *within* each country. No corresponding development of control or supervision at Community level is yet envisaged. There is still no agreement, for instance, on the simple question of taxing interest payments. Unanimity in the Council of Ministers will be required to adopt taxation procedures and Britain, together with tax-paradise Luxembourg, will try to block any rigorous or comprehensive supervision of international loans.

The general liberalisation includes, as a practical necessity, increased freedom for US, Japanese and other external banks and finance companies to operate throughout the Community. France wished to tie wider scope for outside banks operating inside the EC to reciprocal concessions for EC banks in the USA, Japan and others. There was no support for such conditions from other member countries and, in practice, it would be difficult and complicated to deny facilities to US banks which are enjoyed by British banks. In the absence of strong Community-wide financial controls on all banks operating inside the Community, the EC's financial structures will therefore be even more influenced by the deregulated competition characteristic of US finance. Financial agents established in Britain, for example, where public control is minimal, will have much greater freedom of manoeuvre *throughout* the EC.

One serious implication of this liberalisation is that the 'impossibility theorem' may become more directly applicable to the functioning of the EMS. Any tension in the system will now risk provoking much larger and more rapid speculative flows, out of countries which are trying to relax credit or which are threatened by devaluation towards higher interest rates and currencies likely to be revalued. Financial liberalisation, in fact, threatens monetary integration by making the EMS parities more vulnerable to attack and harder to defend. The possibility exists of a forced retreat towards monetary disintegration if either EMS currencies cannot be maintained within the agreed margins, or parity changes become increasingly frequent. The continued non-participation of Britain, whose weight as a financial centre may be increased by liberalisation, would tend to make such an outcome more likely.

The Delors Committee

If the countries participating in the EMS are to maintain stable exchange rates while dismantling controls on capital mobility, then they will have to abandon the other characteristic of the impossible combination, namely independent monetary policies. In that case, the natural response to the integration of private finance would be to develop a single, integrated, monetary policy and to move the Community closer to the use of a common currency. The general logic of this proposition is not in disupte, but what the content of the integrated policy should be and by which path it should be approached remain open questions. In particular, monetary/financial integration involves new constraints on the weaker, southern economies of the EC which have up to now operated foreign exchange controls. What compensation will these countries be offered for accepting more stringent monetary disciplines? Given the importance of the Mediterranean basin to economic development in the whole of Western Europe, this is a key question not just of monetary policy, but of economic policy as a whole.

Exploiting the dynamic of the 1992 programme, the Commission has launched a new initiative towards monetary union, through the report of a committee chaired by the Commission President himself, Jacques Delors. On the basis of the report a new attempt is being made to build unified monetary institutions in the Community. However, the report proposed a very difficult path towards monetary unification without offering substantially greater prospects of social control over credit and finance. The ideas of the Delors Committee to a large extent continue the neo-liberal line of policy which has dominated European construction in the last decade.

The report envisages a transition from the present EMS to full monetary integration in three stages. In the first stage there would be no institutional changes but monetary co-ordination among member states would be closer and more continuous than at present. Britain would participate in the exchange rate mechanism, and all countries would accept more persistent constraints on their economic policy in order to stabilise exchange rates over longer time periods. Until now, if there has been a conflict between the given exchange rates and broad economic policies, the latter have prevailed in the medium term, with the parities being changed to accommodate policy divergence. Although parities would still be changeable in the first stage envisaged in the report, it would more often be economic policies which would be required to adapt. The second and third stages would be based on a new treaty which would transform the existing national central banks into the components of a European System of Central Banks (based loosely on the US Federal Reserve System) and transfer monetary sovereignty from member states to the Community. The second stage, based on full achievement of the 1992 programme, would use parity changes only as a last resort and give the Council of Ministers the right to recommend changes in national government budgets. In the final stage, parities would be fixed irrevocably so that there would essentially be monetary unity, eventually expressed by a single currency. The European Central Bank System would manage the Dollar and other external reserves of the monetary union and the Council of the European Central Banks would decide on a common monetary policy to be operated jointly by all its national components. At the same time the EC Council of Ministers would have effective power to limit the budget deficits of national governments. Effective economic unity would be a precondition for the final stage via the integration of national markets.

Although the Delors Committee may have broken the stalemate in European monetary co-operation, there are several problems with the agenda proposed, which is basically inspired by free-market doctrine. In a somewhat schematic way one can distinguish two views on the role of the central bank in a modern economy. The first view would be that the central bank is one of the instruments of economic policy and should manage the credit system in accordance with the priorities of the government's general economic strategy. This view would be consistent with an interventionist approach to the economy and with the objective of public control over private agents. The second, opposed view of central banking (more in accordance with neo-liberal positions) is that the central bank is not an instrument *of* government but a control *on* government, with a responsibility for avoiding the inflationary finance of government deficits. According to this free-market view, the main danger to financial stability is not the activities of market agents but the workings of elected government, which make necessary an independent check on public spending.

Now it is very much this second view of central banking which prevails in the report of the Delors Committee. The Council of the proposed central banking system would enjoy a great deal of political independence. Its position vis-à-vis national governments would be reinforced by the requirement that they give up not merely monetary sovereignty, but also budgetary autonomy – despite the fact that this is not strictly necessary for monetary unification. The Council would also be able to act as a check on spending at Community level which, the report recognises, would have to be at a higher level than present in order to give more weight to EC economic policy.

Finally, the report takes a view of the process of monetary unification which minimises the use of monetary power to control private credit and finance. A long-standing discussion in the Community has concerned the 'chicken-and-egg' issue of which comes first – economic integration or monetary integration. The report comes down heavily in favour of putting economic integration first: the completion of the 1992 programme is made a pre-condition for the second stage of monetary co-operation; and effective market integration, the desired result of 1992, is a pre-condition of the third phase. National governments will have to accept full integration of their private financial sectors into EC-wide and, in practice, global financial networks, with a corresponding loss of public control, *before* any Community banking institution starts to operate in a way which might constrain the workings of private finance.

The political costs of this kind of agenda could be very high for weaker EC countries. A leap towards a single monetary policy would be made particularly difficult by the absence of effective compensation – in the form of either a strong EC budget to operate fiscal transfers to weak economies, or a European central bank to balance the interests of debtors and creditors, since these would only emerge after policy had converged. The link between money and credit policy and the whole process of economic and social negotiation would mean enormous strains on the latter. It should be remembered that the EMS up to now has essentially worked as a short-term stabiliser: when a serious conflict arose over the medium term between a member country's exchange rate and the direction of its other economic policies it has been the exchange rate which gave way. The 1980s have in fact seen some degree of convergence of medium-term monetary policies, simply due to the pressure of external constraints and this will perhaps continue if these constraints tighten, but the limited convergence of interest rates and inflation rates so far achieved is a long way from the full alignment of national policy stances envisaged in the report. If such an alignment proves too difficult, then the process of financial liberalisation could still threaten the existing EMS.

Every monetary system is a combination of private and social elements, since money is tied both to private exchange transactions and to a necessary agency for overall social control. But the balance between these elements is variable, especially during a phase of internationalisation where private transactions and regulatory mechanisms are moving away from the nation state. The Delors Committee consistently minimises the elements of social control and widens the scope of private decision-making, even to the extent of putting tight limits on the political power of elected authorities.

It is typical of the report that it does not put much emphasis on the role of the ECU, beyond arguing that existing restrictions on the private use of ECUs should be removed. This tends to close off one possible path of development for the EMS which would put the social dimension of monetary systems to the fore: international use of the ECU could be encouraged, challenging the decadent hegemony of the Dollar within and around Europe. The first consequence would be to ease the constraints on national economic policies, not by reversing internationalisation, but by transforming the international financial environment in the direction of greater stability. Instead of being compelled to respond to violent swings in US interest rates and financial markets, member states would finance their foreign exchange needs in ECUs, issued by the European Central Bank in accordance with European priorities. Private capital flows would be less destabilising because European private credit markets would use the ECU as a medium and would be subject to close regulatory supervision developing out of the stable and highly organised national credit systems of France and Germany today. Attempts to bypass or undermine this regulation through the use of Dollar-denominated financial instruments would be extremely dangerous for the agents involved as creditors would be deprived of the guarantees attached to ECU-assets. Agents would also have to assume, for the first time, a serious exchange rate risk because European central banks would no longer automatically shield the Dollar from the consequence of inflationary credit policies. Internationalisation of European monetary systems would continue because the ECU would be a recognised parallel currency and its use inside each member state would be gradually extended, displacing national currencies. This gradual process would be compensated by the growth of European institutions, and would permit exchange rate depreciations by hard-pressed governments during the transition.

The Delors Committee did not work in a political context which would have enabled it to adopt ambitious perspectives. Its thinking was conservative, both because it was composed of the heads of central banks, and because its aim was to push Germany and Britain into accepting some institutional change rather than perpetuating the existing stalemate of monetary integration. As a result, its recommendations essentially extend the free-market policy orientation of recent years: political change in these two countries will probably be necessary for a more extensive approach to monetary co-operation to become a political possibility.

The Need for Stability

The economic malaise of West European countries is not the result of financial or monetary disorders. In fact the main line of causation runs the other way – it was the emergence of serious obstacles to the established path of economic growth (problems of productivity, a general squeeze on profits) which seem to have provoked inflation and other forms of financial disturbance. This makes it unrealistic to expect that reforms of money and banking would, in themselves, resolve the crisis of unemployment or restore economic advance.

Nevertheless the performance of financial sectors does seem to have aggravated Europe's difficulties in two important ways. The first is through volatility – the wide, often dramatic fluctuations that have characterised all financial markets and all forms of credit. The most serious example is the boom and bust in Latin American debt, which has impeded the process of economic development in Latin America, as elsewhere in the third world, while weakening the whole system of international credit. Huge swings in exchange rates are another important case: it is probable that these fluctuations have seriously obstructed international trade and investment flows. The absurd stock-market follies of 1987 are the most dramatic example, although not, in the event, as damaging as was feared. The speculation and inflationary credit expansion linked to the wave of takeovers and mergers on the stock exchange may turn out to be more costly. The second major malfunction is very high credit costs – real interest rates have now been at historically high levels for a decade. Their consequence is to discourage, in particular, long-term investment activity while leading to an adverse shift in the distribution of income.

In both cases – volatility and high interest rates – it does in fact seem to be a matter of financial malfunction rather than the simple reflection within the financial sector of problems arising elsewhere, because there is no good non-financial explanation for either phenomenon. Economic life in general has certainly not been easy to predict in recent years, but there is no real economic justification for fluctuations as violent as those observed in exchange rates, for example, or in stock-market prices. Nor is there a good non-financial explanation for continuously high interest rates: the supply of loanable resources has been abundant and, while demand has been increased by the US government deficit, interest rates rose well before President Reagan's spending spree. So the evidence points to internal problems of the financial sector which has become increasingly unruly through deregulation and internationalisation.

Although more stable and less costly credit and finance would not by themselves regenerate West European economies, they are a necessary condition for regeneration because, without them, economic agents will not be able to plan for structural change over longer time-horizons. The present preoccupation with short-term developments, whether opportunistic or defensive in nature, will continue unless there is reform.

The necessary reform of financial systems, however, has to respond to a profound internationalisation of financial relations which has undermined previously effective systems of public control and there does not seem to be any way of getting the genie back into the bottle by restoring these obsolete national control mechanisms. It is in this context that the EMS takes on its full significance as a collective exercise in international financial stabilisation which has already achieved a recognised success. So far, however, the EMS is a purely defensive arrangement and it is endangered by the extensive further liberalisation of private finance included in the 1992 programme. Further development of the EMS – hardly conceivable without full British participation – requires, firstly, a much stronger institutional framework, that is, a European Central Bank with supranational powers; and, secondly, a coherent external policy, that is, a well defined and united bargaining position vis-à-vis the USA. Although the Delors initiative has opened up some scope for monetary advance in the Community, it has by no means produced an adequate response to the internationalisation of credit which continues to erode the effectiveness of national monetary policies without, as yet, a real prospect of renewed social control at an international level.

Further Reading

See the Committee for the Study of Economic and Monetary Union, *Report on Economic and Monetary Union in the European Community* ('Delors Report'), Luxembourg 1989; M. Aglietta et al., *International Money and Financial Integration: the European Dimension*, Kluwer, Boston (Mass.) 1989; M. de Cecco and A. Giovannini (eds), *A European Central Bank?*, CUP, Cambridge 1989; R. Masera and R. Triffin (eds), *Europe's Money*, Clarendon Press, Oxford 1984.

4 EC Industrial Policy and 1992

Most accounts of the 1992 programme present it as above all a strategy for enterprise. It is claimed that the programme will produce benefits for consumers and increases in employment, and these gains have even been quantified in a very speculative way. In the first instance, the tangible advantages of the programme will accrue to those companies which are actually or potentially engaged in business activities across national frontiers in the Community. For such companies one can point to clear benefits – lower transport costs, reduced administrative formalities, wider access to both private customers and public purchasers, greater ease of establishment for branches in other member countries. The 1992 programme has been sold primarily as a programme for business, and it is its response to the current cult of the business enterprise that has produced its remarkable political and public relations success.

The relationship between these advantages for the corporate sector (or part of it – some companies will lose from the programme, particularly local enterprises without international links which are exposed to more intense competition) and the wider project of European construction is not, however, as straightforward as the usual presentations of the programme assume. In the official accounts, the benefits to business from 1992 will contribute to the competitiveness of European industry vis-à-vis its great rivals in Japan and the USA. From the official point of view, market completion is basically consistent with the other main theme of EC policy towards industry, that is the construction of a

European technological community. This reinforces and interconnects West European R&D and is seen as the other major method of strengthening European companies against the global challenge of US and Japanese industry.

A logical weakness of this stress on European competitiveness is that it presupposes the survival of clear lines of demarcation between the industrial spaces of the rivals concerned: to promote the competitiveness of European as opposed to US industry it is first of all necessary to identify the former and distinguish it from the latter. The 1992 programme will inevitably tend to have the opposite effect – at the same time as it removes partitions between national industrial spaces within Western Europe, it will accelerate the wider process of economic internationalisation, in particular by a further assimilation of the industrial spaces of Europe and the USA. Far from reinforcing existing EC industrial strategies, centred on European competitiveness, the 1992 programme is radically inconsistent with them because the only real specificity of Europe as an industrial region was, in practice, its division into distinct national spaces – which the 1992 programme is designed to eliminate.

Growing concern about this aspect of 1992 has provoked a discussion of a European 'identity' because an identifiable European industry is increasingly seen as being compromised by the globalisation of economic relations. The 1992 programme seems particularly to undermine the Community's industrial identity since it promotes European unification by methods that actually advance this process of globalisation.

It will be argued in this chapter that a European industrial identity cannot be brought about as a well-defined system of enterprises with close and continuing links to the territory of the EC. As a result a coherent industrial strategy must begin by rejecting the uncritical reinforcement of the business sector, which is the common element of all the present policies. What is required is an enrichment of the objectives of industrial strategy, so that it is aimed at more than the promotion of an increasingly meaningless 'competitiveness' in relation to external forces: instead the criteria for industrial intervention should be internal, designed to promote industrial structures in accordance with the Community's social and cultural development. This should be accompanied by a greater economy of means, so that business enterprises only receive public support when they make a tangible contribution to public objectives, in particular to closing the huge gaps in economic development and industrial culture between the different regions of the EC.

The Industrial Policies of the Community

Industrial policy at EC level has gone through several phases, characterised by very different types of policy action and justified by very different, even opposed, arguments. But there is a clear connecting theme which runs through all the phases – the overriding political objective of integration. The Commission has always formulated policies in the light of this central political project, to which specifically industrial objectives have been subordinated. This is only to be expected, given the political role of the Commission, but it does mean that the industrial rationale which is offered for various EC policies needs to be critically assessed in order to extract a political logic which is not often made explicit. The same, of course, is true for all the initiatives and activities of the EC: their economic content has always been seen by the Community's leaders as a means towards the political goal of a united Europe – a means which has been employed because a more direct political approach was blocked. The success of the Community and its repeated development at the expense of national sovereignties, has owed a great deal to the strength of the economic interests it has brought about in this way.

Nevertheless, this use of economic interests to sustain the political project of integration is limited by the fact that the two processes involved have a different logic: the growth of economic interdependence among EC countries is part of a global trend towards internationalisation which by no means respects the geographical boundaries implicit in European political integration. This contradiction, although present from the beginning of the EC, was latent for a long time because the early stages of economic internationalisation and of political integration reinforced each other: the exceptionally rapid growth of the West European economies meant that trade between EC members grew much faster than trade with non-European countries, so that economic internationalisation was centred on Europe. With the end of the long boom, however, Western Europe ceased to be the most dynamic region of the world economy.

This is without doubt a definitive change: a strong resumption of economic advance in the EC is possible, but it is neither likely, nor indeed desirable, that north-west Europe should grow as fast as other regions. Lower-income countries with expanding populations can provide more scope for high rates of investment and have more need for a rapid growth of output. The rich, congested industrial areas of the EC have less need of *quantitative* growth and require more *qualitative* development of their existing productive systems. This slow-down in the growth of output, however, does not alter the trend towards a greater internationalisation of economic life: the continuing strength of this trend is illustrated by the fact that world trade has continued to grow fast even during the economic troubles of the past two decades.

As a result, there is now a clear disjunction between the growth of economic interdependence on a global scale and the construction of a specifically European entity, whose outlines now seem to be dissolving in a process of 'dilution' – exactly analogous to the process which is dissolving national economies as distinct entities. The dilution of the EC economy can proceed even more rapidly than that of national economies because, unlike the latter, it has little real, social or historical identity but is a recent, institutional creation. In this new context the contradiction between economic internationalisation and European political integration becomes quite manifest, producing major problems in the Community's industrial strategy.

The earliest industrial policies of the EC, those associated with the European Coal and Steel Community (ECSC), were interventionist and *dirigiste* – at the time of the Treaty of Paris, memories of the great depression were still sharp and economic planning enjoyed a prestige it has since lost. In addition to this, there was particular suspicion of the steel and coal corporations because of their role in the events leading to war. Ironically, the very far-reaching powers which the Treaty gave the Community to intervene in the coal and steel industries were unused for almost 30 years. In the 1950s, the surprising strength of the EC economies prevented the anticipated crisis in European steel and it was not until 1979, at the end of the spectacular European investment boom, that the Commission invoked its ECSC powers to fix prices and production levels in the steel industry.

The social content of the ECSC was also a sign of the time, which emphasised, to an extent never subsequently equalled, the claims of those who lost out in the integration process. Since it was clear that the introduction of common prices for coal and steel could undermine producers in high-cost districts (Belgian coal mines in particular) specific and well funded social measures to compensate and retrain displaced workers were an integral part of the industrial strategy. The contrast with subsequent policies, and above all with the 1992 programme which was driven through before, and possibly even without, accompanying social policies, could not be more marked.

Nevertheless, the economic procedures of the ECSC were of secondary importance to the founders of the Community: the key question was the political objective – namely to resolve the vexed question of German heavy industry, via an internationalisation of control. In the event, the economic and political sides of the project were mutually reinforcing – the boom in European manufacturing produced such a buoyant demand for steel that the hastily designed institutions of the Coal and Steel Community proved a great success. The dynamic of the West European economy thus triumphantly vindicated the political initiatives of the European federalists – a pattern that would be repeated for the following 25 years.

In contrast to the *dirigiste* ECSC, active industrial strategy was virtually absent from the Treaty of Rome, setting up the European Economic Community (EEC), which seemed rather to endorse a free-market approach to industry; industrial strategy virtually disappeared from the Community's agenda until the 1970s. The reason for its reappearance was, once again, the primacy of political over economic considerations in the work of European construction. German negotiators certainly tended to resist economic intervention in the name of their national government (which was committed, at least in principle, to a free-market economy), but more important than the economic doctrines of the Germans was the fact that the question of economic mechanisms hardly arose. This was because, at the time, trade between European countries was relatively marginal to their economic life. No contradiction was perceived then, for instance, between French indicative planning and the free exchange embodied in the EEC, because European trade did not seem important enough to threaten the character of national economies. The competition rules written into the Treaty of Rome are less an expression of economic liberalism than of political federalism – their aim was not to maximise economic efficiency but to outlaw discrimination between economic agents of different nationality. In other words, the competition rules, which were the main component of the EC's approach to industry for the next fifteen years were essentially an attack on *nationally* organised restrictive practices rather than an assault on departures from the norm of competition as such. This is illustrated by the frequently noted contrast between a tough approach to price-fixing and other restrictive practices between enterprises (Article 85 of the Treaty) and the more lenient view taken of dominance by a single firm (Article 86). In the first case – collusions and restrictive agreements – it was national cartels that were the target of EC law, since they would work to exclude supplies from other member countries. The *size* of companies, in the second case, was not seen as a problem, and was even welcomed since EC policy-makers have always wanted to see the emergence of giant European enterprises, operating on a continental scale like those of the USA.

In this phase, from the Rome Treaties of 1957 until the first oil shock of 1973, there was no important industrial intervention outside the spheres (atomic energy and agriculture) where the Treaties had given the EC specific responsibilities. The main form of action was legal – the attempt to establish a new, Community-wide, framework of competition rules. Once again, economic trends were favourable to the integration project: with rapid growth, the domestic markets of each member country could be opened up with a minimum of damage to vested interests. In this favourable climate, the EC's Court of Justice established its authority in the field of competition law through a series of judgements which undermined national price cartels.

In the phase which followed (see Appendix D), EC industrial policy swung back towards interventionism, although the political project of European unity was still the decisive factor in policy formation. In the 1970s industrial crises in all member states led to an explosion of interventionism at national level: national governments responded to rising unemployment and widespread excess capacity with a series of state-sponsored measures designed to give assistance and protection for the afflicted sectors – employment or investment related subsidies and tax exemptions; the refinance of loss-making companies, often through public ownership; increased use of public purchasing to feed orders to companies with idle capacity. The political colour of governments made little difference to the patterns of intervention: in Britain, a Conservative government nationalised the Rolls-Royce aero-engine company and refinanced British Leyland, while Labour nationalised shipbuilding; in Italy, the state-owned industrial holding companies pursued an anarchic expansion through the take-over of unprofitable private businesses, Germany reinforced support for its steel and shipbuilding enterprises; similar rescues in France took the form of industrial 'plans', rapidly formulated for the most precarious sectors. Although this intervention was largely pragmatic, socialist parties and trade-union movements planned to go further, with comprehensive programmes of state-led industrial reconstruction, such as the strategy adopted by the British Labour Party in the early 1980s or the huge nationalisation programme actually carried out by the Socialist-Communist coalition in France in 1981-2.

From the point of view of the EC Commission the proliferation of such interventions was a serious threat to integration since it tended to fragment Community-wide industries into nationally defined regimes. One possible response was to challenge these developments on legal grounds. The law, however, was an inadequate means of control: firstly, because EC Treaties actually provide for derogations from competition and free-trade rules in cases of emergency; secondly, and more importantly, because a national government enjoying strong political support for a job-saving industrial rescue might successfully defy Community law and thus imperil the whole institutional structure.

In this context, the Commission combined efforts to limit and rationalise national industrial policy with the introduction of its own, Community-wide interventions. Only in the case of steel, however, was a full-scale EC policy implemented, largely because of the special status of steel under the ECSC Treaty. The Treaty of Paris gave the Commission powers, in the event of crisis, to set minimum prices and to assign production quotas for each company. After a series of failed attempts to organise a voluntary steel cartel these powers were used in 1980 by the Commissioner for Industry, Etienne Davignon. The management of excess capacity is never an easy task and the usual problems of such exercises arose: the most efficient producers complained that Brussels was cheating them of the fruits of their competitive strength; others felt they were bearing an unfair share of capacity cuts; the scale of the capacity reductions required to restore some balance between the supply and demand for steel was repeatedly underestimated. Nevertheless, the plan did avoid an acute collapse, making time for the gradual elimination of sufficient capacity to permit the removal of controls in 1988.

In other spheres the EC was unable to introduce such policies since it lacked the legal power to impose a collective solution and could only try to persuade the major companies involved to stabilise prices and reduce output. In heavy chemicals and shipping the Commission failed to organise price rings and production quotas because the companies could not come to agreement. Unlike national governments, the EC was unable to use extensive subsidies as an instrument of industrial policy because it did not have the resources to finance them. So it had to find other instruments for its industrial interventions. One obvious tool was protectionism, which had the political advantage, from the Commission's point of view, of uniting the member states against outsiders. There was a general increase in protectionist measures by the EC, and also by the USA, from the late 1970s. Stagnant markets in the advanced capitalist countries had transformed the nature of industrial competition. From a relatively benign rivalry for the biggest share of increasing sales, international competition became a struggle for survival as each producer could only increase its market share by depriving other producers of their customers: under such pressure protectionist measures tended to multiply, although without disrupting international trade in the way that happened in the 1930s.

The concern of the EC Commission was to prevent such measures from affecting trade within the Community and to channel protectionist sentiments against other countries. At stake was its control over the commercial policy of member states, in principle already complete but in practice precarious because of numerous derogations which allowed separate national trade measures. The most complete protectionist regime established by the EC was through the Multi-Fibre Agreement (MFA) which puts ceilings on imported textile and clothing products from outside the Community; after the economic recessions of the 1970s these imports were still allowed to grow but at a much slower rate than in the past and each renegotiation of the MFA since has slowed down the penetration of low cost textiles and clothing imports from newly industrialising countries and Eastern Europe. The MFA takes the form of a 'voluntary' agreement between the EC and some of its trading partners (although what can Hong Kong do if it is told, 'either accept the following export ceilings or lower ones will be imposed'?). Because of this 'voluntary' form and the exceptional difficulties of some parts of the Community textile industry, the MFA has so far been seen as consistent with GATT, the main world trade agreement, although there have been demands for its removal in the present round of trade negotiations within GATT.

Other protectionist moves have been made by the Commission, but in a less systematic way. In particular, Japan has been induced to restrict 'voluntarily' its total exports of manufactured goods to EC countries. In imitating the USA, the Commission has been building a battery of 'anti-dumping' procedures and penalties, which can be brought quickly into effect when EC companies complain of unfair competition. Once again, mainly Japanese products are involved, but it is doubtful whether there are many genuine cases of dumping (that is, selling exports below their cost). The problem is rather that Japanese export prices, calculated in the normal way, are often below the costs of their European competitors.

Beyond the two cases of steel and textiles, no thoroughgoing, crisis-management industrial strategies emerged at EC level because of the difficulties of reconciling divergent interests in member countries. However, the EC did gradually succeed in countering the challenge which *national* industrial strategies from the late 1970s presented to the project of integration: a combination of political and legal pressures produced some kind of order among proliferating national industrial interventions. Member states were induced to inform the Commission of intended measures and to modify those which had a particularly damaging effect on intra-EC trade. It was especially important that member governments accepted a code restricting employment and investment subsidies and subjecting them to overall Community priorities.

Once again, however, global economic forces were working to sustain European integration. The threat to the Community from national industrial policies declined because it proved impossible to overcome industrial stagnation by these methods. On the one hand, the leading industrial companies in each country were to a large extent multinational and ready to resist policies which curtailed their freedom of manoeuvre. On the other hand, new patterns of industrial trade, characterised by intense international exchange within each branch of activity made efforts to demarcate a distinct national industrial space difficult and costly. The attenuation of international interdependence, which was a precondition of coherent national strategies, risked either obstructing the process of technology diffusion or narrowing the range of products supplied to the market and thus inhibiting the growth of demand. In the 1980s, new financial pressures also worked against the widespread use of industrial subsidies – the interest rates at which European governments could borrow rose to levels well above inflation rates for the first time in twenty years and debt service became a serious financial problem for governments for the first time since the second world war.

In this new context, national governments themselves moved away from protection and subsidy to accommodate loss-making industries towards strategies which made international market forces the main guide to restructuring.

In Britain the re-election of Mrs Thatcher's Conservative government in 1983 confirmed this shift, with the defeat of Labour's programme for protection and widespread industrial interventions. In Italy the big, state-owned, industrial holding companies, IRI and ENI, were run according to new priorities: the absorption of ailing private sector enterprises was stopped and deficits were eliminated by labour-shedding, plant closures and privatisations. The key change was in France because it was here that industrial strategy had gone furthest in the direction of state-led reconstruction on a national basis. The left-wing government elected in 1981 used the slogan of a 'recovery of the home market', and envisaged a reduction in the level of specialisation of French industry, to reduce dependence on imported technology. A vast nationalisation programme was rapidly implemented to permit the realignment of big industrial companies with this strategy. But the general reversal of French economic policy in 1983, from expansion to austerity, also involved a reversal of industrial strategy – the main priority for the big state-owned companies was now to eliminate losses, even if this meant abandoning other objectives cherished by the government. In fact these large French companies wanted to restore profitability by reinforcing their international connections (rather than becoming more independent) and by a substantial wave of labour-shedding, previously blocked by right-wing and left-wing governments alike.

In Germany, industrial policy was more consistent. Some subsidies were used to defend hard-pressed sectors such as coal and shipbuilding, but the export-dependence of German industry was so high that restructuring strategies centred on the home market have never obtained significant support. Since the late 1960s German industrial companies have pursued a policy of restructuring through international investment and reinforced specialisation; government policy has tried to control the pace of this process and to mitigate the resulting unemployment, rather than impose a different strategy on industry.

The early 1980s saw the end of attempts in Western Europe to restructure industry through national programmes aimed at relaxing the pressure of foreign competitors on domestic producers. Governments now sought to strengthen national enterprises within an environment of international competition which was seen as beyond their control. In this context, labour-shedding in manufacturing industry was increasingly accepted as a means to restore the health of enterprises, and industrial subsidies, which were in any case much harder to finance, were suspected of delaying necessary adjustments to new technologies and market conditions. National industrial strategies had come up against serious obstacles and, in the following years, would decline as a threat to the cohesion of the EC. At the same time the climate became more favourable for industrial initiatives at Community level.

The Technological Community

The EC Commission responded to the new concern with competitiveness and industrial adaption by developing a group of initiatives intended to strengthen Europe's technological performance. The rationale of the new policies was provided by the global competition which policymakers increasingly accepted as an unavoidable reality. In language which sometimes became quite dramatic the Commission portrayed a Europe in industrial decline and threatened by dangerous rivals: on the one hand, the super-productive industrial systems of the Japanese menaced the home and export markets of European industry across a wide range of products; on the other hand, the USA, whatever its problems in other spheres, had a long lead in key technologies such as computers which might be decisive in the competitive struggles of the future. Without an adequate response technical and therefore economic or even political dependence could become the fate of European countries.

Until the 1980s, technological co-operation within the Community had been limited to a few areas: nuclear energy, aerospace and agriculture. The COST programme, established in 1971, brought together the EC Commission with both member and non-member countries in Western Europe to sponsor applied research in a number of fields. COST represented a first response to a perceived threat of US technical dominance, but it was small and spread over many research areas.

The relaunch of technological collaboration in the

Community, once again on the initiative of Etienne Davignon, began with an agreement in 1981 between the Commission and twelve giant European electronics companies – German, British, Dutch, Italian and French. Effort was to be focused on information technology (IT) which was regarded as a critical area of European weakness. As always in the policy statements of the Commission, the solution lay in integrating the fragmented and disorganised efforts of the member states into a coherent whole. National technology policies in Germany, Britain, France and elsewhere already absorbed a lot of resources, but their programmes needlessly duplicated some research while lack of communication among researchers and enterprises prevented the exploitation of complementarities.

Davignon's initiative resulted in the ESPRIT programme for co-operation in IT as a way of breaking down the partitions between national research and development activity.[1] ESPRIT remains the largest such programme, but it has also become the model for several others, in biotechnology, telecommunications and other fields. In essence, ESPRIT sponsors research co-operation across national frontiers within the Community (and more widely, since EFTA countries also participate). Individual projects are loosely monitored to ensure that they fall within the remit of the programme, but the main control consists of giving only partial financial support (usually 50 per cent) so that the companies and other participants concerned must have sufficient belief in the project to put up half the money. A 'European' element is built in by requiring projects to involve partners (enterprises, universities, research institutes) in at least two countries. Within this flexible set of arrangements a substantial transnational research and development programme has been produced. In 1987 the Commission obtained the Council's agreement to fund a substantially expanded 'technology framework programme' based on a large number of projects already under way, of which several had already produced results. The 'framework programme' runs to 1992 and contains a new phase of ESPRIT with a large number of smaller initiatives modelled on it.

Alongside these official EC programmes, the intergovernmental programme EUREKA has been developed in response to a French initiative. EUREKA works by collaboration among West European governments, with each enterprise involved in a project having to seek as much sponsorship as it can from its own government.

The programme, proposed by the socialist government of France in 1985, reflected that government's experience of the increasing constraints it has encountered in trying to carry out an active industrial policy at national level; the French sought to avoid these constraints by projecting their industrial strategy on to the European plane. Like ESPRIT, the justification for EUREKA lay in a luridly depicted competitive threat from Japan and the USA. The 'Star Wars' Programme, which was interpreted less as a serious military proposition than as a way of pumping public money into the research and development efforts of major US companies, was a particular stimulus to West European R&D co-operation.

EUREKA has a sharper commercial edge than ESPRIT and the other EC programmes: the key actors are enterprises, with public sector agencies only having a limited role; and the research projects which are sponsored are closer to commercial exploitation. ESPRIT had been designed to avoid too direct an impact on the competitive position of particular companies – the projects it supports are supposed to be 'pre-competitive', that is, some distance away from direct application so that public sponsorship or research should not impinge too much on the competitive development and marketing of new products. EUREKA is much less inhibited on this question and makes the market potential of the research undertaken a criterion for selecting projects: projects are chosen on criteria close to those applied by the companies themselves and as a result there has been a strong response from the private sector. EUREKA is also much better funded than the EC technology programmes because the sponsors are national governments, not the financially hard-pressed Commission. As with ESPRIT each project must involve partners in more than one country and the companies concerned must put up around half of the money. The projects proposed by companies are selected by a small secretariat and then ratified at an inter-ministerial conference, but the conference only attaches the EUREKA label specifically to research and development projects. Each participating company then seeks public support from its national government, which remains free as to whether, and to what extent, it is prepared to subsidise. (Britain, lukewarm on European policy as usual, has failed on several occasions to back British companies for agreed EUREKA projects.) EC institutions are by-passed in these procedures and intergovernmental squabbles on funding are avoided. Perhaps for these reasons alone EUREKA has developed very quickly: by June 1988 some 200 projects had been endorsed, at a total cost of nearly five billion ECUs; this compares with just over five billion ECUs earmarked as the EC's total research budget between 1987 and 1992. However, the programme is no longer as focused on the correction of specific weaknesses in European technology as was intended in the original French proposals. This has attracted criticism from the European Parliament: the decentralisation of control over the programme to the companies themselves and to national governments has certainly accelerated its implementation, but at the cost of a reduced impact on the general direction of European research and development.

There were at first some difficulties with the existence of two separate European technology programmes – ESPRIT and its analogues under EC control; EUREKA, an intergovernmental programme with much better funding. There was some practical danger of duplicating research projects, but more important from the Commission's point of view was the political danger of being marginalised in a major exercise in European co-operation. However, the Commission did succeed in restoring a degree of order to the situation: the EC obtained representation on the EUREKA secretariat and assumed responsibility for avoiding wasteful overlaps in the different programmes.

So EUREKA can now be regarded as an integral part of the group of programmes making up the Technological Community. In operational terms these initiatives have been successful, and a large number of joint ventures and collaborations have been generated in the field of industrial technology. While most of the projects have not yet culminated in marketable products or the implementation of new processes, the financial contribution of the companies involved is a good guarantee that results of some value will be obtained; a large and growing flow of public finance has been secured, especially for EUREKA, but also for the Community's own programmes.

In political terms the Technological Community again appears to be a success since it has made use of the increasing concern of national governments with technical change. Most public research expenditure remains at national level and only a small fraction of private sector research and development has been affected by the European programmes. (The 'framework programme' accounts for about four per cent of total civil research and development in member countries, with EUREKA adding a similar share.) But the dynamism with which the programmes have been presented and developed has made the EC and European co-operation central to the debates on technological adaptation. It is significant here that the Community has sought to create private interests linked to technical co-operation. Discussion of European integration has often, following J. Tinbergen, made a sharp distinction between 'negative integration', brought about by competition and the market, and 'positive integration' through the adoption of common public policies. In fact, the development of the EC has been more complex than this: since the Schuman plan, 'positive' – that is, political – initiatives have been taken in order to construct private interests which will support the integration process. The Technological Community follows this political tradition: the programmes sponsor not only research but also, in effect, international co-operation itself, with the aim of establishing associations of private and public sector agents committed to the process of European construction.

In both administrative and political terms, therefore, the Technological Community is a successful response to the changing preoccupations of industrial policy. What can be questioned, however, is the basic economic coherence of the strategy. The Technological Community, like the 1992 programme itself, is presented as a means of overcoming a crisis of competitiveness in Western Europe, but under closer examination this economic rationale is very difficult to sustain.

The External Threat

The clearest and most emphatic statement of the competitiveness argument can be found in the document of 1983 which introduced the ESPRIT programme. Subsequently the argument was toned down, but it has never been abandoned and the evidence presented at that time is still invoked in support of the Technological Community and other EC strategies including the market completion programme itself. Although it has escaped serious challenge, both the premise and the logic of this argument are extremely dubious.

According to the argument, Europe's economic problems, including high unemployment, result from a loss of industrial dynamism. The competitiveness of European industry, in relation to Japan and the USA, is in decline, particularly in the high-technology sectors which will be of most importance for long-term growth. Unless competitiveness is restored Europe will face not only economic stagnation and persistent unemployment but even political subordination. The essential strategy for restored competitiveness and technological renaissance is integration: Europe's expenditures on research and development are high but their effect is curtailed by fragmentation of research efforts and the lack of communication among technologists. The combination and strengthening of Western Europe's research activity is thus the key to the future. Such was, and largely remains, the economic assessment behind the Technological Community: virtually every one of its constituent propositions is open to question.

To begin with the supposed industrial decline, it is not clear that Europe's industrial problems have much to do with external competition. Certainly the slowdown in economic growth in most industrial countries has intensified international competition, but this seems to be a consequence not a cause: when demand stagnates, the costs of competitive failure rise because the markets gained by one producer are lost to another. Internationally, this intense competitive pressure creates the conditions for protectionism. When Europe enjoyed the highest growth rates in the world neither internal nor external competition appeared to be a major problem and industrial tariffs were rapidly reduced – being abolished within the Community and brought down to very low levels against other countries. Certainly the trend towards trade liberalisation slowed in the 1970s and was even, in some cases, reversed by the use of industrial policies to create non-tariff barriers to trade, but such developments expressed the general industrial malaise rather than an industrial problem originating outside the Community.

In any case, it does not seem likely that the EC as a whole faced a general constraint on economic activity as a result of external trade, except for the years immediately following the oil crisis of 1973-4. There were, without doubt, sensitive sectors such as steel or textiles, but Western Europe's overall performance as an exporter of manufactured goods has never really been in question. Individual countries within the EC have certainly faced external constraints on economic expansion – this was notably the case for Britain in the 1970s, for example – but constraints on particular countries do not imply an overall external constraint on the EC as a unit. This constitutes another weakness in the EC Commission's argument – it has to assume that competition within the Community (benign, progressive) is in a completely different category to competition with outside countries (dangerous, threatening Europe with stagnation and dependence). Of course the distinction is purely political, since the economic processes involved in the two kinds of competition are identical. In fact, the main external constraints on member countries have not arisen from trade with non-members but from their very unequal performance in intra-EC trade, with Germany tending to be in surplus and most of the others in deficit.

It is again problematic to attribute unemployment to a lack of external industrial competitiveness, as the analysis of the Commission usually does. The relatively poor employment performance of West European countries vis-à-vis the USA is not a reflection of their lack of international competitiveness. When US industry completely dominated international trade, in the 1950s and 1960s, US unemployment was well above that in Europe. Indeed the relative industrial position of the USA has continued to decline, even as US employment has expanded rapidly. The actual relationship is the opposite: the improvement of international competitiveness has tended to destroy jobs in Europe.

On the one hand, industrial companies have automated their factories and shed labour very fast precisely because they have had to sustain international competitiveness – so industrial productivity has grown more rapidly in Western Europe than in the USA, even as industrial employment fell much more rapidly. On the other hand, international competition *among* European countries has also affected the personal services and similar sectors which are usually sheltered from such pressure in Japan or the USA. The lack of homogeneity in European society, and the important differences in wage rates from country to country, force personal services, distribution and other non-industrial sectors to maintain their competitiveness – as a consequence, sheltered sectors have not been able to absorb excess labour in Western Europe to the same extent as in the USA. European economies have therefore had to defend their international competitiveness more consistently and more thoroughly than the USA – largely because they are in competition with each other. But the result has been to encourage labour-shedding and inhibit job creation, not the reverse.

There are also problems with the evidence, produced by official EC studies, of a technological decline in Europe. For the most part this evidence has been derived from trade data, but the classification of commodities into high-technology and low-technology products is extremely hazardous when each product goes through many different processes and when the application even of very sophisticated techniques can be rapidly reduced to a routine factory operation. The kind of trap involved can be illustrated by the fact that Ireland appears in the trade statistics as one of the biggest computer exporters in Europe: of course, this is not due to the high level of Irish technology but to the presence in Ireland of US multinationals, attracted by low wages and tax breaks, assembling computers designed elsewhere.

Questions of timing can also have a huge effect on comparisons of competitiveness. It is easy to confuse a strong cyclical effect, which will soon be reversed, with the emergence of a new trend. Just such an error occurred in the main EC Commission analyses of European competitiveness which examined data up to 1982 or 1983. In the early 1980s there was a deep recession in the USA, which reduced European exports, but at the same time the Dollar was rising very fast on the foreign exchanges, inflating the value of US exports. The result was to give a quite misleading impression of US industrial strength and European weaknesses, as all these factors turned out to be cyclical: the US economy started to expand, pulling in record imports from other countries; while the Dollar, after rising fast until early 1985, has fallen even more rapidly since (see Appendix C). 1982 was, in fact, a very exceptional year because West Germany was running a current account deficit – something which has happened in only two or three years out of the last 40 – and Germany's trade performance is obviously central to that of the EC as a whole.

The strength of the German economy has to be underestimated in order to portray an industrial decline in Western Europe. It should be remembered that West Germany, not Japan or the USA, is the world's biggest exporter of manufactured goods. Precisely because of its sustained success in international competition, the German economy is highly export-dependent and suffers from any slow-down in world trade, but there is no real evidence that German competitiveness is under threat or that German industry has lost its impressive ability to adapt to changing technologies or markets. The industrial analysis and strategies formulated by the Commission tend to reflect French rather than German thinking. A concern with the weaknesses in French industrial structure has thus been projected onto the European level, even though German industry can be treated as a dangerous rival from a French point of view, but has to be seen as the most important asset from the point of view of Europe as a whole.

Japan and the USA

A further weakness in the 'competitiveness' argument is that it compounds two very different questions – economic relations with the USA on the one hand, and with Japan on the other. The drama of the 'crisis of competitiveness' really derives from this confusion. Europe's industries can be regarded as in 'decline' relative to those of Japan, but a threat of economic or political domination can only be made plausible by referring to the power of the USA.

It is certainly undeniable that some aspects of US hegemony are a threat to Western Europe, but these threats are basically political, military and (to some extent) financial not industrial. The continuing long-term decline in the relative strength of US industry aggravates the problem of American hegemony because it has become increasingly difficult to reconcile the management of the US economy with the global role of the USA as leader of the Western bloc. Similar considerations apply to the exercise of US financial power which is based on the role of the Dollar: it is the loss of American industrial supremacy which makes the Dollar's status as a world currency problematic because it is no longer easy for the USA to discharge its debts by exporting goods as it could in the 1940s or 1950s.

The main area in which a continuing industrial challenge from the USA can be detected is at the interface of civil and military production: the aerospace sector, for example, which benefits from massive military procurement; some electronics companies whose research spending is financed by the Pentagon with a view to the development of new weapons systems; the development of high-performance computers, again with military objectives and, as a result, colossal government subsidies.

Europeans may be justified in regarding much of US military spending as disguised industrial policy. It has been pointed out, for example, that the EUREKA initiative was to some extent a response to the American SDI programme – an alternative focus for the technology strategies of European companies which, it was feared, might otherwise align themselves with the US programme and accept US priorities.

The question, however, is not about the *existence* of a military-industrial complex in the USA, which was pointed out by Eisenhower 30 years ago, and dates from the Second World War. The key issue is whether, and to what extent, the complex continues to reinforce US industrial competitiveness. Here there seem to be grounds for considerable scepticism: most civilian production benefits to an ever smaller degree from military research, while the few giant companies which are most dependent on Pentagon funds devote their resources to the elaboration of 'baroque' technologies, too costly and over-specialised to be of any economic value. The concentration of publicly funded R&D in the USA on military projects, and President Reagan's increases in military spending have certainly not prevented the continuing loss of market shares, home and abroad, by US companies – even in such sectors as machine tools or consumer electronics where the spin-off from military research might be thought to be substantial. In the past the relationship between big US companies and publicly funded research seems to have been less parasitic and more creative: both the emergence of electronic computers and the first application of computer technology to manufacturing owed a great deal to Defense Department sponsorship. Today the economic effects of militarisation appear to be completely negative: a distortion of priorities and the massive misallocation of material and human resources.

It is significant that a clear European presence has been maintained even in the aerospace sector itself, through exercises in European co-operation of an essentially civil character. The European Space Agency has sponsored the Ariane rocket which is now, partly because of the problems of the US space shuttle, the main launcher of commercial satellites; and Airbus Industrie, a consortium of West European aerospace companies, has won a large share of the international market with successive models of its medium-range passenger aircraft. (British participation in both projects has been half-hearted and irregular.) Both of these activities are, admittedly, dependent on continuous financial support from the European governments concerned (especially France and Germany), so it is misleading to describe them as commercial successes, although this is often done. The economic logic then of both exercises is questionable, since it is not clear how much they really contribute to the adaptation of European industrial structures.

Nevertheless, Ariane and Airbus indicate that US technological supremacy is far from being the overwhelming threat which EC Commission studies have suggested, since that supremacy has been successfully challenged even in the aerospace sector which is the core of the 'military-industrial complex'. In 1986 the USA, for the first time, imported more goods with a high-technology content than it exported. This situation is unlikely to continue, since it reflects the excesses of Reaganomics as much as the longer-term problems of the US economy, but it does make the notion of Europe being excluded from the development of modern technology seem somewhat alarmist.

The advanced educational systems of Western Europe produce large numbers of scientists and technologists including many of those at work in the USA, and this will continue provided that education continues to improve and that good employment opportunities are created for those specialists. The sharp reductions in public support for scientific and technical education and research, which are favoured by free-market conservatives, are probably the main threat to Europe's technological status today because such policies obviously discourage the maintenance and development of the necessary skills.

As opposed to industrial competition, direct assertions of US political power can certainly cause economic difficulties for Europe. One example was the attempt to block the natural gas pipeline from the Soviet Union by the 'extra-territorial' application of US legal restrictions to US subsidiaries in Western Europe. A similar case is the use of COCOM restrictions on technology transfer to Eastern Europe. These restrictions, a clumsy embargo intended to deprive the Warsaw Pact of new military technologies, complicated commercial relations between Eastern and Western Europe. A further example is the US-Japanese agreement on integrated circuits which was signed in 1986: far from being an expression of US industrial strength, the agreement was designed to rescue US producers of electronic components, such as Texas Instruments, which had been world leaders a few years previously but were now unable to meet Japanese competition in a glutted market. The agreement required the Japanese to limit their penetration of US markets and to increase their imports from the USA. European interests were affected, because minimum prices were established – at a level designed to maintain the profitability of US producers – and those minima were supposed to apply to the whole world. European electronics companies buying components from the Japanese therefore had to pay higher prices. In practice, the damage to European companies was probably slight and the agreement was judged, in 1989, to be incompatible with the GATT treaties on free trade. It is likely that US computer companies themselves were the main losers, because it became difficult for them to buy cheap components but the case does illustrate the use, or abuse, of US political power in ways which can harm European economies. The firm, united refusal of such measures seems the appropriate response, as in the case of the Soviet pipeline where the USA was unable to enforce its embargo. Such cases, however, are the exception which proves the rule that in the sphere of industrial production and competition for world markets a US threat to Europe is hard to find.

Turning to the Japanese challenge, opposite considerations apply. It is impossible to deny the efficiency of Japanese industrial systems or the competitiveness of Japanese manufactures. What is not clear, however, is whether these industrial strengths constitute any kind of *threat* to West European economies or societies. In the absence of the hegemonic political and military role played by the US government, what precisely is the danger to Europe from Japan's industrial success? Any such danger is presumably strictly economic – the competitive pressure of Japanese products on sectors of European industry or, at the macroeconomic level, more intense constraints on countries with balance of payments problems due to an overall growth of Japanese imports. Both types of problem exist, but it is hard to regard them as central questions in the adaptation of European industry. In fact, the European reaction to Japanese industrial success has been characterised by an exaggerated neo-mercantilism, both at Community and at member state level.

Straightforward protectionism has been used to relieve the pressure on European industries, particularly automobiles where all EC producers impose quotas on Japanese imports. In itself this is a perfectly logical policy although it is completely inconsistent with the view taken of trade *within* the Community which can, of course, have exactly the same effects. Protected from the Japanese, the British motor industry still fell victim to European competition. (The use of *national* quotas against Japanese cars also, necessarily, fragments the EC market since it means that goods admitted to one member country – Denmark or Ireland, for example, which have no motor industries to protect – are then unable to circulate freely to the others. In principle, the quotas should be scrapped as part of the 1992 programme but three highly 'protectionist' countries, France, Italy and Spain, form a blocking coalition in the Council of Ministers and will not give up their own restrictions except in exchange for tight overall EC quotas which countries like Germany are reluctant to accept.)

The limits of this straightforward protectionism are reached when European producers are unable to match the quality and price of Japanese goods even with the time and resources for adjustment that a sheltered home market provides. In this case, to go on protecting home producers imposes a very high cost on the consumers or firms which are potential customers for Japanese imports. This is what happened during the notorious French attempt to exclude Japanese video recorders, an attempt which is nevertheless being repeated at Community level in the case of Digital Audio Tape, which is being kept off EC markets by a dispute about copying. In the field of consumer electronics in general the superiority of Japanese products has been so great as to make simple protection seem futile. In such cases, however, agreements are still possible to transfer the new techniques and products to European companies – the revival of consumer electronics in Germany and the Netherlands in the 1980s has been based on such transfers. In the absence of agreement the very strength of consumer demand for Japanese imports can become an advantage since they can be taxed at a level high enough to finance adaptation and restructuring in the European industries affected.

In other words, European producer interests are not completely disarmed, even when Japanese products are overwhelmingly superior and even in the absence of industrial collaboration which is usually the best solution. In fact such collaboration has been the rule: European companies can adopt aspects of Japanese production systems and modernise their product ranges, while the Japanese obtain secure access to European markets and diversify output away from the congested and costly industrial regions of Japan. Without significant military or political power, the Japanese cannot simply impose their will in such cases, but are constrained to reach this kind of agreement. It would be to the general advantage of European countries to have a common and united policy on the Japanese investments involved. This can avoid a Dutch auction to attract the plant to one region or another and ensure that genuine technology transfer is taking place, not just the location of an assembly-only, 'screw-driver' factory in Europe to avoid possible trade restrictions. The cost of divergent national policies is shown by the French-British disputes on Nissan cars: for the British, these are European because most of their value is added in Britain; for the French, they are Japanese because their engines and transmissions are made in Japan.

Beyond such sectoral difficulties, serious but not out of control, there is the question of the overall balance of EC-Japanese trade. Japan has a persistent surplus in its overall trade with the Community: to what extent is this a problem? In many ways the neo-mercantilist approach adopted by the Commission to Japan's commercial success has been exaggerated and even irrational.

There is firstly the basic point that in a multilateral world trading system, bilateral surpluses or deficits between trading partners are not normally a legitimate cause for dispute. Japan needs bilateral surpluses in its trade with other industrialised countries in order to import oil and raw materials, since it has none of its own. The Commission's complaints about the size of Japan's surplus in its trade with the EC considered in isolation, are not therefore consistent with the accepted principles of international trade. It is the overall surplus on Japan's foreign trade which is a legitimate cause for concern, just as the persistent surplus of Germany, a Community member, might produce problems. Japan's position on its current account surplus, which is to some extent the simple consequence of US economic policy, has been accommodating – both in the effort to reduce the surplus and in avoiding financial dislocation by the way the surplus is invested.

Nevertheless, Japan has also agreed, in response to the Commission's pressure, to limit its total exports to the EC. The absurd aspect of the Commission's commercial policy towards Japan is its continuous drive to foster, quite artificially, Japanese imports of EC goods. Since, in most cases, European products are not competitive on Japanese markets the campaigns centre on highly differentiated, luxury products – French perfume or Scotch whisky – and efforts to stimulate their conspicuous consumption among the more prosperous Japanese. Apart from the waste involved in encouraging this kind of consumption at considerable expense it is also quite probably useless in easing the pressure of Japanese competition on world markets because the imported luxuries substitute for Japanese products which are then exported. In any case, the Community is not constrained by an imbalance in its external trade since the EC as a whole has a substantial current account surplus. The most pressing constraints on member countries arise from the West German surplus, which is almost as big and even more persistent.

A final example of the distortions in the Community industrial strategy which are caused by this kind of mercantilism is the case of high-definition television (HDTV). The big European electronics companies have been subsidised, through EUREKA, to develop a set of standards and technical specifications for HDTV. It is very logical for European countries to agree on common norms and specifications in such cases, in order to avoid the emergence of inconsistent and incompatible systems in different countries. A new emphasis on the role of the EC in defining common standards, and agreement by individual countries to accept them, is one of the most obvious benefits of the 1992 strategy. In the case of HDTV, however, the choice of technical standards has been designed to limit the entry of Japanese firms onto the European market. It is hardly conceivable that Japanese companies can be excluded from the market for the new generation of TV sets, but there will apparently be a determined effort to lock them out of the markets for TV cameras, transmitting equipment and so on. The dangers of this kind of practice are difficult to assess in advance. The emerging European system may be as good as its producers claim, in which case the fiasco of the European video-recorders will not be repeated. However, there may also be a serious risk that users of HDTV equipment, that is broadcasting companies, film companies and other producers in the cultural industries will be handicapped by expensive and retrograde technologies which, after a few years, have to be expensively ditched.

No argument is being made here for free trade: trade

intervention is justified both to protect the potential losers from international competition and to prevent the initial technical or marketing advantage of the winners from being perpetuated by the cumulative effects of initial success. However, the types of intervention presently favoured by the EC, which identify European interests with those of a few big electronics companies, narrow the possibility for negotiated solutions to conflicts with Japan, and even result in a Malthusian rejection of Japanese industrial excellence.

Recently there has been an interesting change in the way the Commission talks about Japan (see Appendix C). It is proposed to strengthen 'the third side of the triangle' – to enhance Japanese-EC interactions which are still very thin and underdeveloped compared with either US-Japanese or US-EC relationships (the other two 'sides of the triangle'). The basis for this notion is a new assessment of the problems and opportunities arising from Japan's industrial success. In particular there is the suspicion that the very large trade and investment flows between the USA and Japan might be an advantage for the USA and one way of overcoming its industrial stagnation. This is certainly a more realistic approach, but it is hard to reconcile with the Commission's repeated declarations about the crisis of European competitiveness.

A Widening Technological Gap?

One aspect of rapid economic growth in Western Europe was a technological 'catching up' effect: industrial productivity could be increased very rapidly by introducing American methods and techniques. As a result, productivity in the 1950s and 1960s grew much faster in Europe than in the USA. In the 1980s, however, policy-makers in the EC have suggested that the gap is widening rather than narrowing – hence the supposed need for a European 'technological renaissance'.

Independent assessments have not confirmed this view of technological decay. Margaret Sharp's attitude in 1985 was that Western Europe's problems were not general but confined to specific sectors (electronic components for example) and certain countries (such as Britain). Two years later Pari Patel and Keith Pavitt reached the same conclusion, 'There is no justification for assuming general European technological backwardness.'[2] Recently, even official French studies have repudiated the notion of a serious technology gap. This is significant because it was French analyses in particular which inspired the EC's new policies on research.

Even the widely accepted judgement of European weakness in electronics requires some qualification. European companies have indeed been out-performed in consumer electronics, and they also lag behind in the production of very large computers. But Europe's lack of specialisation in standard electronic components may not be the major disadvantage often suggested: this kind of production can be rapidly adopted by some newly industrialising countries, making it unprofitable in higher-wage economies such as Western Europe or the USA. On the other hand, EC countries are relatively strong in other activities, such as the production of software, and in some applications of information technology. The recent, more optimistic assessments of Europe's position have even been put down to the success of EC research policies which are said to have transformed the situation. Since these policies have not had sufficient time or resources for a major impact, it is much more likely that Europe's backwardness was exaggerated in earlier studies by the Commission.

Even where there is a technology gap, it is not clear that the reinforcement of co-operation within Europe is a logical response. It seems just as valid for the sectors and industrial groups concerned to seek closer links with US or Japanese partners to overcome technical or organisational lags, rather than to develop closer relations with another European company which suffers from the same weakness. Ironically, the strategy of some French companies provides good examples of this approach, as in the link-up of Bull with the Japanese computer giant NEC or the take-over by CGE of the telecommunications activities of ITT. The notion of parallel, largely autonomous industrial technologies evolving separately in Europe and the USA (as one might have discussed British and German engineering a century ago) is surely anachronistic. What is at stake is the participation of West European economies in a *globally unified* process of technological change. From this point of view, co-operation within Western Europe can only be a complement to interaction with the USA, Japan and other outside countries.

A Military-Industrial Complex in Europe?

It has been pointed out that much of the strategic thinking behind the Technological Community is French. The dangers of present policy directions can be elucidated by examining French industrial ambitions in Europe, which include France becoming the key supplier of military equipment for a European Defence grouping much more independent, both politically and technically, of the USA than European members of NATO are at present.

French insistence on a more autonomous European position on military questions has the merit of challenging US hegemony over defence policy in the West. But French policy is not necessarily more in favour of disarmament – the maintenance of French nuclear weapons is in fact one of the aims of their proposals for closer military co-operation among European countries. There is an important industrial dimension to the geo-strategic thinking behind French policy. On the one hand, France is a very big producer of armaments but cannot afford to sustain its arms companies by its own military procurement: there is a constant need for arms exports which would be much easier if there existed a tightly organised West European military grouping, with unified views of strategy, and independent of the USA. On the other hand, French traditions in economic policy emphasise a very close connection between industrial and strategic issues which both tend to be seen as aspects of foreign policy and the geo-political rivalry among states. Although French industrial traditions are highly interventionist, and constitute an important source of opposition to free-market doctrines in the EC, it is advisable to look closely at the logic and direction of the interventions which are being proposed.

In fact, French ambitions for a European Defence Community are unlikely to be fulfilled in the near future, and French ministers themselves have recognised this. Some European members of NATO, in particular Britain, remain completely Atlanticist; others are enthusiastic for thorough disarmament. German views, which combine a reluctance to quarrel with the USA and a preoccupation with détente as the basis of improved German security, are opposed to French conceptions and are likely to block the emergence of a coherent European military structure, supplied by a European arms industry.

Nevertheless, some of the industrial initiatives taking place within the Technological Community have a similar character to what might be expected from a more explicitly military type of co-operation. The collective state sponsorship of high-tech companies in France, Germany and Britain has almost the appearance of a surrogate military-industrial complex in Europe – at least an analogous industrial structure even though it does not have a direct military function. In particular, technology and industrial policy are aimed at meeting an external threat and at improving Europe's global competitiveness. Interventions with this rationale are bound to reinforce the strongest sectors of European industry and to sponsor the big French, British, German and Netherlands industrial groups which can most plausibly be regarded as Community 'champions'. The technical leaders benefit more than the followers, the large companies more than the small. The exercise can hardly avoid sustaining the industrial dominance of northern Europe within the EC since the less developed industries of Spain and Greece have little to offer in a race between Europe and Japan. Public expenditure artificially supports the generation of new technology in a spurious competition with the USA and Japan, rather than its application and diffusion. The massive internal disparities and lags in industrial culture which are the real problem in Community industry are therefore neglected, or even aggravated, by policies geared to the external threat.

The 1992 Programme and the European Identity

According to the official discourse of the Community, the 1992 market completion programme is completely consistent with EC industrial policies and even reinforces them. Just as the Technological Community attempts to build globally competitive industrial groups on the basis of European co-operation so also, it is claimed, the market completion programme will promote a process of modernisation and adaptation tending to strengthen Europe's industries against US and Japanese rivals. It is arguable, however, that in reality the 1992 programme, far from supporting other industrial policies, actually results in confusion and incoherence.

A keyword in the interpretation of 1992 is 'internal': the use of this term to qualify the big European market implies that the programme develops and completes the internal, domestic market of the Community, putting European companies on a par with those of the USA and Japan which already benefit from huge, unified home markets. 1992 can be given a neo-mercantilist interpretation, popular in France and to some extent even in Germany, as well as the neo-liberal interpretation which is preferred by the British government. According to the mercantilist view, a strong home market, allowing for the early achievement of economies of scale, and securing a solid profits base, is the key to success in international competition. 'Non-Europe', national rivalries and the fragmentation of Community market have, in this view, deprived European companies of a key element in competitive success, which the 1992 programme will correct.

A first objection to this kind of reasoning is that it does not seem to apply in important cases. Multinationals based in some of the smallest European countries – Switzerland, Sweden and the Netherlands – have achieved impressive results in spite of tiny home markets. Qualitative aspects of a company's home base may be just as important as the sheer size of its domestic market; and it may not always be appropriate to regard firms as being based in countries, rather than particular cities or regions.

More fundamentally, the European market which emerges from the 1992 programme will not be 'internal' in the sense which the neo-mercantilist interpretation requires – that is, it will not be an economic space in which a distinct set of 'European' enterprises enjoy a privileged position relative to their non-European competitors. In fact the programme will work in the opposite direction: by reducing the *national* advantages which British-, German- and French-based companies have at present, it will tend to put US, Japanese and other outside multinationals (already operating freely in Western Europe) on a completely equal basis with the Europeans. This is the case for at least three of the major items in the 1992 programme, which will open European economies to the rest of the world as much as to each other. Capital market liberalisation will give outside banks and financial institutions much greater mobility within the Community while limiting the privileged access to credit of nationally based competitors. The removal of technical and regulatory barriers to internal trade again offers as much advantage to US companies as to European ones. Indeed, both these reforms concede to long-standing US demands for greater access to European markets. The opening up of public procurement, with more competition and greater transparency in the award of government contracts will again improve the prospects for outside suppliers. For example, more open competition in the European telecommunications sector will make it easier for US and Japanese companies or their subsidiaries to expand their sales (of exchanges, terminal equipment and 'value added services').

Only one major aspect of the 1992 programme seems to favour internal economic agents – the removal of fiscal frontiers. This is because goods from outside will still have to go through tax procedures at the frontier. Even in this case, however, European companies will enjoy an advantage only in comparison with companies located outside and exporting into the EC; outside companies producing inside the EC will also benefit from tax harmonisation measures.

The neo-mercantilist interpretation of 1992 as the creation of a clearly identified home market for European industry is impossible to sustain, given that no measures will be taken to protect the unified market from outside forces. Rather, the 1992 programme will tend to accelerate the continuing globalisation of European economic relations by making the economic system more homogeneous. The frontiers separating European enterprises from those outside will be increasingly hard to define. As a consequence, Community industrial policy, conceived at present as the reinforcement of an identifiable group of 'European' industrial companies, will start to become problematic. How will the 'Technological Community' be interpreted, for example, if most of the major participants have close technological links with the US or Japanese companies which are supposed to be their main rivals and are increasingly involved in production or marketing in the

USA or the Pacific rim.

The repeatedly frustrated search for 'European' companies is a long-standing theme in EC policy discussion. The USA provided the industrial model for the original architects of the Community: the vision behind most EC industrial policy has been of large enterprises, operating on a continental scale and as mobile across Europe's internal frontiers as the US giants are across states. In practice, imitation of US models was combined with a convergence of the USA and Europe, so that from the start US-based companies themselves were the most active in producing and selling from one European country to another. Measured by the intensity of their intra-European activities, Ford and General Motors are among the most 'European' car manufacturing companies and IBM is the most 'European' computer company.

Efforts to construct more authentically European rivals to the US giants have frequently failed. Initiatives such as the Unidata computer link-up of Siemens, Philips and CII or the Dunlop-Pirelli merger did not have enough industrial logic to sustain them. By 1980 the most important fusions of companies from different countries still dated from before the EC – Royal Dutch Shell and Unilever, for instance.

Today the climate for co-operation, joint ventures and even mergers between companies in different European countries is much more favourable. The real significance of ESPRIT, EUREKA and the other technology programmes has not been so much their effect on research and development as their attempt to encourage the interlinking of activities and interests among French, German, and other companies. The psychological impact of 1992 has also encouraged a wave of transnational mergers and takeovers in Western Europe. But these phenomena are only an aspect of a much wider process of financial reorganisation on a trans-Atlantic or global scale, in which deals involving European and non-European enterprises are just as important as those inside Europe. In spite of the 'europhoria' around 1992, the internationalisation strategies of big companies in France or Britain do not follow a European logic but a global one. The need to spread risks, to secure technology transfer, to exploit new products in the widest possible market, all lead companies to regard intra-European co-operation as only one aspect of their plans for international expansion. Similarly the integration of financial markets around the world induced companies to raise finance, including equity finance, in the USA and Japan as well as in Europe. Once again the dream of 'European' companies seems about to fade – the links between big companies and their home countries may be weakening but this is not leading to close links between these companies and the EC as a whole. A 'European identity' may be a necessary side of the integration project, but that identity will not be constructed by the initiatives of the corporate sector.

It was suggested above that the strength of EC industrial policies derived from the ineffectiveness of national interventions. This was the case, in particular, in the employment crisis of the 1970s and 1980s when national efforts at industrial reconstruction failed, largely because of the very high degree of international economic interdependence. The logic determined by this interdependence is visible in the EC's attempt to rationalise the use of subsidies by member states. EC policies themselves, however, are also exposed to the process of internationalisation. An image has been projected of a well-defined European economy, locked in a life-and-death struggle with its US and Japanese rivals, and policy has been formulated in response to these perceived threats. But in reality the economic forces of these zones increasingly interpenetrate – the result is a basic incoherence in EC industrial policy. The Technological Community aims at strengthening European industry against the external challenge while 1992 makes it more difficult to make an operational distinction between internal and external economic forces.

The contemporary cult of business enterprise exacerbates this incoherence by directly aligning industrial policies with the goals of corporate strategy. Since these strategies necessarily attach a very limited importance to European integration, it becomes more difficult to orient policy towards integration or, indeed, other political objectives. The danger arises that real problems of industrial structure and industrial change will be neglected at Community level.

A European Company Statute

The first requirement for a more consistent EC policy is to

adopt a more objective approach to industrial enterprises, rather than assuming a fictitious coincidence between the interests of companies and the political goals of the Community. Such objectivity could become one of the strengths of the EC, since it is increasingly difficult for member states to avoid a close entanglement of their governmental processes with the decision-making of giant companies, because the investment and employment choices of these companies are now so important in political terms. The size of the Community, and the need of multinationals to have access to EC markets, tilt the balance back from corporate power towards the public authorities at EC level, always provided that the EC is not engaged in the neo-mercantilist promotion of its 'own' multinational champions against those of the outside world. The 'European enterprise' will not arise from a spontaneous solidarity between the Community and companies which happen to have their headquarters within its frontiers.

Companies operating inside the EC, regardless of where they are based, can be constrained to respect common, politically defined, standards of behaviour regarding payment of taxes, respect for the environment, provision of information, recognition of unions, consultation with employees and so on. The use of Community company law, already fairly developed on competition issues, can gradually produce this kind of common regime, beginning with companies above a certain size. This is a possible line of development from Commission proposals for a European company statute: companies would be able to opt for registration with the EC rather than with national authorities and such registration would have automatic validity throughout the Community. The conditions imposed on these companies would set a standard for all companies operating in more than one member state, to begin with only a recommended standard but becoming legally binding as EC law develops. The great advantage of a common set of standards is that it avoids giving privileges or imposing penalties on the companies of particular member states. This legal approach can, of course, only produce a limited commitment of companies to European political objectives but this commitment is likely to have more substance than an increasingly problematic attempt to distinguish 'European' companies from the rest. As so often, British governmental and employer resistance are the main cause of delay in the introduction of European company status, even though the constraints presently envisaged, affecting employee consultation, are minimal.

Certainly, legal structures will not obviate the need also for specific interventions in industry to encourage investment, training, job creation, research and so on. Such interventions are proliferating in all industrial countries and at every level of government. But EC law can provide a framework for such interventions which should be of a clearly instrumental nature, embodied in contracts between the enterprises and the authorities concerned: that is, specific measures of public support are explicitly linked to specific actions by the companies which receive it, rather than subsidies simply enhancing profitability in the interest of 'competitiveness'.

The Diffusionist Model

The argument for the use of contracts and general legal constraints in relations between EC institutions and industrial companies owes much, it can be freely admitted, to the ideas of free-market theorists – although very little to the practice of free-market politicians who generally preserve intimate relations between big business and government. These are formal aspects of industrial policy, though none the less important for that. The scale of the EC economy is such that transparency and objectivity in public policy require the respect of formal rules. The informal, corporatist development of industrial policy under Etienne Davignon could only work by privileging the very largest companies in the formation of policy, and has resulted in structures which continue to favour the strongest and most powerful economic agents.

The content of industrial policy and the aims which it should pursue involve a different set of choices. Firstly it is necessary to insist that choices *are* available. The rhetoric of the 'competitivity' argument denies that there is any real choice: either Europe responds to the external threats or economic and political disaster will follow. If, however,

European unemployment and the danger of social regression arise from internal problems then there is much more scope for discussion as to which policies to follow.

Although individual member states certainly face external constraints, and although individual sectors may be insufficiently competitive with US or Japanese rivals, there is no empirical basis for the overriding imperative of competitivity in official EC discourse. At the same time it should be accepted that in future the industrial space of the Community will necessarily be extremely open to outside trade and investment, because European integration will encourage the extension of relations between member states and outside countries and develop them into relations with the Community as a whole. This openness is unlikely to face a serious challenge in the future because it is seen as necessary for the diffusion of new technologies and new products on a global basis. Continuing globalisation is embodied in the strategies of multinationals which, regardless of their country of origin, will not confine their activities to Western Europe. These trends do not rule out trade intervention by the EC but they do mean that the aim of such intervention will be to influence the balance between European and outside interests, not to restrict the scope of trade and investment flows.

One possibility for European industrial strategy is to emphasise the internal diffusion of industrial advance as a complement to global diffusion processes. As opposed to the present drive for competitiveness, which must tend to increase disparities between strong and weak economies in the EC, a diffusion strategy would enhance Community solidarity by reducing existing gaps in technology and industrial culture. It would also tend to multiply the value of the Community's human and material resources by stimulating general improvements in quality and efficiency, rather than strengthening the strongest links in the chain, as do present interventions.

A diffusionist approach could also be designed to address the serious industrial problems which are not linked to external competition but are either internal to the Community or general to all advanced industrial countries. One aspect of the general industrial malaise is a widening gap between the technical advances of the 1970s and 1980s and the prevalent organisation of industrial enterprises: for most of the post-war period this organisation has centred on highly specialised production lines, where semi-skilled workers turn out long series of standardised products; new techniques and processes have put the advantages of assembly-line working into question, either by permitting complete automation or by revaluing batch methods of factory production. Secondly, market changes have tended to destabilise the established forms of productive organisation: as the initial demand for mass-produced consumer goods has been saturated, it has become insufficient for producers simply to achieve high output volumes; a wide product range, style and quality, marketing and service, and the ability to adapt output quickly to changing tastes, have all become increasingly critical to industrial success. Thirdly, and perhaps as a result of these technological and market developments, there has been a slowdown in the growth of productivity – a phenomenon which appeared first in the USA in the late 1960s and has since affected most industrialised countries. The slowdown occurred before industrial investment started to decline (although it was aggravated by falling investment) so that it is not merely a result of recession but appears to reflect fundamental problems in the productive system which emerged at the end of the long boom of the 1950s and 1960s. Finally, the loss of momentum in industrial development has undermined established patterns of bargaining and the existing social compromise. In the 1960s the key wage bargains were struck between manufacturing employers and the unions organising semi-skilled line workers, especially in automobiles. In the typical deal wage increases were traded against increased output volumes. The growing complexity of industrial processes and consumer markets meant that established bargaining procedures were less effective in maintaining an industrial compromise which answered the needs of either employees or management. The consequent loss of consensus aggravated the difficulties of adaptation in the industrial system.

To focus on such issues is to suggest that the central question in European industrial policy is not how to parry the external threat but how to move towards a more complex, more finely adjusted, type of industrial system. The potential of new industrial technologies is to give a much closer match between consumer needs and the goods and services which are sold by enterprises. At the same time productive processes, less oriented towards the crude maximisation of output and subject to more sophisticated control can meet social priorities, such as environmental protection, much more adequately. As the assembly line, operated by workers confined to narrowly specified tasks, becomes a thing of the past, much more involved and committed employees can become an active force in industrial change, with a correspondingly enhanced position in the enterprise.

The kind of industrial and social changes needed are well beyond the capacity of business enterprises and spontaneous market adjustment, as two decades of unemployment and instability now show. With the collapse of the previous model of development, and a huge increase in system-wide uncertainty, defensive strategies have prevailed in European companies: restructuring has been dominated by cost-cutting rationalisation; new technologies are used mostly to shed labour; competition has become a struggle for survival rather than a race to introduce new goods and services. Public policy towards industry has increasingly tended to ease constraints on business enterprise – through tighter controls on trade unions, reductions in company taxation and a series of moves towards market liberalisation and deregulation which culminated in the 1992 programme itself. But none of these measures has corrected the bias of company strategy towards short-term adaptation, and the current wave of industrial takeovers provides another illustration of this: huge conglomerates are being constructed which often have very little industrial rationale beyond the attempt to increase shares of static markets; to finance the deals companies are being loaded with debt, compromising their ability to undertake investment. Meanwhile the avoidance of predators has become a major concern of industrial managements, leading them to raise dividends and curtail internal growth.

If spontaneous market forces cannot resolve the problems of industrial development, neither can the problems be solved through a comprehensive scheme of industrial adaptation imposed by the government. Economic policies can, however, accelerate the process of industrial adaptation and limit the damage produced by defensive reactions to uncertainty and instability. The policies required go well beyond industrial policy as such: macroeconomic and monetary stability are required to lengthen the time horizon in investment decisions and correct the present imbalance between productive and financial spheres. Stronger regulation, especially of employment, is needed to exclude regressive forms of competition such as an increasing reliance on casual labour.

In the specific area of industrial policy, the diffusionist perspective would seek to generalise the successful introduction of processes, products and services – multiplying the impact of local adaptations and preventing wasteful and dislocative disparities in the rate of industrial advance. One field of application could be competition policy. The EC Commission, in the context of 1992, has asserted more control over competition policy in the Community, including the regulation of takeovers and mergers. Until now the main theme of EC competition policy has been to promote market integration. It is becoming equally urgent to develop effective supervision of competitive and anti-competitive practices within the emerging integrated industrial space. The aims should be to exclude regressive and damaging forms of competition, such as predatory takeovers, and to prevent the abuse of dominant positions.

In technology policy diffusion should be the main target, rather than the struggle for world technological leadership. Long delays in the spread of new techniques and products from the most advanced to the most backward regions and enterprises are themselves an important obstacle to industrial adaptation. At the same time they erode Community solidarity and expose the weakest economies to deflationary competitive pressure. The sponsorship of technology transfer and the spread of improved managerial practice seem a more appropriate role for EC intervention than the finance of research and development in big French and German industrial groups. (A very small programme, SPRINT, already exists to encourage technology transfer.) Some of the existing policy instruments could be adapted for this new role. As with ESPRIT and EUREKA there could be sponsored agreements among private companies or public sector agencies. Sponsorship would only cover part of the costs of each project to ensure that the participants had a genuine interest in it and would manage it efficiently.

More rapid and wider diffusion would make significant contributions to overall economic development. In spite of the contemporary cult of high technology, it is often the wide deployment of new techniques, not the initial innovation, which is of decisive economic importance. It is certainly advantageous to have a strong computer industry, for example, but there are greater advantages in introducing computers into all the other industries and then making good use of them. In fact the actual production of information technology (IT) equipment is frequently unprofitable because of intense competition among suppliers selling into a buyers' market. Widespread use of the equipment by people with a good knowledge of its possibilities, may make a more secure contribution to income and employment. The growing importance of service activities reinforces this argument. The reliability, speed, range and quality of services can be enormously enhanced by telecommunications and computers, but this is much more a question of diffusion than of technological research as such. So far only a few service sectors, such as banking and finance, where the introduction of IT was encouraged by huge profits, have been deeply affected. Whole branches of service activity continue with relatively primitive technical support, even in the richest European countries.

A further line of policy follows from the 'diffusionist' approach – the development of permanent structures to encourage a rapid response to new productive possibilities. Associations of enterprises across national boundaries are one possible channel, but public sector institutions supporting industrial development form a key part of the networks needed to make rapid diffusion and adaptation an in-built characteristic of the Community's economy. Skilled people, mobile between sectors and across national frontiers are another necessary support for this kind of adaptability.

In recent years policy-makers have made the business enterprise into an absolute value of economic life, the only agent capable of bringing about economic development and the only conceivable location of productive activity. The unequal balance of forces on the labour market, where workers have been desperately seeking enterprises to employ them, has encouraged this tendency, as has also the resurgence of free-market ideologies in conservative forms which insist on the discipline of the company as well as of the market. Economic policy has increasingly focused on support for companies, (EC industrial policy, as we have seen, being no exception). The theme of competitiveness, in particular, has implied the promotion of European champions to struggle for success in global markets. The diffusionist perspective, which centres attention on internal problems of economic development and the huge gaps in levels of productivity within the EC, brings out the limits of enterprise as an economic agent – the lack of communication within and between enterprises, and the difficulty of aligning private business with social objectives. For a diffusionist industrial strategy, concerned to enrich the economic interactions between the regions of the Community, it is essential to extend the range of agents and policy partners to include associations of all kinds, public sector agencies, individual workers and their organisations. Companies continue to be key actors on the economic scene, but their value is relative; they are assessed by their capacity to further the overall tasks of economic and social development. Such a reorientation is the necessary political condition for a more constructive and effective industrial policy within the Community.

Notes

1 EC Commission, 'Towards a European Strategic Programme for Research and Development in Information Technologies', COM (82) 287, May 1982.

2 M. Sharp, 'Europe: Collaboration in the High Technology Sectors', *Oxford Review of Economic Policy*, vol. 3 no. 1, 1987, pp.52-66; P. Patel and K. Paritt, 'Is Western Europe Losing the Technological Race?', *Research Policy*, vol.16, 1987.

Further Reading

On European industrial policy in general, A. Jacquemin (ed.), *European Industry: Public Policy and Corporate Strategy*, Oxford, 1984. For EC policy in particular, D. Swann, *Competition and Industrial Policy in the European Community*, London, 1983.

On R&D the official view is in EC Commission, *First Report on Science and Technology in Europe*, COM (88) 647, 1988 and policy is surveyed in *European Documentation*, 2, 1988, 'Research and Technological Development Policy'. On competitiveness, the original Commission report, *The Competitiveness of Community Industry*, 1982, was updated in *European Economy* 25, September 1985. The most recent assessment is in *European Economy* 39, March 1989, while mergers are studied in *European Economy* 40, May 1989.

5 The Social Dimension

British discussion of the 'social' dimension to 1992 is made more difficult by a point of vocabulary: in the Community and generally in continental Europe, the term 'social policy' has a much wider content than in Britain, covering not only social security and welfare issues but also, critically, industrial relations and collective bargaining. In fact, the two areas overlap in many West European countries where social welfare systems are administered by employers and trade unions rather than directly by the state (and therefore become a central aspect of bargaining between them). It is in the sense of industrial relations and employment law that the 'social' dimension of the Community is most significant, since there are at present few prospects of integration for welfare systems because levels of income and standards of security are too far apart. Employment contracts, the rights of workers and the legal framework of collective bargaining are obviously affected by the process of economic integration accelerated by the 1992 programme. Thorough-going competition between enterprises in the EC would seem to require similar, if not equivalent, labour market procedures. In the absence of common ground rules, competition might tend to become a matter of undercutting or undermining workers' rights in the more advanced countries.

This kind of undercutting, an indirect form of labour market deregulation, has in fact been the objective of the neo-liberal forces which have dominated Community policy-making for most of the 1980s. According to the neo-liberal view, no positive Community employment regulation is needed to replace the national regulatory system which might be called into question by the 1992 programme;

indeed it is regarded as a major virtue of the programme that it permits the circumvention of labour market controls. The doctrinal justification of this neo-liberal stance has been provided by the search for labour flexibility and the theories which attribute unemployment and instability to rigidities in the labour market. In the last decade such theories have been influential all over Europe, not least because of widespread unemployment. Feeling the balance of market forces tilt in their favour, employers have found the constraints of regulation and centralised bargaining irksome. Although many governments have been more or less influenced by neo-liberalism, it has been the British government which has fought hardest and most consistently against any type of labour market control or convention at EC level.

In the short run the neo-liberal forces led by the British government have won undeniable victories. Social and employment legislation within the Community has been virtually blocked for a decade, and the previous process of labour market intervention, based on Christian Democrat and Social Democrat consensus, brought to a halt. The culmination of neo-liberal success was the adoption by the Council of Ministers in 1986 of a British-inspired document establishing flexibility as the aim of Community policy and displacing the more interventionist perspectives of the Commission.

In this context the political conflict around the social dimension of the big market takes on its full significance. In themselves the various reforms envisaged in different versions of the social dimension are unlikely to have a major impact on employment relations, but they would represent an important change in policy direction, away from neo-liberal themes and opening up new possibilities for future advance.

A Flexibility Offensive?

Since the mid-1970s, the member states of the European Community have lost three million (net) jobs. The fashionable view, captured in the term 'Eurosclerosis, is to attribute this poor job creation performance to artificial inflexibilities and rigidities in the European labour market which have prevented market mechanisms and price signals operating with the necessary speed and fluency. In support of this view the experience of the USA during the same period is invoked: where labour markets are claimed to be highly flexible, creating 18 million (net) new jobs for a labour force of about the same size as the Community.

In some quarters the gradual loss of flexibility in European labour markets is attributed to the behaviour of trade unions and excessive government regulation. In particular, by preventing wages from adjusting to market conditions, trade unions are accused of keeping wages too high and thus pricing workers out of jobs. Government regulations in the form of legally based rights and employment protection schemes are regarded as leading to high labour costs, resulting in redundancies and the discouragement of hiring. In addition to government regulation, social security systems are regarded as responsible for involuntary unemployment and acting as a disincentive to work. Under the policy banner of labour market flexibility, the removal of these purported 'sclerotic' rigidities has become a central theme in the neo-liberal agenda for the Community.

Labour market flexibility itself can be a confusing term since it incorporates, or has been used to denote, different and even opposed concepts. There is at least a consensus that it involves three interrelated matters. One is macroeconomic flexibility which refers to the responsiveness of the general wage level in a country to increases in unemployment (or inflation). At this level, if wages are 'sticky' and do not respond to supply difficulties such as higher prices or productivity problems then the result may well be a fall in employment. From this point of view, those elements in wage formation arrangements which reduce wage elasticity should be removed.

Mobility, taken to mean movements of workers between occupations, industrial sectors and geographical regions, is the second element of labour market flexibility. Once again the role of wages is perceived as an important element of this process. If an industry falls into recession leading to a decline in product prices, wages need to fall by an equal amount to avoid unemployment in the industry and/or to give the incentive to workers to switch to more buoyant industries. Similarly, if a region is experiencing an economic downturn, then pay levels should fall, thereby establishing wages differentials between depressed and prosperous regions to encourage labour and capital mobility.

The third and probably the most important aspect of labour market flexibility is enterprise level flexibility. Atkinson's model of the flexible firm is probably the most useful typology of the different initiatives pursued at this level.[1] Three different forms of flexibility pursued by firms are observed: (i) numerical flexibility which allows firms to adjust their workforce (on hours worked) in line with changes in demand. For the most part, this type of flexibility is achieved through increasing the number of part-time, temporary and seasonal workers; (ii) functional flexibility concerns the elimination of job demarcation and/or the creation of multi-skilled workforce so that employees can be deployed over a broader range of tasks to meet variations in output; (iii) financial flexibility, at least in the Atkinson model, is defined rather cryptically, but it appears to refer to developments in performance related to pay, profit-sharing schemes and other innovatory payment schemes.

Labour Market Flexibility in Practice

The theme of labour market flexibility has greatly influenced policy makers in almost every West European country, but to what extent has it guided actual employment policy? This section gives an overview of the flexibility initiatives introduced by the member states at the three different levels outlined above. As regards macroeconomic flexibility, the main impediment to pay levels adjusting swiftly to changing employment patterns is considered to be wage-fixing arrangements. These arrangements include such measures as statutory minimum wages and indexation agreements. The wage-fixing systems of the member states are outlined in Table 1, and the differences are most striking. Some countries, like Italy and Belgium, have legally binding minimum wage and indexation arrangements, while others such as Germany and the UK leave these matters to collective bargaining. Since the early 1980s the trend in almost every member state has been towards relaxing wage-fixing arrangements, though the pace of the movement in this direction varies considerably.

Despite being the least regulated, the UK – by denouncing ILO conventions no.94 on labour clauses (public contracts), no.95 on the protection of wages and no.26 on minimum wage-fixing machinery – has gone further than any other

Table 1: Wage Fixing Systems of Community Member States

Country	Pay increases of Employed persons 1986 Trend National	Real	Negotiating Level	Minimum Wage	Indexation
Belgium	3.0	1.8	Interprofessional agreements (2 years) taking account of wage-moderation and competitiveness	Statutory minimum wage since 1975	Indexation reduced since Royal decree 178 of 30/3/86 – 2%
Denmark	3.1	0.6	National agreements taking account of government recommendations	Agreed minimum wage in very few agreements	Indexation suspend since March 1983
Spain	8.6	0.6	Local & sectoral collective agreements (1-2 years) major state involvement	Statutory minimum wage	No official indexation mechanism but safeguard clauses
France	4.3	1.9	Sectoral agreements and agreements at company level (1 year) major state involvement	Statutory minimum wage (SMIC) (Law of 2 January 1970)	No official indexation but safeguard clauses which are tending to disappear
Greece	15.2	–5.9	Central agreement for private sector and sectoral agreements in a number of branches	Statutory wage since 1982	'A priori' indexation since May 1983
Ireland	6.6	3.6	Sectoral agreements and agreements at company level (12-18 months)	Minimum wage rates fixed by joint (*) labour committees	No wage-indexation mechanism
Italy	7.6	1.8	Three year sectoral agreements taking account of 1983 protocol	Agreed minimum wage in each industry	Automatic indexation since 1957 in low year since 1983
Luxembourg	4.2	3.3	Sectoral negotiations major state involvement	Statutory minimum social wage since 1944. Statutory minimum income since July 1986	Return to automatic wage indexation in Jan 1986
Netherlands	2.2	2.2	Sectoral agreements and agreements at company level (1 or 2 years) Considerable state intervention limited, however, by law of April 1986	Statutory minimum wage since 1986	Automatic indexation tending to disappear from agreements and be replaced by a single payment
Portugal	17.2	4.6	Sectoral agreements (1 year)	Statutory minimum wage	No indexation mechanism
FR Germany	4.0	4.0	Sectoral agreements (1 year)	No statutory minimum wage	Prohibition of sliding scale
UK	7.7	3.6	Negotiations at sector and company level	Minimum rates fixed by Wages Councils (*)	No indexation mechanism

(*) Wage committees statutorily authorised to fix minimum rates for workers not covered by collective agreements.
Source: European Commission 1987.

member state. But the other member states have introduced *some* reforms: for instance, where minimum wages are fixed by law, the rules governing these arrangements have been amended downwards; equally in all the countries where indexation rules exist, either on the basis of legislation or contained in collective agreements, these arrangements have been weakened – sometimes, as in Italy, after major industrial unrest. So, it would appear that the European pattern has been towards streamlining wage-fixing arrangements to increase macroeconomic flexibility.

In terms of encouraging labour market mobility West European countries have done little to make industrial or regional wage structures more flexible. Again Britain seems to be the only country seriously pursuing this option. However, national legislative action has been taken in a good many countries to encourage *enterprise level* flexibility. Moves have been made to liberalise the comprehensive legislation restricting fixed-term contracts which was introduced throughout Western Europe during the 1970s. In West Germany, for instance, legislation was passed in 1985 extending the maximum duration of fixed-term contracts from six to eighteen months and also removing the need for any particular justification for such workers. Spain adopted similar measures in 1984; in the same year Italy increased opportunities for offering fixed-term contracts to young people and in 1986 liberalised their previous restrictive regime.

Regulations governing the recruitment and dismissal of employees ('hiring and firing rules') are identified as a major source of rigidity by the advocates of flexibility doctrine. However, there has been no general West European drive to dismantle these 'hiring and firing' regulatory regimes. Britain has gone further than any other member state by removing legal provision in unfair dismissal cases from employees with less than two years service. As a result of this change over a quarter of adult men in full-time jobs and more than a third of women in full-time employment now have no legal protection in this area. Most other member states continue to have more heavily regulated 'hire and fire' systems, although legislation in France and Spain, for example, has made dismissals somewhat easier for employers.

Little evidence exists to suggest that enterprises are systematically moving towards the flexible firm model developed by Atkinson. In the sphere of numerical flexibility, part-time work has increased considerably and continues to do so. Since 1984 three quarters of the net employment created in the Community has been part-time. Approximately thirteen per cent of the Community's workforce now consists of part-time workers, but (as table 2 shows) wide differences exist between the member states in terms of the share of part-time jobs in total employment, ranging from five per cent in Italy to 23.7 per cent in Denmark. As far as, temporary employment is concerned, figures for the member states suggest that although this form of work has increased everywhere except Italy it remains relatively small in terms of total employment.

Some dispute exists as to whether the increase in part-time work is the result of structural shifts in the economy away from manufacturing towards certain types of service activity or whether it is due to new managerial practice. In present economic circumstances, it can hardly be disputed that enterprises have increased the number of part-time workers in order to adjust the level of labour inputs to meet fluctuations in output. But for enterprises to introduce numerical flexibility in any systematic manner, working systems would have to be more flexible. Throughout the Community there is a trend towards 'annualised hours' arrangements which allow workers to vary the time at work from week to week. Beyond initiatives in this area, and with the exception of some significant developments in West Germany, virtually no other general or systematic attempts have been made to loosen up working arrangements. As a result, the relative increase in numerical flexibility is probably best explained by the broad sectoral shift in employment from manufacturing to services. The reasons why this form of employment varies so much across Western Europe can be attributed to differential growth rates in those types of service activity where atypical forms of work tend to be overrepresented; to different institutional environments, particularly in terms of legal regimes restricting the recruitment of part-timers; and to certain indigenous factors such as a 'cultural' preference for part-time jobs.

Table 2: *Share of Part-time Employment in the Community – 1986*

as % of total employment

B	DK	D	GR	F	IRL	I	L	NL[1]	UK	EUR 10[2]
9.4	23.7	12.9	5.8	11.8	6.2	5.0	6.6	21.0	21.6	13.3

[1] Employees only
[2] Estimate

Source: EC Labour force survey

Contribution of Part-time Employment to Total Employment Creation

	B	DK	D	GR	F	IRL	I	L	NL	UK	EUR 10
Percentage change in employment 1983–86 (%)											
Total	1.8	7.2	1.7	1.4	−1.1	−4.4	3.0	4.6	3.1	3.9	2.0
Contribution to the change in total employment (% points)											
Full-time employment	0.9	5.5	1.2	1.7	−2.4	−4.3	0.6	4.6	2.4	0.9	0.5
Part-time employment	0.9	1.7	0.5	−0.3	1.3	−0.1	2.4	0.0	0.7	3.0	1.5

Source: EC labour force survey, own calculations.

No systematic analysis has been undertaken to assess whether functional and financial flexibility are on the increase. Studies of individual member states as well as cross national comparisons suggest that the trend is to break down task demarcations in order to establish more multi-skilled jobs, and other more general research tends to reinforce this conclusion. Loveman shows that across the Community firms are now spending much more on training, which he interprets as evidence that the need to increase skill levels has become a preoccupation of enterprises.[2] Johnson and Storey, as well as Sengenberger and Loveman, demonstrate that the demand for more skilled workers has increased with the expansion of small firms in every Community country.[3] Again the indications are that the drive towards creating a more multi-skilled workforce is happening at different speeds across Europe, with West Germany and Italy in the lead. These developments cannot simply be regarded as evidence of employers intensifying occupational segmentation by creating a new 'core' group of highly skilled workers. Some commentators in fact suggest that the motivation behind such developments is to meet the requirements of fragmented and differentiated product markets.

Financial flexibility is one of the most dominant trends in personnel policies pursued by American companies, but it is hard to assess how prevalent this practice is in Europe. Several member states have introduced tax concession schemes to promote initiatives in this field, although the research indicates that this practice is more widespread in Britain than in other member states. It is safe to assume, given the prominence of this issue within European personnel management circles, that financial flexibility initiatives will grow in popularity over the next few years.

Overall then it can be concluded that in every member state some type of initiative has been introduced to make aspects of the labour market more flexible. At government level, the objective of flexibility initiatives has either been to make wage formation more responsive to employment conditions or to relax some of the legal restrictions governing certain features of personnel policies at enterprise level. But the scale and pace of these flexibility initiatives differs considerably across the member states. Britain has gone further than most in implementing labour market flexibility, and as a result now has the most deregulated industrial relations system in the Community. Most member states have been reluctant to follow the British example, preferring instead to introduce flexibility on an ad hoc, pragmatic basis.

The total economic significance of firms' flexibility strategies is difficult to assess. In some cases it would appear to be a question of purely defensive measures which lower costs and reduce risks for individual enterprises but without improving the adaptability and responsiveness of the economy as a whole. This would be true, for example, of measures which – through casualisation – transferred the risks of demand fluctuations to employees without in any way reducing these risks or the real costs they impose. On the other hand, enterprise strategies may also contain elements with more positive implications for aggregate economic performance, such as increasing the skill base of employees, introducing new technologies and improving product quality and design. In concrete cases, a complex combination of both kinds of measure can be found, with 'positive' strategies more obvious in Germany or Italy and defensive ones more prevalent in Britain.

Despite a variety of trends and initiatives, no clear or uniform Community patterns have emerged on labour market flexibility: attempts at obtaining greater flexibility have been specifically national in character. Differing economic and political circumstances, distinctive industrial relations traditions, norms and conventions (such as the extent of unionisation), the presence or absence of social consensus and co-operative structures, and the type of wage formation arrangements, have interacted to determine the nature of the flexibility measures implemented.

This diversity of national experience calls into question the neo-liberal demand for a set of Community policies to be applied across the European labour market to remedy the supposed problems of rigidities and inflexibilities. Labour markets inside the Community function in highly specific ways which resist the application of a single strategy. The advocates of the neo-liberal view often overlook the fact that the introduction of flexibility and deregulatory initiatives in Britain was considerably eased by the relative absence of employment legislation and the lack of central institutions, structures or norms governing industrial relations. In other member states the reverse is the case, with the industrial relations system being composed of a dense array of national institutions and legal arrangements. To be effective a Community labour market flexibility policy would require root and branch changes to such industrial relations systems, since it is a basic premise of this approach that the employment relationship should not be conditioned or constrained by non-market external influences. Without a doubt, such far-reaching policy changes would be highly disruptive and might not yield beneficial results. In simply practical terms then, it may not be feasible to implement a Community wide labour flexibility programme.

The problems with this policy model in any case go beyond its practicability or feasibility. A number of underlying incoherences and limitations detract from the case for labour market flexibility. In the first place, the evidence suggests that increased income inequality rather than more efficient labour markets is the most direct impact of flexibility initiatives: for example, the first order effects of deregulatory policies introduced by the Thatcher government have been to widen earnings differentials and not to lower unemployment. Strong social and moral arguments can be deployed against this approach because of the way in which it places the burden of adjustment on poorer sections of the population, but economic arguments can also be mustered. Since fully fledged flexibility strategies tend to build up a reliance on low pay and casualised work, the result could actually be the discouragement of competition between firms on the basis of technology, production methods, marketing and so on. In a Community context this could mean cost reduction becoming the central dynamic in the member states' labour markets, which would work against the Community's need to be competitive on the basis of product markets requiring a high input of quality skills.

A variant of this argument which has become prominent in the discussion about whether a social dimension should accompany the 1992 project is the notion of 'social dumping'. An ill-defined term, social dumping appears to refer to two different but related processes. A completely liberalised internal market without any labour market regulations may encourage the poorer countries to hold down wages and social benefits to limit imports from the richer member states and at the same time increase their exports to those countries. Such a strategy would involve exporting domestic unemployment. According to those most alarmed by this possibility,such action would inevitably force the richer countries to check real wage growth and streamline existing labour market regulations, consequently triggering a price and cost reducing war inside the Community.

Compounding this problem, the second process of social dumping would involve a sizeable shift in production from northern to southern Europe as companies chase after low-wage investment sites. It is feared that the combination of these two processes would destabilise European economies by shifting the concern of governments and managers away from product and processes innovations (which could lead to more sustainable and long-term economic improvements), towards cost reducing strategies (a more defensive and short-term route to gaining competitiveness). In this scenario of social dumping, the main casualties of the competitive regime would be workers and their families who would experience a lowering of their incomes.

Social dumping along these lines may well occur in highly labour intensive industries which are price sensitive, but it is doubtful whether this process will have the systematic effects alleged by some, simply because the 1992 programme itself will not have as rapid or as great an effect as is claimed. To begin with, labour intensive industries are in decline throughout the Community, limiting this effect to a fairly confined range of industrial sectors. Secondly, international investment decisions are taken for a multiplicity of reasons, with wage considerations being only one. When the higher levels of productivity of north European countries are taken into account, the labour cost advantages of the southern member states do not appear so large. While the fears of social dumping are not unfounded, this dynamic will probably not emerge on the widespread scale as sometimes suggested. The limited scope for social dumping, however, does not invalidate the claim that a Community labour market flexibility programme will reduce the incentive for firms to compete through innovation in production methods or by seeking new markets. Obtaining competitiveness through cost reducing strategies will be seized upon by many enterprises as a viable commercial route. While some firms may prosper from such a course, it will certainly be detrimental to the Community's economy as a whole. Unregulated labour markets tend to have a demoralising and anomic effect on the workforce, actually undermining the ability to use effectively new technologies and product systems which depend on the active engagement and co-operation of employees. In other words, the pursuit of short-term gains may undermine the needs or requirements of a longer-term, sustainable model of development.

The flexibility model also contains the danger that many of the proposed reforms might be introduced in a contradictory and self-defeating way. To obtain greater functional flexibility, enterprises may establish groups of core workers which will tend to insulate these employees from market pressures and thus undermine the key objective of macroeconomic flexibility of making wage formation responsive to demand and supply. This is in fact what happened in Britain for most of the 1980s: despite massive unemployment, pay increases for certain groups of workers remained stubbornly above inflation as enterprises strove to retain their skilled workers. Mobility provides a further example: among employers preference has emerged for internal sets of skills specific to the firm; but by establishing such internal labour markets, employers may be undermining the traditional model of highly standardised certification for occupational skills which of course facilitate the transferability of qualified workers. A further example of potential tensions between different flexibility initiatives is the encouragement of 'portable pensions' at the same time as offering fiscal inducements for profit related pay; this strategy simultaneously weakens and strengthens the financial solidarity between workers and employing enterprises.

The introduction of a sweeping range of flexibility initiatives, in order to remove purported labour market rigidities may not result in the smooth working of market forces but in the creation of a new range of imbalances and tensions. At their most extreme, these influences could result in increased instability within the Community's labour market. As Piore points out, 'experience suggests such anarchy will produce an instability that sooner or later would be replaced by a structured set of relationships between labour and management. If these relationships are going to emerge, it would seem better to establish them in a deliberate and reasoned way than to let them emerge in a political reaction after relationships have become embittered and potential structures have become discredited by the excess with which they have become 'associated' '.[4] In other words, the preferable strategy both in economic and social terms is to establish certain arrangements in an effort to make coherent the dynamics of the Community's labour market, rather than leaving them to be determined by unrestricted competition. In a nutshell this is the case for a social dimension to the 1992 project.

A Social Dimension to the 1992 Programme

A social dimension to the 1992 project would consist of legislation, collective norms, conventions and public policies to guide and influence the development of the Community labour market. A number of basic principles underpins this kind of arrangement. In the first place, the search for economic efficiency and competitiveness inside the Community would be conducted in a manner which does not undermine or call into question established social protection and employment rights. Workers should not have to bear an excessive burden from structural adjustment and change. Besides, the social dimension should operate as a facilitating and enabling arrangement to encourage socially preferable strategies for employee relations such as increasing the skill base of employees, giving employees a voice in technological or organisational change. This type of action is imperative for the Community since it will only be able to remain a relatively high-wage economic area so long as it competes on the basis of high-skilled product strategies.

Although the social dimension should be strong enough to influence labour market outcomes, it would be a mistake to attempt to harmonise industrial relations institutions and conditions across the member states towards a single, monolithic model. Table 3 below outlines the extent of the diversity in social regulations in the Community. Just as this diversity places an enormous constraint on introducing a fully-fledged flexible programme, so it also limits the extent to which regulatory arrangements can be standardised and made uniform across the Community. The field of health and safety is an exception: because it involves workers' safety, Article 118A of the Single European Act does in fact allow the establishment of harmonised health and safety measures on the basis of qualified majority voting. In general, the social dimension should be about the creation of a range of policies, laws and rules in the context of institutional diversity inside the Community. The various component parts of the social dimension (namely, legal regulation, a social charter, social dialogue and labour market concentration initiatives) are worth examining in more detail.

Legal Regulation: an Overview of EC Social Legislation

To avoid being abstract, the possible scope and nature of employment law in the context of 1992 should be understood in the context of current Community labour market statutes and their precursors. Before the 1970s, Community social policy was mainly concerned with encouraging the free movement of workers between the original six member states. But with the completion of the first 'negative' phase of European integration in the late 1960s and with a growing desire on the part of some Community leaders at that time to give the Common Market a 'human face', pressure built up for social policies of a more *dirigiste* kind. As a result of this pressure, the member states issued a communique from the 1972 Paris European Council meeting declaring that they were equally committed to establishing a social union as to establishing economic and monetary union.

This declaration gave the Commission the green light to develop a new range of active social policies, a direction it had been wanting to follow for some time. Subsequent attempts to establish positive policies and legal statutes on labour and employment affairs fall into a number of fairly distinct phases. In the first phase, the motivating logic behind the Commission's social initiatives was to obtain greater

Table 3: *The Diversity of Social Regulations in the Community*

Country	Separation law/agreement State intervention	Co-ordination between the levels of agreements	Dominant level of agreement
B	Overlapping of laws and agreements. State involvement depending on problems	The inter-industry agreement provides a minimum basis. Additional advantages granted by firms or at sectoral level	Inter-industry and sector
DK	Autonomy of the two sides of industry, but considerable involvement in wage policy	The inter-industry agreement provides a framework for sectoral agreements	Sector
D	Law supporting negotiation. Principle that State abstains from involvement	Increased co-ordination between sectoral and company agreements	Sector
GR	Two sides of industry closely linked to parties. Almost exclusively State regulation		Sector
E	Autonomy of two sides of industry. State participation in tripartite agreements	Interlocking between levels inter-industry agreement provides the framework for the sectoral agreement which in turn provides a framework for company agreements	Sector
F	Importance of the law – centralised system – increasing autonomy of two sides of industry (Auroux laws)	Attempt to introduce a strict division between the levels (by the Auroux laws)	Sector

IRL	Principle of non-intervention by the State, but increasing involvement	The inter-industry agreement provides a framework for the sectoral agreements, complemented by a company agreement	Sector
I	Law of support for negotiation. Recent reduction of State involvement	Move towards strict complementarity of sectoral and company agreements	Sector
L	Overlapping of laws and agreements		Sector and company
NL	Overlapping of law and agreement; recent reduction in role of State	It is less and less the case that the inter-industry agreement provides a framework for the sectoral agreement	Sector
P	Principle of autonomy of the parties involved; role of State still important		Sector
UK	Law not very important, but individual contract highly developed; State abstentionism; principle of bipartisan agreements		Sectoral and occupational category

harmonisation between member states' employment systems in order to equalise competitive conditions within the internal market. In 1974, as part of the Fifth Directive on Company Law, it proposed that a more or less uniform model of worker participation be introduced by all member countries. This proposal was met with immediate opposition from many of the member states and from most employers' organisations and some trade unions. Not only did they regard specific clauses as deficient, but they also objected in principle to the idea of having to uproot long established and finely tuned institutions and practices of industrial relations, simply to conform to some arbitrarily devised Community standard.

Faced with virtually unanimous opposition from the member states, the Commission had no alternative but to withdraw the proposal for reformulation. The main significance of this episode, however, is that it raised early on the question of the extent to which the Community should try to harmonise the employment and industrial relations systems of the member states. Working from an integrationist perspective, the Commission regarded social or labour market harmonisation as a legitimate and worthwhile objective since it believed this could result in the Common Market working more effectively. But in pursuing this policy, it appeared unaware of, or at least insensitive to, a basic tenet of comparative labour law which suggests that transplanting industrial relations practices across national boundaries is fraught with problems. As one commentator pointed out, 'We cannot take it for granted that rules or institutions are transplantable; ... any attempt to use a pattern outside the environment of its origin continues to entail the wish of rejection. Labour law is part of a system and the consequences of change in one aspect of the system depends upon the relationship between all elements of the system. Since these relationships may not be similar between the two societies, the effects of similar legislation may differ significantly between the two settings.'[5] This reinforces the point that the scope for uniformity and standardisation in industrial relations institutions and arrangements seems seriously restricted in the medium term.

It is interesting to note that despite endless rounds of negotiations no agreement has yet been reached on a

Community model for worker participation. Since no fully-fledged policy aimed at harmonisation in any labour market area has ever been implemented, the evidence suggests that there are strict limits to such a goal. Applying undiluted integrationist principles to social policy was going to create difficulties from the outset. Recent policy documents from the Commission suggest that it is finally beginning to recognise these limitations.

At the time when the member states rejected the first draft Fifth Directive, the Commission was already devising alternative and, it hoped, more acceptable proposals. However, as a result of the economic recession in the 1970s, in all the member states, this task was largely put aside. By the late 1970s a new set of priorities had come to dominate Commission thinking on social policy. In particular, as many multinationals and other large companies were either streamlining their operations or closing them down altogether, the Commission became concerned that such restructuring should take place in an orderly fashion and that workers should be afforded some protection in these situations. The themes of worker protection during corporate reorganisations became a major goal of the Commission's social policy proposals.

In this new phase, the Commission fared much better with its initiatives. Between 1976 and 1980 three directives were passed by the Council of Ministers which established Community-wide legislation on workers' rights in situations of mass dismissals, transfer of undertakings and insolvencies. By and large, however, these directives only paralleled the existing or forthcoming national legislation of the member states. Only the Transfer of Undertakings Directive could possibly be construed as obliging certain member states to introduce legislative provisions that went beyond the scope of their corresponding statutes, although there is evidence to suggest that certain member states have failed to incorporate fully these provisions into their national laws. Under the Community legal system, member states are free to implement directives in a manner which accords with their legal custom and practice and pre-existing law in the same area. Some member states are accused of using these legal ports of entry to soften or limit the possible impact of directives in the labour and employment fields rather than making the necessary adjustments to ensure that national law fully complies with Community law.

As well as these worker protection directives, the Commission was also successful in these years at getting the member states to establish several Community statutes on equal opportunities. Specifically, the Council of Ministers adopted the Equal Pay Directive (1975), the Equal Treatment Directive (1976), and the Equal Treatment (Social Security) Directive (1978). The motivating factor behind these pieces of legislation was to give legislative expression at Community level to the growing demand within European society that the rights of women at work needed formal status. These directives can be regarded as a body of quasi-supranational law since, as a result of their enactment all the member states, (with the exception of Greece), have had to change their national equality statutes.

Many of these changes were made voluntarily by the member states, but again evidence exists to suggest that either by accident or design several member states failed to make the necessary revisions to national law required for full compliance with these equality directives. On numerous occasions, the Commission has successfully launched infringement proceedings against certain member states at the European Court of Justice for not properly implementing these statutes. (Britain has been found guilty of not complying with European equality laws more than any other member state.) By acting effectively in its capacity as guardian of Community law, the Commission has ensured that there is greater adherence to these laws than otherwise would have been the case. Nevertheless, the general conclusion of academic research on this issue, as well as expert legal opinion, is that the Community's equality legislation should have had a bigger impact on the member states. Among the main factors which have been identified as holding back the influence of European equality legislation are: obscurely and clumsily written clauses of some of the directives; the method of adaptation into the statutes of member states enabling some member states to soften the impact of the Community directives on their employment environments; and the painfully slow time for infringement cases initiated by the Commission to be dealt with by the Court of Justice.

The Community's legal presence in the area of women's rights has been significantly extended by a number of Court of Justice rulings unrelated to Commission infringement cases. Because Article 119 of the Treaty of Rome obliges member states to introduce equal pay for equal work, Community citizens have the legal right to use European law in national courts to claim non-compliance with this principle either by a member state or an individual enterprise or organisation. This legal right arises because Article 119 is part of the original Treaty and therefore has what is known in 'Eurospeak' as *direct applicability*, the situation where European law gives individuals fundamental legal rights which can be evoked in any court inside the Community. Normally backed by an equal opportunities interest group, people from several member states have, by citing Article 119, used this right to bring anti-discrimination cases before national courts and ultimately the European Court. Primarily because the European Court has interpreted Article 119 fairly broadly, a number of rulings have been made which not only caused the relevant member state to change in some way its equality laws, but also reinforced the Community law vis-à-vis other member states.

While individuals face the same long delays as the Commission in getting their cases heard by the Court of Justice, this practice – still only in its infancy – may be a more effective way of ensuring that national law corresponds to Community law in the equal opportunities field. Despite the efforts to carry out its responsibilities as guardian of Community Law, the Commission simply does not have the resources to execute this task properly. Individuals and pressure groups with a more intimate knowledge of possible legal loopholes in national laws with regard to Community statutes and of possible violations of such statutes by commercial organisations may be better placed to uphold European equality legislation.

It should be emphasised that as yet it is only the field of sexual equality which is open to this type of initiative 'from below'. Although there is some legal dispute on the issue, the general view is that with the obvious exception of the free movement of workers, no other aspect of Community labour law has direct applicability. Where a member state is considered not to have implemented a piece of labour legislation properly,individuals or pressure groups have no legal recourse to challenge such 'defective' laws either in national courts or at the European Court of Justice. In this situation, the only option for individuals is to inform the Commission of a possible infringement of Community law by a member state and hope that the Commission itself will initiate proceedings.

From the Commission's point of view, the years 1976-80 were on the whole successful as it was able to oversee the establishment of a broad range of Community social legislation. No doubt encouraged by this experience, it produced a new range of legislative proposals to be adopted by the member states. Concerned with the growth of atypical forms of employment, particularly with part-time and temporary work, the Commission centred these new proposals on giving workers in such jobs throughout the Community a floor of basic legal rights. In addition it produced two draft recommendations (which have no legally binding status): one covering the reorganisation of working time; the other, flexible retirement systems. The purpose of these proposals was to encourage the member states to introduce their own new initiatives in these areas in the hope of reducing labour supply, thereby cutting the unemployment figures.

With the exception of a revised version of the Flexible Retirement Recommendation, none of these proposals has been adopted by the Council. The main hurdle barring their passage has been the use (or threatened use) of the veto by the British Conservative government which came to power in 1979. Under the leadership of Mrs Thatcher, this administration has taken the view that Community regulatory employment legislation only fuels rigidities and inflexibilities in labour markets, jeopardising the competitiveness of European companies. In addition, because of the Conservative government's 'minimalist' stance towards European integration in general, it is reluctant to see the powers and scope of the Community developing in many policy areas, including monetary policy for example, as well as the social dimension.

Following its fundamental objections to the Community

extending its role beyond the creation of a free market, the British delegation has opposed every Commission proposal for further social legislation or any other type of interventionist labour market policy which has come before the Council. For instance, it has vetoed the non-binding Recommendation on the Reorganisation of Working Time, even though major modifications had been made to the proposal to incorporate the British objections to an earlier version. As well as being instrumental in blocking the various proposals on working time, the British government has also resisted the Commission's attempts to establish Community legislation giving workers certain information and consultation rights in complex organisations – widely known as the (draft) Vredeling Directive; it has also blocked the aim to create minimum Community provisions in the area of parental leave and leave for family reasons.

It is true that some other member states had reservations about several of these measures, but because they could count on the British Government to oppose them, they discreetly and conveniently kept quiet during the relevant debates in the Council of Ministers. The British therefore became the villains of the piece while the other member states avoided any potential domestic political clash with opposition parties or trade unions.

The effect of the British government's stance was that virtually no proposals for social legislation were ratified by the Council in the early 1980s. The only exception was a number of health and safety proposals: because these draft directives were based on scientific and medical research, and as they mostly parallelled national law, no opposition was mounted against them. Overall, the opposition to the Commission's proposals – spearheaded by the British government – meant that developments in social policy came to a virtual standstill.

The Commission's attempt to develop a body of employment legislation has met with mixed success. On the positive side, it successfully established important statutes in the spheres of equal opportunities, employment protection, and health and safety. Several factors account for the success of the Commission in these areas. In the first place, by being able to evoke a clause in the Treaty of Rome, specifically in the sphere of equal opportunities, the Commission rendered impotent any possible legal opposition from the member states. Secondly, some of the legislation paralleled or only extended to a small degree existing laws in the member states, thus no threat was being created to existing national provision and practice. Thirdly, those directives which can be considered quasi-supranational were adopted mainly because it had become accepted almost everywhere in the Community that a strong legal framework was required on that particular issue. Finally, given that most of the directives were passed in the 1970s, when two of the 'big three' – Britain and West Germany – had social-democratic governments, it is clear that the political climate inside the Council of Ministers was then more conducive to this type of action.

On the negative side, a good many of the Commission's proposals for labour legislation remain at the negotiation stage, having failed to be ratified by the Council. To some extent the Commission must be held responsible: by forwarding proposals which were excessive in terms of the degree of harmonisation being sought, or which were incomplete and complex initiatives, the Commission was virtually guaranteeing that these would not get passed by the Council. But the most important factor has been the British government's uncompromising use of the veto inside the Council to block social policy proposals with which it disagreed. To this negative list, we can add the problem that the process by which Community statutes should be transferred into national laws is not operating properly, reducing the impact of EC labour legislation at the ground level.

A Social Charter for the Community?

Attempts to relaunch Community social policy have been hampered by the failure of the Single Act to introduce majority voting on employment issues, with the exception of health and safety. Consistent with its record, the British government has made full use of the power it obtains from the need for unanimity. Nevertheless, the Commission, supported in particular by the socialist government of France and by West European trade unions, has sought to use the impetus of the 1992 programme to break the deadlock on social policy. Presentations of these initiatives vary, from a simple set of 'accompanying measures' subordinated to the 1992 programme and merely designed to support market-led integration, to large-scale, if somewhat cloudy, notions of a European 'social space' which would have an equivalent status and value to the economic space which 1992 is intended to construct. The most ambitious proposal has been for a European Social Charter, which would lay down minimum rights for employees in all EC countries.

In its strongest form the charter would be practically a European Labour Code with direct applicability in all member countries. A similar proposal is for a European Social Constitution, based for example on the European Social Charter of the Council of Europe, and again directly enforceable in member state courts. Such a reform, flatly subordinating the complex labour law of each country to that of the Community, would be a major step towards federalism and there is little sign of sufficient political support to push it through. Nor in fact are Community institutions ready for the corresponding tasks: if the Constitution or Code went far beyond very wide generalities, it would greatly limit the impact of national legislation and transfer competence over a vast judicial area to the Community. From labour organisations' point of view this rapid integration would be of dubious value. It would tend to consolidate and generalise gains won in the past in north European countries, but it might well inhibit further legislative advances in individual countries while there would as yet be no possibility of a continuing reinforcement of employees' rights by Community institutions. Experience of labour law in federal states, for example Canada, has indicated some of these difficulties, which would be multiplied in the much more heterogeneous case of Western Europe. The emergence of a genuinely unified system of employment legislation is likely to be a very long-term process which gradually extends the existing areas of direct applicability, such as equal opportunities, into new fields of social policy.

The Economic and Social Committee (ESC), whose recommendations of February 1988 have become the basis of initiatives towards a Community Social Charter, explicitly rejected the notion of a European Labour Code. It preferred instead a document with directive status, which constrains the content of employment practice in the different member countries while leaving open the legislative procedures which could be used. In this form the recommendations won very broad support from the ESC with, once again, the British as the main exception. (The vote was 135 to 22 with 13 British representatives, mostly employers, among the minority.) The proposed charter would lay down basic rights in the areas of social security, trade-union organisation and collective bargaining, training, information and consultation of employees, annual holidays and so on for all employees in the EC. In addition there would be specific measures in response to the 1992 programme: control on the cross-frontier use of short-term labour contracts; rights to consultation and information in the case of transnational mergers; and the continuing application of existing collective agreements and employment regulations when public procurement is opened up to Community-wide competition.

In the following month, the European Parliament went much further, adopting by a majority of 238 to 34 a proposal for a directly applicable Community labour statute which would place tight constraints on employers, including minimum wage provision. (It should be noted that this vote was before the European elections of 1989 which produced a Parliament significantly more favourable to organised labour.)

Nevertheless, the Commission and sympathetic governments made little headway towards the Charter in early 1989, against the resistance of employers in general and the British government in particular. In an attempt to maintain consensus it was suggested that the Charter should have no binding legal force: instead of having directive status, it would simply be a recommendation or a 'solemn declaration' by member governments. The obvious danger is that it would be a dead letter – like the OECD's code of conduct for transnational companies, or the Community's code of conduct for European companies with investments in South

Table 4: *Fundamental Social Rights: Summary of the contents of the Social Charter*

The preamble emphasises the importance of the social dimension in the light of the 'impending completion of the internal market' and extends the notion of social rights to all citizens of the EC whether working or not. The implementation of these rights should not prejudice those which are more advanced already existing in individual member states.

Title I – Fundamental social rights

Right of freedom of movement (paras. 1-8) covers rights to freedom of movement, freedom to pursue an occupation, equal treatment, recognition of qualifications, frontier regions, subcontracted labour, social protection and public works contracts.

Employment and remuneration (paras. 9-11) covers freedom to pursue an occupation and access to placement services free of charge.

Living and working conditions (paras. 12-13) covers improvements in these areas, including working time, employment contracts, employment regulations (governing areas like redundancies and bankruptcies), annual paid leave and weekly rest periods.

Social protection (paras. 14-15) covers access to social security cover and minimum income for the unemployed.

Freedom of association and collective bargaining (paras. 16-18) covers freedom of association, union recognition and right to strike, settlement of disputes and contractual agreements between employers and workers. Para. 18 urges the development of the 'social dialogue'.

Vocational training (paras. 19-20) covers training opportunities, training and retraining systems and the freedom for every EC citizen to enrol for occupational training on the same terms as any national of the member state where the course is to take place.

Equal treatment (para. 21) covers intensification of implementation of equal treatment between men and women.

Information, consultation and participation (paras. 22-23) covers 'appropriate lines' for such rights, especially for workers in multinationals and in cases of technological change and restructuring. Particular attention to transfrontier workers.

Health and safety (para. 24) covers further harmonisation in this area, with particular regard to public works.

Children and adolescents (paras. 25-27) covers minimum employment age (16), equitable remuneration, training and labour regulations.

Elderly (paras. 28-30) covers living standards, minimum income and social protection.

Disabled (para. 31) covers integration into working life, including training, accessibility, transport and housing.

Title II – Implementation

(Paras. 32-35) Member states to take appropriate steps to guarantee these rights. Commission to draw up action plan and related instruments and to report back regularly thereafter on implementation of these rights to the Council of Ministers, European Parliament and Economic and Social Committee.

Africa, neither of which is considered to have had a real impact on company or government behaviour.

The Adoption of the Charter

Finally, after considerable 'behind the scenes' negotiations, eleven member states – with the exception of the UK – signed a solemn declaration on the Social Charter at the Paris Summit Meeting in December 1989. This decision morally and politically commits them to guarantee the social rights contained in the Charter. However, it does not legally commit them to the various clauses since the term 'solemn declaration' is outside Community legal vocabulary. Consequently the Social Charter will not be implemented in the manner of a social constitution as some have advocated. Instead, the Commission has produced a social action programme outlining the specific proposals which the member states should enact to fulfil their obligations by signing the solemn declaration. In many respects it is the action programme and not the Charter itself which will influence the direction of Community labour market policies in the future. As a result it may be worthwhile looking at the programme in a little more detail (see Appendix F).

The action programme sets out 47 separate proposals to put into operation the labour and social rights encoded in the Social Charter. These various proposals can be divided into two categories. One group aims to promote greater policy co-operation between the labour market institutions of the member states and the Community's central bodies. These policy initiatives range from fairly low-key proposals to increase the flow of information on labour market matters to schemes to establish concerted action by member states on such things as training and equal opportunities. For the most part, proposals in this category command wide support from the member states.

Potentially these 'concertation' initiatives could bring significant benefits to the member states. One recent study in employment policies in Europe suggests that cross-national contact in this field is one of the most effective ways of ensuring that specific measures reach their maximum feasible potential in terms of their actual impact on employment practices.

The other category is made up of proposals to establish a Community legal or regulatory framework with regard to labour market affairs. The various proposals in this category can be further divided into other subsets: one set of legal clauses simply aims at updating and revising already established Community statutes; another group of proposals aims at aggregating existing national labour laws on such things as part-time and temporary workers, working time and so on. Although member states will be obliged to introduce some reforms and some new measures, these proposals will not entail any 'root and branch' changes to the regulatory environment in the specific areas at national level. Probably these proposals are best regarded as consolidating and making uniform at the European level already well established arrangements prevailing in most member states.

A further cluster of clauses, mostly in the health and safety field, will create supranational European labour regulations. But since the member states agreed to accept the principle of majority voting in the areas of health and safety when they signed the Single European Act, it is likely that there will be no major opposition to these measures. A final group of proposals, for example, on information and consultation and employment clauses in public contracts aim to give the Community some type of regulatory presence, but the precise form of this regulation has not even been outlined. The rationale for not stating the type of regulation wanted is to allow further discussion on the issues.

The action programme will not therefore amount to the enactment of a full-blown European industrial relations policy in the Community. Its actual impact will be threefold: in the first place, it will strengthen and make more coherent the policy networks which have emerged around the Community's labour markets; secondly, it will encourage the Europeanisation of national labour law; finally, it may influence the framework or ground rules for future industrial relations practices in the Community. Probably the most positive way to describe the programme is that it establishes the first foundations for a European system of labour market regulation.

The Social Dialogue

In the realisation that even if the Charter or similar reforms did take place, the Community's influence over European labour market developments would be limited to a relatively restricted range, additional measures have been proposed. In particular, it has been suggested that to complement legal regulations, the Community should also develop a range of informal, or at least non-statutory, norms and conventions to govern the European labour market. The notions of labour market norms and conventions is a recurrent theme in French thinking where it is taken to mean institutional and social arrangements which establish patterns, standards and expectations for employee relations practices and attitudes. The idea that employees should have the right to be consulted on issues such as technological change, or that women should not be discriminated against can be regarded as norms and conventions.

One way would be to develop the Social Charter through negotiation between employers' and employees' representatives at Community level. Complementing and reinforcing this approach to the charter, the employers and trade unions (the so-called social partners) could be given an 'institutional place' within the Community's decision-making framework beyond that which they already possess. The purpose of this body would mainly be: to monitor and assess the extent to which the social rights in the Charter are being observed by the member states and commercial organisations; to attempt to extend the remit of the charter by agreeing to new additional principles to draw up operational guide-lines for the implementation of the informal social rights; to maintain direct links with national institutions and arrangements for collective bargaining, so as to facilitate the rapid transfer of information on industrial relations developments between the member states and to exhort these national bodies to act on agreed Community labour market policies.

Of course the idea of increasing the role of 'social partners' inside the Community decision-making structure is not new. In the late 1960s and early 1970s, the Commission established several industrial sector committees comprising representatives from the trade unions and employers with the hope that these would produce labour agreements. These social partners were also drafted on to a wide range of advisory and policy committees at the Community level. Generally, these initiatives were not all that successful: only one insubstantial agreement covering agriculture workers came out of the sector committees that were set up. By the late 1970s, the general consensus was that these committees had lost their way, meeting infrequently and discussing little of any importance. Although the social partners have appeared more comfortable in the advisory committees, they tend to adopt a passive role in many of the discussions.

Given this rather lack-lustre record, the idea for an institutional involvement of the social partner fell into abeyance for a number of years. On taking office in 1985, however, Jacques Delors revived the idea by proposing the establishment of *social dialogue* as a way out of the stalemate on social policy. Essentially, the social dialogue concept involved the trade unions and the employers' organisations at the European level (ETUC and UNICE) taking over the initiating role from the Commission for employment and labour policy. More specifically, it was envisaged that all the social partners could perform this 'policy initiating' role by holding discussions on particular issues or themes, with the objective of concluding joint agreements which would then be used as the basis of proposals for Community labour legislation.

Unquestionably the social dialogue concept was a clever piece of thinking on the part of Delors. For by incorporating the employers' organisation more fully into the decision-making process the constant complaint made by the European business community that the Commission's social proposals ignore the commercial needs of European companies would no longer stand. Of course, for this project to work not only required the social partners to co-operate fully, but also to adopt a more visionary approach to Community affairs than hitherto had been the case. It was on this crucial step that the project stumbled.

To get the social dialogue idea running, Delors initiated a set of discussions with trade unions and employers known as the Val Duchesse talks. However, from the very outset UNICE, the employers' organisation, made it plain that it would only take part in the talks provided the Commission gave an undertaking not to produce proposals for legislation from any agreement that might emerge. For the sake of saving the initiative the Commission agreed to this stipulation, but of course this undermined the central purpose of having a social dialogue. Although several agreements, or more precisely 'joint opinions', have emerged from these talks, they have not led to any meaningful action being undertaken by any Community institution or by the social partners themselves. As a result, the Val Duchesse talks seem to have fallen a long way short of Delors' original objectives.

Given past experience, then, formidable barriers exist to establishing an arrangement which gives the social partners an institutional place inside the Community structure. The most significant obstacle currently is the opposition of European employers to participation in any body which may open the way to European collective agreements. In this situation the Commission effectively has only two options: one possibility is to scrap the proposal and thus limit, if not abandon altogether, the creation of Community norms and conventions; alternatively, a range of concessions and incentives could be designed to induce the employers to participate fully in the arrangement. The main concession could be for the Commission to agree that a social dialogue would not involve the establishment of binding European collective bargaining and that in the short-term no legislative action would be taken on any agreements arising from the discussions. But what should also be made clear is the intention to establish labour market norms and conventions *with or without* employer involvement.

'Concertation' Initiatives

A third key component of the social dimension should involve concertation initiatives, which essentially bring together the labour market and training institutions of the member states either to launch co-ordinated action or to develop independent Community measures. Over the years, these concertation initiatives have mainly focused on the free movement of workers. For example, the Community finances exchange visits between different national employment recruitment agencies in order to ease the process of transferring vacancies and applications across frontiers. SEDOC (the European system for the international clearing of vacancies and applications for employment) was established to facilitate this process still further. In the context of 1992 concertation initiatives in this field are being significantly increased so that a genuine 'occupational area' is created within the Community.

Concertation initiatives have also been embarked on in the sphere of active labour market policies, but these appear less developed than those schemes aimed at increasing labour mobility. So there should be a strong case for the Community to take on a more prominent role in this area. Taking the issue of training, we have already argued that if the Community wishes to remain a high wage economy then it must remain a highly skilled economy. But skill levels and training systems vary considerably across the member states. In the more successful economies such as Germany the key ingredient appears to be a symmetrical relationship between public training institutions and private enterprises: the public institutions provide clearly structured and comprehensive training which meets the needs of enterprises, and in turn the enterprises act as a place of learning as well as for production. The result is a large supply of workers with high quality occupational skills. In the not so successful economies, not only does there appear to be an asymmetry between the public and private sectors, but each area appears internally incoherent: in Britain, for example, the training system lacks structure, with a noticeable absence of any large-scale programmes to provide high quality training; at the enterprise level there is a wide variance in the amount and level of training provided for workers. As a result Britain appears to be caught in a 'low skills equilibrium' trap.

The Community, standing above the member states, seems to hold a key position to harmonise upwards member states' training systems and provisions, but so far it has been unable to perform this role adequately. The problems surrounding the Eurotechnet programme are indicative of the general problems which the Community has faced in this area. Eurotechnet was initiated by the Community in 1987 with the objective of encouraging the member states to establish innovatory and experimental training schemes in the new information technologies. From this network of pilot projects it was hoped that improved networks of training in these new technologies would emerge across the member states. However, in many member states only limited resources were committed to this programme, undermining the project's entire purpose. In Britain, for instance, *no* new schemes were set up. Instead, the already operational Information Technology Training Centres were put forward as the British contribution to the initiative. Although the programme was heralded as a success, the actual practical benefits arising from the Eurotechnet were relatively few.

If the Community is to act institutionally to upgrade the training system of many member states, then this situation has to change. More extensive and profound connections need to be established between the training agencies in the various member states. A wider range of collaborative projects with more funding and with more commitment from the member states have to be developed. Perhaps more importantly, the Community institutions must be given the capacity to set standards, minimum arrangements and policy guidelines for the provision of training. For instance, the enabling legislation must be introduced to implement the commitment in the Social Charter to making vocational training open to all in the Community: now that a social guarantee has been established across the member states in relation to the provision of training for young people who want it, the Community must ensure that the content and quality of that training reaches a certain level. Much more has to be done to create relevant training provision for women who will play an increasingly prominent role in the Community's labour market as a result of demographic changes, new working practices and different industrial needs.

The Community will need to perform this *dirigiste* role in skill formation because private sector-led training is incapable of producing the quantity and quality of training to meet the needs of advanced productive structures. As Streeck argues, 'most firms will most of the time have a tendency to invest less in training than they should in their own interest':[6] in other words, unless training is regarded as a public good, benefiting the whole of society, profit-seeking firms will always tend to be free riders seeking trained workers without themselves investing in their training. The Community needs a presence in the European labour market with regard to training so that institutional pressures are created towards a high skills equilibrium. The general point is that the Community needs to perform a role which facilitates and enables the private sector to pursue commercial strategies based on the use of highly skilled labour.

Conclusion

By the end of the 1980s the recently fashionable analysis of labour markets in terms of flexibility has started to seem somewhat threadbare. In the USA – the home of flexibility theory – employment has certainly grown fast, but wages and working conditions have deteriorated, inequalities widened and huge macroeconomic imbalances threatened a new phase of stagnation. Britain, the other country committed to labour market deregulation, was hardly a better advertisement for neo-liberal strategies: a substantial, if inadequate, reduction in unemployment was also threatened by balance of payments disequilibrium while the lack of training and shortages of qualified labour were approaching the dimensions of a national crisis.

In this context, the continued rejection by the British government of social legislation at EC level seems less intractable. The questions will soon be not whether a social dimension is needed, but what kind of labour market regulation is required. Here, there is no generally accepted model to replace the previous flexibility approach but a few observations can be made. Firstly, a reconstruction of the wage bargain seems to be a necessary condition for full economic recovery since the bargaining patterns of the 1960s and 1970s excluded too many workers from the benefits enjoyed by the more qualified and well organised sections of the workforce; they were also focused too narrowly on wage levels as the only object of bargaining, and were too crude to relate complex productive efforts to the range of monetary and non-monetary rewards for which they were exchanged. The very highly qualified West European workforce, and increasingly complex economies, undoubtedly require more sophisticated and advanced patterns of bargaining – this is the grain of truth in flexibility theory. But, as opposed to the flexibility model, which implicitly relied on the fear of unemployment as the basis of employee motivation, it now seems increasingly implausible to expect a fuller and more responsible engagement of workers with their tasks without a correspondingly developed level of participation in the definition of these tasks, including the objectives of the enterprise itself.

The institutional implications of this point of view are not easy to derive. Institutionalised bargaining structures will continue to play a key role in regulating conflicts, perhaps also acquiring new functions in communication between more differentiated production units and the diffusion of new practices. A greater degree of decentralisation, however, seems quite likely and there are certainly limits to the role that can be played by Community institutions, even though European employers are likely to see new merits in centralised control as skill shortages accumulate and the balance of power in the labour market tilts against them (in spite of continuing unemployment). So it is possible to anticipate new interest in a social dialogue at European level, especially if there is a clear will to legislate within EC institutions.

The direct value of a Community Social Charter should not be exaggerated, but it could consolidate existing gains and help to prevent damaging and retrogressive forms of competition. Beyond that, its value would be to open up new possibilities for industrial bargaining to be pursued at national, sectoral or enterprise levels. The Charter has also, as we have seen, acquired a symbolic value – as a repudiation of neo-liberal doctrine – which makes its enactment in any effective form politically significant in itself. The development of *directly applicable* employment law in particular areas such as health and safety, equal opportunities and perhaps the treatment of migrant workers can reinforce this kind of effect.

On the other hand, the EC's positive contribution to a new model of employment relations will require more subtle policy instruments – co-ordination of national and regional initiatives, localised interventions and legislation of the 'directive' type which tries to generalise good practice without imposing specific procedure to be followed in all cases. The challenge is to demonstrate, in accordance with West European traditions, that enhancing the status of employees, extending their rights and raising their level of qualification are not sources of economic 'rigidity' but on the contrary the best way of constructing a more productive and genuinely flexible economic system. In such a weakened form, however, the Charter might lose the support of its original proponents (who see little point in a document which fails to constrain actual employment practice), while not necessarily winning over the opposition.

A similar stalemate was reached in another proposal with a significant employment relations aspect – the introduction of a European company statute. In itself this is simply a legal simplification: companies could register at Community level rather than in individual member states and this registration would be recognised throughout the EC. The social aspect of the project is that this form of registration would carry a set of obligations – including employment practices – which would be intended to set a standard for all companies in the Community. Once again, the aim would be to influence the actual effect of company behaviour, not the details of their procedure: requirements for employee consultation, for example, would not prescribe the German co-determination model in particular but impose a general obligation to consult employees which might be fulfilled in different ways. However, sufficient political support does not yet exist to carry through the European company proposal. Political change, in Germany and, above all, Britain, appear to be the key to renewed progress.

Notes

1 For a fuller description of the flexible firm model as developed by Atkinson, see 'Manpower Strategies for Flexible Organisations', *Personnel Management*, August 1984, pp7-13.

2 See G. Loveman, 'Structural Change and the Composition of Manufacturing Employment', Department of Economics, MIT 1988.

3 See S. Johnson and D.J. Storey, 'Small and Medium Sized Enterprises and Employment Creation in the EEC Countries – Summary Report', Commission of the European Communities Programme of Research and

Actions on the Development of the Labour Market 1986; and W. Sengenberger and G. Loveman, *Smaller Units of Employment: a Synthesis Report on Industrial Reorganisation in Industrialised Countries*, International Institute of Labour Studies, Geneva, Discussion Paper OP/3/87.

4 M. Piore, 'Perspectives on Labour Market Flexibility', *Industrial Relations*, vol.28 no.3, 1986, p158.

5 R. Blanpain, *Comparative Labour Law and Industrial Relations*, Kluwer Deventer, 1984, p5.

6 W. Streeck, 'Skills and the Limits of Neo-liberalism: the Enterprise of the Future as a Place of Learning', *Work, Employment and Society*, vol.3 no.1, 1989, p.94.

Further Reading

The best official Commission documents on the social dimension to 1992 are 'The Social Dimension to the Internal Market', *Social Europe*, Special Edition no.3, 1988; and 'The Social Dimension of the Internal Market', Commission Working Paper, SEC 1988, 1148 final. For a critical assessment of the issue, see P. Teague, *The European Community: the Social Dimension*, Kogan Page, London 1989. For further information on labour market flexibility see R. Boyer, *In Search of Labour Market Flexibility: European Economies in Transition*, Clarendon Press (OUP) 1988, and J. Grahl and P. Teague, 'Labour Market Flexibility in Germany, Britain and France', *West European Politics*, vol.12 no.2, April 1989.

6 The Regional Dimension

Although the Treaty of Rome established the removal of regional economic and social disparities as a key objective of the Community, it did not set out specific interventionary instruments or policies towards this goal. To the architects of the Treaty, the reduction of regional imbalances would be one of the many dynamic gains brought about by the creation of a common market. But nobody can seriously claim that this objective has been realised: even the most ardent supporters of the Community concede that wide differences in economic and social conditions and economic performance persist among the regions of the EC. In fact the divergences may well have widened since the signing of the Treaty of Rome even though a Regional Development Fund was established in 1975. To a large extent this is explained by the recruitment of poorer countries from the Mediterranean basin into the Community, and by the slow down in economic growth since the 1970s.

With the 1992 programme liberalising markets even further, regional disparities may well be accentuated and not relieved. Under open market conditions, Portuguese or Greek industry has little chance of competing successfully with companies from northern Europe. However, the member states appear to have relaxed the text-book assumption, which prevailed in the early years of integration, that regions tend towards income equalisation as a result of goods and factors of production moving freely. They have now agreed to a programme of economic and social cohesion to accompany the central, market liberalising initiatives. Essentially, the programme of economic and social cohesion reorganises and gives more resources to the Community instruments aimed at alleviating regional economic and social imbalances. But this programme is not strong or extensive enough to ensure that the 'less favoured regions' do not lose out as a result of 1992, and still less to close the gap between rich and poor member states.

In our account of the regional dimension of 1992, the first part of the chapter outlines the extent of regional disparities inside the Community. Then there follows a discussion of the dynamics of spatial polarisation in contemporary capitalist economies, to highlight the difficulties less favoured regions face in attempting to close the gap with the richer ones. Next the record of the Community's main regional policy instrument (between 1975-86) – the European Regional Development Fund (ERDF) – is examined. The fourth section assesses the programme for economic and social cohesion linked to 1992 to assess whether it will be able to reduce regional disparities in the context of open markets in Europe. Finally the conclusion brings together the main arguments of the preceding analyses and some comments are hazarded on the possible course of regional development in the 1990s. For a guide to the major landmarks in the development of Community regional policy, see Appendix E.

Reducing Community Regional Imbalances: the Scale of the Problem

The officially recognised poorer regions of the Community are Portugal, Greece, Ireland, southern Italy, and about half of Spain, as well as Northern Ireland and the French overseas *départements*. Dominated by agriculture, poorly endowed with economic infrastructure, and held back by low productivity, the per capita income of these regions is less than 75 per cent of the Community average. Obtaining economic and social cohesion inside the Community is a daunting objective given the differences that exist between these poorer regions and the richer member states: no matter what indicator is used a considerable gap is revealed between the richer and poorer parts of the Community. For instance in 1987, GDP per capita, measured in current prices and purchasing power standards (PPS), was about 46 per cent below the Community average in Greece and Portugal, 37 per cent below in Ireland and 25 per cent in Spain. On a regional basis, the gap is even wider with the ratio of GDP per capita between the five richest and the five poorest regions in 1986 estimated at about one to six. Unemployment rates can vary between three per cent in prosperous regions and over 30 per cent in disadvantaged areas; endowment in basic economic infrastructure shows a ratio of one to twelve between parts of Portugal and Denmark. The list could easily be continued.

To reduce this gap in the economic and social conditions inside the Community will necessarily involve the poorer regions or countries growing at a faster rate than the richer member states over a long period of time. Realistically, for this to happen, the less favoured regions will not only require substantial additional financial resources from the Community, they will also have to improve and modernise their own productive structures, but catching up is going to be difficult – the effects of the economic recession in the Community since 1973 have left the less favoured regions in poor shape to close on their richer partners. During the 1960s, when economic growth was high, investment as a percentage of GDP reached 29 per cent in the less advanced regions, but in the wake of the economic downturn these ratios gradually dropped to a low of 19.8 per cent in 1985. The situation has improved marginally since then, but the current level of 21.8 per cent is still far below the late 1960s/early 1970s figures. A similar pattern occurred in the efficiency of investment: in the 1960s countries like Spain and Greece experienced above average efficiency rates, but after 1973 there occurred a sharp fall in these rates, intensifying regional disparities.

Compounding these problems of the quantity and quality of investment, the four less advanced member states had more difficulties than the other member states in containing real unit labour costs, particularly during the last part of the 1970s. Between 1974-79 productivity in these four countries increased on average by about 3.1 per cent, while real wages increased by about 4.1 per cent. So real unit labour costs increased by one per cent on average in the less advanced countries, against a rise of 0.3 per cent for the Community as a whole. The result was that profit levels declined more sharply in these countries than in the richer member states, thereby creating a cold climate for investment. Other macroeconomic factors also appear to have contributed to the poor investment performance of the less advanced countries: a shortage of national savings for instance, (partly due to growing public deficits) and lower foreign capital inflows help to account for the decline in investment shares.

The recession considerably widened the gap between the poorer and richer parts of the Community in terms of both economic conditions and economic performance. Although the process of catching up appears to have resumed in recent years for Spain and Portugal (but not for Greece and Ireland) since these countries enjoyed higher economic growth than the Community, the outlook is far from favourable. The four less advanced member states would need to grow much faster

Table 5: *Growth Differential Rates for Convergence*[1]

	GR	E	IRL	P	EUR 4[2]
		(1) Historical record			
1961-73	3.1	2.1	−0.2	2.9	2.3
1974-79	0.6	−0.9	1.0	−0.5	−0.6
1980-87	−1.0	0.0	0.0	0.0	−0.1
1988-92[3]	−1.0	1.4	0.3	0.7	1.0
		(2) Growth differential required for reducing the prosperity gap to 90%[4]			
1992	10.6	3.9	7.1	10.8	5.6
1997	5.2	1.9	3.5	5.3	2.8
2002	3.4	1.3	2.3	3.5	1.8
2007	2.5	1.0	1.7	2.6	1.4

[1] Measured as percentage point difference with EUR 12 of annual growth of GDP per capita.

[2] EUR 4: GR, E, IRL, P.

[3] Based on medium-term projections 1988-92, October 1988.

[4] In order to obtain some orders of magnitude of the differential required, the real convergence objective is fixed at 90% of the average of EUR 12. This perspective is only put forward as a numerical example and is in no case to be considered as a policy standard.

Source: Commission services.

than the Community average, if they are to become as prosperous as the north European countries in the medium to long term. If the four were to expand annually at a rate one per cent above the average of the twelve which is currently the case with Spain, then it would take more than 30 years to close the prosperity gap. If the time period was shortened to fifteen years, then the differential growth rate would have to be of the order of three per cent; so if the Community on average grew at about three per cent, the poorer member states would have to grow at about six per cent to catch up.

The table opposite outlines what the growth differential would need to be over different time periods for the four less advanced countries to catch up to 90 per cent of the Community average.

This gives some statistical background to the problem of closing the prosperity gap inside the Community. Whether or not regional disparities are actually reduced can only be assessed in the context of the internal dynamics of the Community's economy, and its patterns of industrial and structural adjustment. Judging by current trends, reducing disparities is going to be a difficult task.

The Spatial Dynamics of Contemporary Capitalism

Economic development and structural change have always had a strong geographical character. The emergence of mass production industries in Europe for instance had an obvious spatial dimension. A few decades ago regions in different European countries – the West Midlands in Britain, the Ruhr Valley, Dusseldorf and Freiburg in West Germany, Lorraine, Picardie and the Rhone Alps in France, and Lombardia in Italy – had similar industrial structures based on manufacturing. Now that employment in these mass production industries is in decline these regions are once again experiencing similar, though less benign, developments in terms of deindustrialisation and high unemployment. As these once prosperous regions have gone into decline, new centres of economic and commercial activity have emerged.

The more successful regions display a variety of economic structures, which are interpreted in different ways. One of the most widely discussed theories is that of new industrial spaces based on flexible specialisation. In this model, the use of new technologies and multi-skilled workers links industries to external commercial support structures which encourage innovation and product differentiation at the same time as discouraging price competition. The 'Third' Italy (between the industrial north and the Mezzogiorno) and the Baden Württenberg region of West Germany are the most often cited examples of this flexible specialization model. This is an interesting development, particularly as it represents a considerable decentralisation of economic activity and income generation in the countries affected. The difficulty lies in generalising this kind of productive system so that it does not become the basis of new spatial polarisation of employment and income. Geographical complexes consisting of high technology enterprises along with their associated group of input suppliers and dependent sub-contractors represent another, often identified, new regional economic area. The most celebrated instances of this kind of development are the 'M4 corridor' of south-east England, Cité Scientifique in southern Paris and Grenoble in South-east France, and California's Silicon Valley and Route 128 outside Boston in the USA.

Hall suggests that the emergence of these high technology regions is the result of universities and other research establishments generating intellectual external economies, spawning and sustaining a host of small firms through the valorisation of innovations and other scientific research developments.[1] A third discernible trend, though less easy to define than the first two, is the regional bunching of particular services industries, providing an immense variety of interacting business, financial and personal services. This regionally specific constellation of service activities can take a number of forms – in Paris, the advertisement industry appears to represent the key dynamic; in Madrid it is the fashion business; while in London it is finance.

All of these new spatial paradigms offer lessons for regional policy formation, although they also present risks of new types of polarisation and new patterns of exclusion. They are sometimes treated, quite unrealistically, as a spontaneous solution to the decline of Fordist mass production as a source of employment and the decay of Europe's industrial heartlands. This interpretation regards those spatial shifts as aspects of the transition to a new 'flexible' economy which, it is believed, can adapt enterprises to the uncertainties involved in economic internationalisation and to rapid changes in the level and direction of consumer demand. 'Flexible firms' are seen as using new technologies to counter purported rigidities in previous labour process. Governments influenced by neo-liberal doctrines are therefore reinforcing these enterprise strategies and their new patterns of location. In practice, however, much of this change seems to be defensive.

As a result the evidence so far is that the deindustrialisation of the 'mass production' regions combined with the emergence of the new regional growth centres is leading to renewed spatial polarisation. Regional development is now highly uneven and differentiated: peripheral and less favoured regions are characterised by high unemployment, the relative absence of good jobs in high tech industries and in producer service industries. By contrast, the prosperous regions not only have the lion's share of the good jobs, but they have also the indigenous economic and commercial infrastructure to maintain their dominance over the less favoured regions.[2]

Because of this pattern of development in the Community most industrial employment is concentrated in the richer, northern member states, with the poorer parts of the Community having relatively few of these types of occupations. The main neo-liberal solution to this problem is, unsurprisingly, to allow the market to work more freely. In particular, it is argued that if the market is working freely then sufficient incentives will emerge for people in depressed areas to move to more buoyant economic locations and/or for companies to move to backward regions to take advantage of the surplus labour situation, the low cost of factory sites and so on. This thesis is examined in more detail below.

Solving the Regional Problem Through the Market

Bringing People to the Jobs

In the 1950s and 1960s emigration was the principal way of resolving the regional problem. During this period hundreds of thousands of workers moved from mainly agricultural areas of southern Europe to the industrial centres of northern

Europe. To a large extent, the key dynamic in this process was the emergence of large enterprises based on Fordist principles requiring large numbers of unskilled workers. Migratory flows helped to sustain the massive industrial expansion taking place in the richer parts of Europe, and at the same time relieve some of the unemployment and other social problems in the poorer locations. As a result of these migratory movements as well as the spillover of economic expansion into southern Europe the gap narrowed between the richer and poorer parts of Europe. However, this pattern of mobility more or less ceased in the 1970s when the economic crisis reduced employment opportunities in Germany, France and elsewhere, and immigrants from outside the EC, such as Turks and North Africans, were subjected to tight controls.

With the relaunch of economic integration in the context of the 1992 project the hope is that labour mobility will also take off once again and help alleviate regional imbalance. If economic growth increases significantly through the 1992 project, it is conceivable that migration to the old industrial centres will increase again, but it is doubtful whether such movements will approach previous levels. This is mainly because future patterns of occupational demand will not encourage mass migratory movements. At one extreme, the new technology-based industries require a level of skill which is out of the reach of most workers in the less favoured regions (excluding Ireland). At the other end, it is questionable whether the unstable and precarious forms of employment expanding in the tertiary sector will be attractive to people in poorer regions in the light of the advances made in social security provisions and benefits in those areas: the current trend is for these positions to be filled by people from underdeveloped countries outside the Community. Job openings in the middle range of the spectrum will probably be filled by the existing unemployed in the respective countries. It would appear optimistic to hope that labour mobility will make an appreciable contribution to the reduction of economic pressures in less advanced regions. In any case, migration was always an ambivalent process for low-income areas: it lowered unemployment and raised income through transfers from the workers who left; but at the same time it tended to undermine this internal development, through the loss of the most energetic members of the population.

Bringing Jobs to the People

A different market scenario for the reduction of regional disparities is that completing the internal market will cause a reallocation of enterprises within the Community. One popular view is that transnational companies and other large firms will move from northern Europe to southern Europe in search of lower cost sites. A variant of this argument – the social dumping thesis – is examined in the chapter on the labour market and found not to be convincing. But it may be worthwhile examining this view from the perspective of regional policy: implicit in this thesis of spatial reallocation of industry in the context of 1992 is the assumption either that certain barriers have prevented enterprises pursuing commercially advantageous locational policies or that corporate strategies have for some reason or another not fully investigated this option.

Little evidence exists to support either assumption. It is hard to argue that any of the invisible barriers to trade identified by the Commission have operated as impediments to companies locating in the less favoured regions. Certainly large firms, particularly transnational companies, complain about the wide diversity of fiscal regimes inside the Community but this can only be regarded as an inconvenience and not a barrier since many already have establishments in different member states. The same argument applies for border controls. The only exception may be the transport sector since several studies have indicated that if frontier checks are removed some haulage companies will move to lower cost regions. In other words, it is hard to conceive the type of barriers that the internal market programme will remove so that a more favourable regime for cross-border investments is created – put another way, the Community is already a virtually free investment zone.

The evidence also fails to support the suggestion that the corporate sector has yet to exploit the possible commercial advantages of low cost regional sites inside the Community. A survey of intra-EC investment flows revealed a large presence of foreign companies in many industrial sectors in Greece, Portugal and Spain and that French, German and British firms are heavily represented in each of these three countries.[3]

In Spain foreign controlled companies were responsible for about half of turnover in all major industries and about 46 per cent of employment. In Portugal foreign firms are over represented in manufacturing and financial services and contribute more than proportionately to employment in these sectors. A high degree of foreign ownership is also present in the Greek economy. In many of the more important manufacturing sectors (chemicals, electrical machinery, basic metal industry for instance) the presence of foreign owned companies is particularly high; the economic presence of transnational companies is even more stark with regards to the Republic of Ireland. The thesis that the poorer regions have failed to attract foreign multinationals appears to be unsubstantiated.

A more subtle version, however, of that argument is that with heightened competition after 1992 enterprises will be obliged to reformulate corporate strategies which, for some, will mean turning towards the poorer regions in an effort to secure some type of comparative advantage. Recent research suggests that enterprises are fundamentally re-examining their European corporate strategies in light of 1992, but there are no indications that a shift to southern Europe is about to occur. For established firms in northern Europe to move to Portugal, Greece or wherever, there must be sound commercial reasons for doing so. The table below outlines the factors that influence a company to take such a decision. Against a reading of these factors, it appears unlikely that any significant shift of enterprises will occur from the richer to the poorer parts of the Community. Take, for instance, the case of a German company considering a move to Portugal or Greece: the vast majority of factors – whether infrastructure, geographical location, product market potential, or labour market factors such as training and skill levels – would influence the company to remain in Germany. If the company was in a high labour-intensive sector where wages represent a significant proportion of total costs, then the inducement to move may be greater; but when differences in wage levels are set off against productivity levels, then the divergence between the north and south of Europe is not that great, making a shift less attractive.

Table 6: *Factors Influencing the Location of Firms*

Market potential
- local market demand, growth potential;
- potential for economies of scale.

Macroeconomic context / economic policy
- growth rate of the economy, its capacity to absorb shocks;
- exchange rates, credit rates, taxation (income/company taxes);
- industrial policy: R&D, subsidies, energy policy;
- commercial policy: import constraints, non-tariff barriers.

Labour market
- labour costs;
- qualification of the workforce;
- labour market legislation: working-time, redundancy legislation;
- social climate: industrial relations, flexibility, trade-union activity.

Geographical situation
- proximity of clients, suppliers;
- transport costs (and communications).

Infrastructure
- energy costs (electricity, gas, water);
- industrial sites (costs and expansion potential);
- services (banks, insurance, ...);
- educational institutions (universities, research institutions, etc.).

Type of activity
- product life-cycle;
- labour intensity.

Other factors
- social, cultural and language factors;
- quality of living environment.

In other words, the argument that the 1992 programme will induce a geographical realignment of enterprises from the core to the periphery of the Community lacks a strong foundation – in practice the very reverse may be the case. For

1992 may lead to greater specialisation and concentration of export-based activities in areas of greater economic advantage because it may be easier and more cost-effective to service the internal market from fewer sites.

Overall then there is little prospect that the regional problem can be solved through the creation of open markets in the Community. By definition, this means that intervention is required to reduce regional disparities. For the past fifteen years the Community has devised a range of interventionary arrangements targeted on regional problems mainly in the form of the Regional Fund, but also to a lesser extent the Social Fund. In the following sections we examine the nature and impact of the Regional Fund in particular and the direction of Community regional policies in the context of 1992.

Community Regional Policy

The Social Fund was the only instrument established by the Treaty of Rome which in any sense could be described as a form of regional policy since it was seen, at least in its original form, as a mechanism to help transfer unemployed workers from labour surplus to labour deficit areas. Other than this arrangement no interventions were considered necessary by the Treaty drafters to correct possible regional imbalances. The prevailing assumption was that economic divergences would spontaneously erode as a result of market integration, and this view remained the orthodoxy until the end of the 1960s: apart from collecting data, the Community had no active regional policy. Then, as part of the wider project to redirect Community action towards positive integration and away from negative integration, the idea of a set of European interventionary regional initiatives gained support (see Appendix E).

At the 1972 Paris Summit the move towards an active Community regional policy was given official endorsement by the member states: the final communiqué from that meeting stated 'that a high priority should be given to the aim of correcting, in the Community, the structural and regional imbalances which might affect the achievement of economic and monetary union'. To meet this objective the Commission was instructed to begin the work of establishing a

Community regional policy instrument. In the following year the Commission published the Thompson Report which systematically argued the case for an active Community Regional Fund on economic, political and environmental grounds. It also laid down some operational principles and guidelines for such an instrument: in particular, the report recommended that the Regional Fund should be targeted on areas overdependent on agriculture or suffering from structural underemployment. Ironically, it was the British government above all that pressed for this new instrument, in the hope of winning support for its declining industrial regions. In the 1980s, the British government moved to oppose European regional spending, partly because of its free-market principles, but also because Britain could no longer hope to be a major beneficiary after the entry of the low-income Mediterranean countries.

Although the report was widely welcomed, its actual impact on subsequent developments was minimal. Many of the arguments used in the report were premised on the continuation of high economic growth, but these quickly became redundant under the onslaught of the economic crisis. With the dramatic turnaround in economic fortunes the member states quickly lost enthusiasm for a Regional Fund targeted exclusively on the less favoured regions. A consensus emerged that all member states should in some way benefit from a Community Regional Fund. As a result, when the ERDF was established in 1975 it was organised on the basis of a 'quota scheme' so that each member state would receive some money. Although revised in various forms, this quota scheme was the main mechanism for allocating the ERDF until 1986/7. The table below outlines the quotas arrangements between 1975-86.

In the early years, between 1975-79, the ERDF operated along the following lines: an advisory Committee on Regional Policy made up of representatives from the member states, the trade unions and employers working in conjunction with the Commission established 'indicative guidelines' for the type of national projects eligible for financial assistance; working within these 'indicative guidelines' each member state wrote a Regional Development Programme (RDP) outlining the social and economic context for the proposed initiatives and describing aspects of the organisational arrangements – the develop-

Table 7: *The Quotas of* ERDF *Allocated to the Member States, 1975-84*

Member State	Percentage Quotas 1975-77	1978-80	1981-84	GDP per capita 1981 (EC = 100)
Belgium	1.49	1.39	1.11	105
Denmark	1.29	1.20	1.06	109
West Germany	6.34	6.00	4.65	114
Greece	–	–	13.00	56
France	14.87	16.86	13.64	110
Ireland	6.46	6.46	5.94	67
Italy	40.00	39.39	35.49	89
Luxembourg	0.10	0.09	0.07	116
Netherlands	1.69	1.58	1.24	104
United Kingdom	27.60	27.03	23.80	93

Source: Croxford, et al 1989

ment objectives, the financial systems and the implementation strategies of the proposed projects.

From the outset, however, the operation of the Fund came in for considerable criticism. In the first place, the Fund's administrative and financial arrangements were heavily criticised, particularly as its 250 million ECU budget had to cover 55 per cent of the Community's geographical area and 40 per cent of its population – one Prime Minister called the Fund 'inadequate to a derisory degree'. Another criticism was that as the quota system guaranteed each member state an annual ERDF allocation, no incentive existed for national administrations to prepare comprehensive regional development programmes. National quotas resulted from a political compromise, with little relation to the level of development in each country, with the result that Germany, Denmark and the Netherlands obtained substantial quotas. (These countries do of course have national regional problems, but it is doubtful whether they can be regarded as European problems, since income levels – although below national averages – are much higher than in Italy, Spain, Greece and so on.)

In their examination of the RDP submissions, Martins and Mawson found them to be of a low quality.[4] Not surprisingly, they concluded that most member states saw RDPs as a bureaucratic ritual which had to be undergone to obtain Regional Fund money. The overall result of these shortcomings was to limit the Commission's ability even to co-ordinate regional policies amongst the member states, let alone develop an independent European regional policy. In essence, the national RDPs were a catalogue of separate independent projects in different geographical locations rather than a coherent set of proposals for the development of certain regions. In the final analysis, the ERDF was simply financing 'stand alone' projects in the member states.

These limitations were almost immediately recognised by Community institutions and other independent analysts. As a result, no sooner had the Fund been established, than the process of revising it was put in train. The first reforms were made in 1979 when a small non-quota section, comprising five per cent of the total resources, was introduced into the Fund to give the Commission the capability of funding projects of its choice. In addition, certain administrative and organisational changes were made to make the eligibility criteria more flexible and to improve the co-ordination of national regional policies. While these reforms made some improvements they appeared not to have remedied the central shortcomings of the Fund. In the early 1980s, academic assessments continued to conclude that the Fund was still dominated by national interests, that the 'non-quota' section – the nascent independent *European* dimension to the Fund – was cosmetic and that overall the entire arrangement was too cumbersome to be effective. On several occasions between 1981-84 the Commission proposed further reforms (for example in 1981 it tabled a proposal to increase the 'non-quota' section of the Fund to twenty per cent and to make the structure of the Fund much more adaptable) but these came to nothing.

The 1984 Reforms

After years of persistent cajoling and lobbying the Commission was finally able to get the member states in 1984 to accept a set of reforms designed to correct some of the deficiencies of the ERDF. Three main changes were introduced by these 1984 regulations. In the first place, the 'quota/non-quota' arrangement was abolished and replaced by a system of indicative ranges. Under this new system a member state's share of the ERDF could vary between guaranteed minimum and maximum levels. In other words, member states were no longer assured a fixed amount from the Fund each year. By introducing this element of competition into the allocation of the ERDF, the Commission was attempting to get the member states to improve the quality of their submissions for money. The table below outlines the indicative range for each member state established by 1984 regulation.

Table 8: *Indicative Ranges Introduced by Reformed* ERDF *Regulation (and subsequently amended to include Spain and Portugal)*

Member State	Indicative Ranges Minimum %	Maximum %
Belgium	0.61	0.82
Denmark	0.34	0.46
West Germany	2.55	3.40
Greece	8.36	10.64
Spain*	17.97	23.93
France	7.48	9.96
Ireland	3.82	4.61
Italy	21.62	28.79
Luxembourg	0.04	0.06
Netherlands	0.68	0.91
Portugal*	10.66	14.20
United Kingdom	14.50	19.31
EC total	88.63	117.09

* Following the accession of Spain and Portugal to the Community in 1986 the Indicative Ranges were altered. Consequently, the upper and lower limits for these two countries apply for a two-year period only.

Source: EC Council Regulation (EEC) 3641/85.

Reinforcing this change was a new set of criteria to assess applications for ERDF assistance: in future, applications had to show how their projects would assist the economic development of the region, contribute to job creation both directly and indirectly, and implement Community objectives such as paving the way for further investments in the area.

The objective of this new assessment procedure was to ensure that only applications which furthered the Community interest would be funded. To palliate these changes for the member states the rate of ERDF assistance to individual projects was increased from 30 per cent to 50 per cent.

The second change introduced by the 1984 regulation was a gradual shift from financing single, occasional projects to funding programmes consisting of a number of separate but related projects in the same region. Through the establishment of the programmatic approach the Commission was hoping to increase the impact and visibility of Community assisted regional schemes. Three different types of programmes were established – National Programmes of Community Interest (NPCIs), Community Programmes, and Integrated Development Operations. To a large extent, the NPCIs, which were to receive 80 per cent of the ERDF, appear to be only a modified form of the Regional Development Programmes which prevailed until 1984. In many respects, because the Commission failed to spell out what it expected to be included in a NPCI, it is difficult to be precise about how the two were intended to differ. The impression is that the Commission wanted a NPCI to contain a co-ordinated and integrated package of projects covering such matters as small and medium-size business development, technology transfer initiatives as well as standard infrastructural schemes, rather than a checklist of individual projects which tended to dominate RDP submissions. The revisions did not seriously challenge the right of the member states to devise and develop the type of initiative to be assisted by the Fund, but the Commission's influence over the direction of the Fund and of the type of project or programme that would get funded increased with the introduction of more competition into the overall financial allocation to the member states.

The Community Programmes were introduced to replace the non-quota part of the Fund which allowed the Commission independently to select programmes for assistance. Under the old arrangement, the non-quota scheme received only five per cent of the Fund, but as result of the changes this portion increased to twenty per cent. With more money at its disposal, the Commission developed a more co-ordinated approach to funding schemes. In particular it set up two new initiatives, both to be targeted on the less favoured regions, and which would receive the bulk of the finance. One was the Special Telecommunication Action for Regional Development (STAR) designed to assist the development of modern telecommunication infrastructures in the poorer regions. A budget of 780 million ECUs over a five-year period was allocated to the scheme with each selected project receiving a Community contribution equal to about 55 per cent of the total expenditures. The other initiative set in motion was the Valorisation of Endogeneous Energy Potential (VALOREN). The aim of VALOREN was to improve local energy supplies either by assisting the exploration of indigenous energy resources or the promotion of efficient energy use. A total of 400 million ECUs was set aside for this scheme over a five year period; once again the Community would only contribute 55 per cent of the cost of any funded project.

Integrated Development Operations was the third new programme established by the 1984 Regulation. Consisting of a combined set of public and private measures and investments, the objective of these integrated operations was to 'bring out the potential for indigenous development' and to concentrate financial flows in favour of a region or sector. Modelled on two pilot schemes established in Belfast and Naples in the early 1980s, the essence of these operations was to obtain the maximum feasible level of co-ordination between the institutions and financial instruments working towards regional and industrial renewal.

Although established by the 1984 reforms, these various programmes were not immediately to replace individual project financing. Rather modestly, the enabling regulation stipulated that by 1988 only twenty per cent of the Regional Fund had to be directed towards assisting programmes. The most significant aspect of the reform in the short term was to be the transition from the quota arrangements to the indicative ranges. This change, designed to increase competition for ERDF grants, had an immediate impact – within two years 1,300 extra projects were submitted by the member states. Much of this increase in the numbers of applicants must be ascribed to the ERDF contribution to a project's cast budget rising from 30 per cent to 50 per cent.

Nevertheless, the evidence in terms of the quality of applications also suggests that the reforms have encouraged the member states to adopt a more active and systematic approach to the ERDF.

The Regional Fund in Practice

The Scale of the Fund

The table below outlines the distribution of the ERDF across the member states in the years 1981-86. It shows that although every member state obtained some money from the Fund, the lion's share went to the countries with severely depressed regions – Italy, Greece, the UK and Ireland – but it also shows that the Fund did not expand at a sufficiently fast rate to compensate for the accession of Spain and Portugal. A redistribution of the Fund had to take place with the pre-existing poorer regions losing out so that the two new entrants could get some assistance.

Table 9: *The Distribution of ERDF Assistance, 1981–86*

Member State	Ave. alloc. 1981–84		1985		1986	
	mecu	(%)	mecu	(%)	mecu	(%)
Belgium	16.1	(0.8)	24.5	(1.0)	32.3	(0.9)
Denmark	21.1	(1.0)	13.2	(0.5)	11.1	(0.3)
West Germany	66.5	(3.3)	83.7	(3.0)	82.5	(2.4)
Greece	274.6	(13.4)	409.0	(16.7)	316.7	(9.2)
Spain	–	–	–	–	640.9	(18.6)
France	273.3	(13.4)	309.9	(12.6)	310.0	(9.0)
Ireland	123.3	(6.0)	157.2	(6.2)	126.8	(3.7)
Italy	761.8	(37.2)	871.1	(35.5)	833.8	(24.2)
Luxembourg	2.1	(0.1)	0.0	(0.0)	3.4	(0.1)
Netherlands	21.5	(1.1)	18.8	(0.7)	29.7	(0.9)
Portugal	–	–	–	–	380.8	(11.0)
United Kingdom	485.2	(23.7)	608.1	(23.8)	558.7	(16.2)
EC total	2045.5	(100)	2495.5	(100)	3446.3	(100)

Source: Croxford et al, 1988

The Impact of the Fund – A Snapshot of One Year

Table 10 details the nature of projects assisted by the ERDF in each of the member states in 1986. The table shows that seven

Table 10: *Projects Benefiting from Assistance in 1986*

Member State	Industry, services and crafts Number	Assistance	Infrastructure Number	Assistance	Total (in million ECUs) Number	Assistance
B	14	3.00	24	12.46	38	15.46
DK	41	1.17	32	7.44	73	8.61
D	217	53.50	63	28.92	280	82.42
GR	6	1.72	247	290.36	253	292.08
E	25	11.20	238	629.68	263	640.88
F	135	18.78	115	210.37	250	229.15
IRL	31	21.98	70	102.54	101	124.52
I	571	186.08	829	627.19	1,400	813.27
L	–	–	–	–	–	–
NL	–	–	5	23.19	5	23.19
P	–	–	792	380.85	792	380.85
UK	281	84.12	616	371.64	897	455.76
EUR 12	1,321	381.55	3,031	2,684.64	4,352	3,066.19

out of ten projects approved were located in either Italy, the UK or Portugal and that 87 per cent of the aid went to infrastructural projects. The average ERDF contribution per infrastructure project was about 885,000 ECUs making up half of public expenditure or just over a third of total investment costs. The largest single grant made in this year was 59 million ECUs for telecommunications modernisation in a number of regions in Greece. However, the transport sector, roads and highways, were the type of infrastructure project which benefited the most from assistance, receiving 70 per cent of the total aid to projects.

Only thirteen per cent of aid went to projects promoting productive investment in the industrial, craft, and service sectors. The objective of this part of the Fund is to assist investment projects in economically sound activities intended to help create or maintain permanent jobs. The Fund has always failed to attract large numbers of viable applications in this category. Before 1984, it was a stipulation that about 30 per cent of the Fund was to go to projects in this field, but this had to be relaxed as it was never realised. In addition, many of the operational criteria governing this type of project had to be abandoned as they were proving to be too stringent. The share of grants varies considerably from country to country, but the richer member states benefit the most. In 1986, West Germany received 65 per cent of all the aid from this part of the Fund, next was Italy with 23 per cent of the Fund. The less favoured regions received paltry amounts – Spain 1.7 per cent, Greece 0.6 per cent and Portugal submitted no industrial projects.

In terms of project financing, the funds received by the less advanced countries from the ERDF more or less relate to physical infrastructure initiatives. While the poorer regions of the Community are in need of better economic infrastructure, it seems that ERDF assistance is skewed too much in this direction. If the purpose is to encourage internally generated methods of development then the Fund has to support a wider range of activities.

The Fund's Limitations: the Problem of Additionality

One of the biggest controversies surrounding the operation of the ERDF is the notion of 'additionality'. This notion concerns the problem of ensuring that ERDF grants are really additional to national financial assistance and are not merely refunding national public authorities the money they have already allocated to projects. Although article 36 of the 1984 regulation establishes that in the case of industry, craft industry and services, ERDF assistance should be used to supplement national assistance, every member state uses money from this part of the Fund to offset national expenditure. The British government is accused of being the worst offender as it uses all its receipts from the ERDF partly to refund its own expenditure on regional development initiatives. For instance, when a British local authority receives a grant from the ERDF, it receives money from Brussels, but the government deducts a corresponding amount from the authority's approved borrowing programme. When a firm receives a ERDF grant, the Department of Trade and Industry, will retain the money sent from Brussels since it will have already disbursed a grant to the company in lieu of the Community's cheque.

There appear to be three major (negative) implications arising from this situation. In the first place, the extent and scale of initiatives generated at the ground level by the European Regional Fund is severely constrained. If a British local authority were to receive ERDF money in a manner where it properly supplemented national funds, then it could embark upon other projects to the benefit of the locality and at the same time increase the Community's visibility on regional matters. Furthermore, because the UK government takes into account ERDF receipts when setting the budget for capital spending in the public sector, it has cynically used the Fund as a way to limit public expenditure growth. This virtually reduces the operation of the Fund, in Britain at least, to a bureaucratic farce: public institutions, like local authorities, are obliged to make applications to the ERDF simply to stand any possibility of obtaining funds determined at the national level. The third implication is that the British government is only concerned as to whether applications actually coincide with the eligibility rules governing the ERDF and not with the broader issues of how the applicants may help develop local areas. As a result of this practice the concept of the Community developing an independent regional policy is all but undermined.

When first established the Regional Fund was intended to eliminate the regional disparities existing within the Community. Measured against this benchmark the Fund has failed miserably, but – given the level of the Fund's resources – it is unrealistic and naive to think that it could have succeeded in this task. A fairer assessment would be that although the Fund suffered from a number of organisational and operational drawbacks, in the local context it did bring benefits to certain areas and regions, particularly with regard to physical infrastructural provisions. Overall, however, the operation of the Regional Fund between the mid-1970s and mid-1980s is the story about how a decline in commitment to the European project among the member states held back the emergence of fully fledged Community regional policies. With member states taking a firmly intergovernmental approach to Community affairs, the Regional Fund had virtually no chance of developing into an effective instrument for regional development. The fact that the lion's share of the money went to help finance *nationally* determined projects and that most member states used the money from the Fund to replace rather than to supplement domestic public expenditure vividly illustrates this point. If the problem of regional imbalance is to be resolved in the context of 1992, the political outlook and practice of the member states in this area will have to change considerably.

Regional Development and 1992

Fearful that the 1992 project might cement or even accentuate regional disparities, the Commission proposed a programme of economic and social cohesion. Despite initial reservations from some member states, particularly the UK, the European Council ratified the programme – in fact, the programme was given legal status as it was included in the Single European Act. In its document, *The Single Act: a New Frontier for Europe*, the Commission expanded on what the social and economic cohesion programme would entail: essentially it amounted to the integration of the Community's various structural funds – the European Social Fund, the 'guidance section' of the European Agricultural Guidance and Guarantee Fund (FEOGA) and the European Regional Fund, enlarging their share of the Community budget and targeting these funds on a narrower set of defined objectives. After some resistance the member states endorsed the Commission's plan and committed themselves to doubling the structural fund budget from 7,400 million ECUs in the 1988 budget to a total of 13,000 million ECUs in 1992. This increase represented a significant shift in the direction of Community expenditure since 30 per cent of the overall budget would be allocated to regional development as opposed to eighteen per cent which had been the case in 1988.

In addition to the doubling of its size, the new integrated structural funds were set five new priority objectives to pursue: ('Objective No. 1') developing 'less developed regions'; ('Objective No. 2') converting regions and small areas 'seriously affected by industrial decline'; ('Objective No. 3') combatting long-term unemployment; ('Objective No. 4') combatting youth unemployment; (Objectives No. 5a and 5b) developing 'agriculture structures and rural areas'.

Criteria were established for defining 'Objective No. 1' and 'Objective No. 2' areas. As regards 'Objective No. 1' the qualifying regions are those where GDP per capita registered less than 75 per cent of the Community average in the preceding three years (in geographical terms, this definition incorporated Greece, most of Spain, Portugal, southern Italy, the Republic of Ireland, Northern Ireland and the French overseas départements). Approximately three-quarters of ERDF finances were to be devoted to 'Objective No. 1', which would lead to the doubling of these areas' receipts by 1992. Regions to be included in 'Objective No. 2' areas were to be selected on the basis of a 'synthetic index' calculated by linking together employment participation rates, the proportion of the workforce in industry and the proportion of the workforce who had left industry in recent years.

The programme approach established by the 1984 ERDF regulation is regarded as the principal method for allocating money from the new structural funds. Over time the management-by-project approach will be phased out. Furthermore, as a result of the different funds being integrated not only will the programmes cover initiatives in the regional policy field (infrastructured projects and so on), but they will also include employment and training schemes. The hope is that with a bigger budget and more comprehensive programmes the structural funds will be better placed to have a significant impact on specific regional economies – in the words of the Commission, 'replacement by the traditional sector-by-sector approach with an 'integrated approach' enabling the resources of the different funds to be channelled towards one objective, thus rendering each fund more effective'.[5]

Can the Programme for Economic and Social Cohesion Succeed?

For the structural funds to improve the internal growth conditions in the less favoured regions and countries, they will have to create a positive impact at enterprise, regional and macroeconomic levels. The microeconomic level concerns the formation of new enterprises, helping existing ones to grow and expanding the role played by the commercial sector in regional economic development. Earlier parts of the chapter indicated that the ERDF success at this level was minimal. Clearly, new and innovative ideas and approaches are required to make the new structured funds more effective at this level. One idea aims to place the notion of entrepreneurship at the centre of the regional economic development: entrepreneurship refers to the process of creating more small firms, reducing the local economy's reliance on the public sector as well as transnational companies, and encouraging a more commercially oriented culture. (A variant of this entrepreneurship model for regional development is probably the British government's Enterprise programme.)

This approach has influenced policy-thinking at the Community level. For instance, a Community Programme for Business and Innovation Centres has been established to assist in the creation and growth of small firms, but it is questionable whether this entrepreneurship model should guide the operation of the Community's structural funds. As one commentator pointed out, it would be 'too good to be true' to think that economic development can occur in peripheral regions through the promotion of entrepreneurship.[6] It tends to be densely populated regions close to urban centres which spawn entrepreneurs in large numbers and not poorer regions where the indigenous skills, resources and traditions are powerful obstacles to the successful implementation of such an approach. Assessment of initiatives to promote entrepreneurial forms of regional development inside the Community tend to reinforce this conclusion.[7] In particular because many of these initiatives involve giving fairly generous non-discriminatory grants for the establishment of new small business, the effect has been to generate too many start-ups and to support poor quality entrepreneurialism. Moreover, in terms of wider goals such as employment generation the indications are that entrepreneurialism brings few benefits. It may be ill-conceived and a waste of money to replicate some of these approaches and give lavish handouts to potential small firm owners. Support for the expansion and development of existing enterprises may be much more cost-effective.

Another much canvassed idea is for the Community to concentrate on innovation and high technology oriented regional policies. The rationale for this objective is that the poorer regions have to leapfrog a phase of industrialisation and establish advanced economic structures to have the capacity to compete successfully in international markets. There is certainly a great need to increase the technological base of the less advanced member states – in the chapter on industrial policy we argue strongly for the Community's technological programme to be geared towards diffusing innovation and new technological equipment from the north to the south of Europe. However, technology transfer and other high technology policies alone will not bring about economic and social cohesion. One reason, emphasised by recent research, is that the industrial base in the poorer regions is too small to generate sufficient numbers of worthwhile projects. In other words the less advanced member states may not have the 'absorptive capacity' to sustain a technologically based regional policy.[8] It appears that technologically oriented policies should be but one part of a broader regional package.

Loveman and Sengenberger develop an approach which may be more beneficial for the Community to pursue at the microeconomic level.[9] Instead of focusing exclusively on the formation of new firms or on technological initiatives, the emphasis would be to create support structures to 'create a particular 'social organisation' of the market'. Social organisations of this type are essentially about 'rooting small business in a co-operative social network and tying to it social relations'.[10] The objective of such an arrangement in less advanced regions is to compensate for the financial, personal and technical resources often lacking locally. Three types of social organisation are cited by Loveman and Sengenberger, particularly with reference to small firms. One is the historical example of public institutions which, by conferring exclusive privileges and rights to particular industries to produce certain goods, facilitated the creation of craft-and guild-based industries. Through this public regulation, even protection, market principles were restricted and social and commercial structures were established around a specific industry. While such overt attempts to establish protected markets may not be feasible today, it is suggested that the principle or model of public institutions using their directive capacity to establish social networks to compensate for commercial deficiencies could be explored more effectively than hitherto has been the case.

Another example of the social organisation of the market is the relationship between large enterprises, often transnational companies, and small firms. Although it is conceded that this relationship can be exploitative, it can also be one of 'mutual dependence and symbolic exchange on approximate equal footing'. The Japanese Kanban system is cited as a positive example: the key feature of this system is that as a result of a myriad of inter-firm relations a vertically integrated pattern of production exists in which large enterprises operate as the locomotive for a web of subsidiary commercial networks. The industrial districts of the Third Italy or in southern parts of West Germany are evoked as final examples of market oriented social organisation. A range of small firms, mostly in the same product market (for example, textiles) are interconnected not only with each other, but also with a range of external political and social institutions which promote a commercial culture based on co-operation and non-price forms of competition.

Establishing this 'social organisation' approach as the guiding principle for the Community's structural funds would pay a number of dividends. In the first place, it would allow the funds to play more of an animating and enabling function in local level regional economic development, rather than getting involved in the costly and time-consuming role of directly assisting business formation. Furthermore, it would encourage the Community to adopt a flexible policy approach to regional development as the form and extent of these social organisations will differ across the poorer parts of the Community as a result of different economic conditions and cultural and political traditions. For instance, in the Republic of Ireland, the emphasis may be on establishing networks and arrangements to create better linkages between local enterprises and transnational companies given the predominance of the latter in the Irish economy. However, in Portugal where contacts between individual firms and external agencies appear to be at best rudimentary, the focus may be on upgrading the performance of local institutions such as the *agrupaments dos concelhers* which provide technical standards to industries, and on launching a number of other schemes to encourage inter-firm co-operation on such matters as collaboration over material purchase or marketing.

Region-wide Measures

Of course establishing regionally based social organisations for the market, or to use Walker's phrase 'territorial production complexes', involves more than creating schemes and policies aimed at enterprises.[11] It also entails implementing measures of a broader structural kind such as infrastructural projects and sector-wide programmes. To date, as shown, the lion's share of Community regional money has gone to mainstream infrastructural projects – improving roads, sewage systems and so on. Obviously support for this type of scheme will have to continue since the economic and physical infrastructure in many of the poorer regions is still fairly underdeveloped. But if the Community's objective of internally generated economic development is to be realised then other more innovatory types of initiative need to be developed which have a direct bearing on investment and economic performance. As Comfort suggests it may be the case that structural fund money should be allocated to help develop local recreational and leisure activities such as golf courses, since such amenities are at least as attractive to high technology firms as the improvement of local roads.[12] Put simply, the concept of physical productive infrastructure needs to adopt a broad and flexible definition.

In addition to strengthening the physical economic infrastructure, projects need to be launched which focus on upgrading the invisible factors in regional development. There are two issues in this category which particularly stand out. One is the need to improve the vocational training and the education system more generally to increase the quality and quantity of skills in the less favoured regions. The problem of education and training appears to be particularly acute in Portugal and Greece: it has been estimated that eight million ECUs needs to be spent to bring the Portuguese education system to within 80 per cent of the Community average. Other problems exist in terms of the quality and extent of training given to young people and the absence of training in relation to new technology. Some efforts are being made to counteract this situation: a special agreement has been drawn up between the Commission and the Portuguese Government which provides for a EC contribution of fifteen million ECUs towards the total cost of ten vocational training centres; but activity in this area needs to be more sustained and far-reaching. The organisation and content of training in many of these regions are outdated and need to be overhauled, and closer links should be established between enterprises and training institutions, since without a better trained workforce many of these regions will be destined to remain backward and disadvantaged.

The other factor which may improve the 'invisible' climate for regional development is the creation of a modern business infrastructure, especially through the creation of more business services. Increasingly, the presence or absence of business services is being seen as an important influence on the level of economic and commercial activity in a region. These services give assistance to enterprises with regard to appropriate technology, marketing strategies and financial planning which improves production organisation and product quality and thus increases commercial performance. These business services, however, are not readily available in many of the less favoured regions, depriving local enterprises of an important means to upgrade their businesses. To compensate for this shortcoming, the Regional Fund should help set up technology transfer institutions, provide advance factory units with common commercial services, such as accountancy aid, marketing assistance and so on.

These two examples are by no means an exhaustive list, but are used to emphasise the point that the structural funds should concentrate as much on improving the invisible factors in regional development as on visible factors. Of course this policy direction is not entirely fool-proof: the danger of attempting to create production complexes within less favoured countries is that some regions may fare better than others with the result that development process becomes lopsided. Similarly, a policy of improving the skill base of certain regional economies may have little impact if no suitable employment opportunities are made available. The recent large-scale emigration from Ireland is a salutary example of what happens when such a mismatch occurs. To a large extent, such feedback problems can be reduced if regional development programmes are being implemented against the backdrop of sustained Community-wide, economic growth.

Macroeconomic Aspects of Regional Policy

During the 1960s, many of the regional interventions in European countries were working directly against the spontaneous flow of economic forces. There were powerful tendencies towards a centralisation of capital, labour and economic activity in the established industrial areas. Regional policy in this context was not useless, but it often seemed to be spitting into the wind, unable to alter the basic economic forces for centralisation, and thus limited to exercises in compensating the declining regions. Ambitious attempts to decentralise large-scale production – to the Mezzogiorno for example, or to Scotland – did not result in strong, viable enterprises, able to stimulate more rapid growth in the lower-income regions.

Today, this context has changed completely. Mass production industries are no longer expanding their workforces, while service activities and smaller-scale forms of industrial production are more geographically mobile. Demographic trends have gone into reverse, with population leaving all the main conurbations of Europe. Congestion costs and ecological constraints dictate a more modest expansion of incomes in northern Europe with much more attention to qualitative aspects of economic life, and macroeconomic policy in such countries as Germany or the Netherlands is aimed at only rather slow growth in overall output. Meanwhile, many southern regions are attracting high-income migrants from the north, and lower wage levels in Mediterranean countries are encouraging a relatively rapid expansion of production. As a result, regional policy no longer has the problem of directly opposing spontaneous economic tendencies. Rather the problems are to accelerate the processes of decentralisation which are already at work to increase the number of low-income regions which are able to accept a transfer of economic activity, and to extend the emerging networks for the diffusion of new technologies and products.

This change in context transforms the macroeconomic implications of regional policy. It is no longer a question of a constraint on a highly concentrated growth process. (In Britain, the Conservatives' strategy of reducing regional interventions in order to encourage the dynamic of the south-east has rapidly produced huge disequilibria which are an obstacle rather than an encouragement to economic growth.) Strengthening and generalising the decentralisation process clears the way for more rapid growth and reduces the risks to private enterprise of relocation and expansion in the low-income regions. Similarly, the rehabilitation of blighted zones in the congested industrial regions helps to stimulate the emergence of new, higher quality, service activities in the cities. Regional policy, on a European scale, can help to establish the lines of a new, more sustainable pattern of growth, reducing uncertainties on the location of economic activity and raising the level of investment and thus the rate of economic development. Given the constraining nature of existing regional imbalances, regional policy is ceasing to be a constraint on growth: on the contrary, it is a key element in the move towards a new growth model.

The Diffusionist Perspective

In the discussion of industrial policy it was argued that the Community needs a shift of priorities – away from a logic of global competitiveness, which leads to support for the strongest, most technically advanced companies and towards a logic of diffusion which would emphasise the spread of new techniques, new products and services, and improved managerial procedures throughout the whole economic system of the EC. From the point of view of regional policy this adjustment of industrial objectives is equally critical: it would give the Community industrial and regional strategies which were complementary, rather than counteracting a decentralising regional policy with industrial interventions still tied to the old centralising approach.

A diffusionist strategy, aimed at bringing the whole West European economy much closer to the standards of performance which are obtained in leading companies and in the most favoured areas, would make for a much higher average level of performance in the EC, and at the same time reinforce the cohesion and solidarity of its citizens. In the long-run rapid diffusion procedures would continue to accelerate the application of productive improvements and enhance their value. More importantly still, it would bring dormant productive forces to life, dynamising economic agents and multiplying the number of enterprises and regions which can themselves generate technical advance or initiate developments of the productive structure.

Other aspects of regional policy can also be re-examined in the light of the diffusionist strategy. At enterprise level, a switch is needed from the sterile multiplication of low-quality business start-ups, towards an enhancement of the performance of existing enterprises and their ability to introduce and master new techniques and business practices. But the strategy also implies a shift away from the enterprise as the only basis for regional interventions and the only conceivable partner in regional policy initiatives. For effective diffusion, the social integration and cohesion of enterprises and other agents is more important than their individual performance considered in isolation. The development of integrating institutional structures and cohesive patterns of behaviour, through which knowledge and capacities can be spread, should become the leading theme in regional intervention. As the scale of regional policy is stepped up and the long-term commitment of Commission and member governments is established with conviction, private economic activity can begin to align itself with the new policy directions. At this point regional strategy becomes a key element in the construction of a new pattern of sustainable growth in the Community as a whole.

So far, regional policy has not been of particular importance in the life of the Community. For the most part it has been a political compromise, a limited compensation offered to the weaker countries, but – under the impulse of the Single European Act and the relaunch of European construction – it has been increasingly prominent in Community affairs. The possibility now exists of developing the productive aspect of regional policy so that it becomes more than a channel for redistribution and starts to make a major contribution to economic advance in the EC.

Notes

1 P. Hall, 'The Geography of the Fifth Kondratieff Cycle', in P. Hall and A. Markusen (eds), *Silicon Landscapes*, Allen & Unwin, London 1986.

2 G. Therborn, *Why Some People Are More Unemployed Than Others*, Verso, London 1986.

3 P.J. Buckley and S.I. Papadopoulous, *North-South Direct Investment in the European Communities*, Macmillan, London 1988.
4 M. Martins and J. Mawson, 'The Development of the Programme Approach in the Common Market Regional Policy', *Town Planning Review*, vol.51 no.4, 1983, pp66-82.
5 European Commission, *The Single European Act: A New Frontier for Europe*, COM 173 (final) 1988, p4.
6 R. Martin, 'Industrial Capitalism in Transition: the Contemporary Organisation of the British Space Economy', in D. Massey and J. Allen (eds), *Uneven Redevelopment: Cities and Regions in Transition*, Hodder & Stoughton/The Open University, London 1988.
7 See S. Johnson and D.J. Storey, 'Small and Medium-Sized Enterprises and Employment Creation in the EEC Countries – Summary Report', Commission of the European Communities, Programme of Research and Actions on the Development of the Labour Market 1986.
8 J. Howells, 'Memorandum to Select Committee on the European Communities', Reform of the Structural Funds, Session 1987-88, 14th Report.
9 W. Sengenberger and G. Loveman, 'Smaller Units of Employment: a Synthesis Report on Industrial Reorganisation in Industrialised Countries', International Institute of Labour Studies, Geneva, Discussion Paper DP/3/87.
10 *ibid.*, p87
11 R. Walker, 'The Geographical Organisation of Production-Systems, Environment and Planning', in *Space and Society*, vol.6, 1988, pp409-501.
12 A.M. Comfort, 'Alternatives to Infrastructure? Possible Ways for the ERDF', *Regional Studies*, vol.22 no.6, 1988, pp542-51.

Further Reading

For a detailed discussion of the new spatial dynamics of capitalism, see C. Sabel, 'Flexible Specialisation and the Re-emergence of Regional Economies', in P. Hirst and J. Zeitlin (eds), *Reversing Industrial Decline*, Berg, London 1989; and D. Massey and J. Allen (eds), *Uneven Redevelopment: Cities and Regions in Transition*, Hodder & Stoughton/ The Open University, London 1988. For the most important recent official Commission documents in regional policy see 'The Regions of the Enlarged Community', *Third Periodic Report on the Social and Economic Situation and Development of the Regions of the Community: Summary and Conclusions*, Luxembourg 1987: 'Proposal for a Council Regulation on the Tasks of the Structural Funds and Their Activities Between Themselves and With Their Generations of the European Investment Bank and the Other Financial Instruments', *Official Journal*, OJ C245 of 12/9/87.

7 External Policy and Political Co-operation in the EC

One of the long-standing worries of European unification is that its real success has been in the economic sphere in spite of the fact that the early proponents of unity were much more concerned with political structures and adopted the path of economic integration only as a 'second best' solution when direct political progress towards a Federal Europe was blocked. The resulting imbalance, continuing political separation alongside ever deeper economic interdependence, will be increased by the 1992 programme which again drives economic integration forward while making only minimal moves towards stronger political institutions.

Partly expressing this situation, the term 'political co-operation' itself has come to have a restricted range of meanings in the Community. Usually it denotes the spheres of foreign policy and/or military policy where West European co-operation has remained stubbornly inter-governmental, with national governments being prepared to co-ordinate their policies but not to recognise the competence of a supranational authority. Nevertheless, there are pressures for closer and more permanent integration of external and military policy and these have been increased by the successful launch of 1992, re-opening debate on all aspects of the European project. In particular, there are proposals for military integration and for adoption of a unified strategic position among the members of the Community. It is argued here, after a survey of previous attempts at politico-military unification, that closer military co-operation and the creation of supranational defence structures would not contribute to the security of Western Europe nor to the process of disarmament which is the most effective means of enhancing security. The most important dimensions of political unification are internal: Western Europe needs political structures to establish democratic control over the vast economic system brought about by internationalisation and integration. Nevertheless, although a West European military bloc would be an unnecessary and dangerous development, the Community does need a coherent external policy, outside the military sphere. The advent of perestroika in the Soviet Union, and rapid political liberalisation in Eastern Europe, greatly expand the scope for a constructive and open approach to external political questions by EC members.

Early Attempts at European Political Co-operation

In the aftermath of the Second World War, the main objectives of the European movement that had emerged virtually spontaneously coincided with those of American foreign policy, agreeing on the need to rebuild the war-torn economies of Europe and finally to put an end to the historic national antagonisms which had bedevilled the region for centuries. At this stage, therefore, the economic and political objectives of European integration were running in parallel. Alongside the establishment of such institutions as the OEEC to administer the distribution of Marshall Plan monies and the European Coal and Steel Community (ECSC) attempts were made at creating pan-European political and defence arrangements. The table below details the various bodies and organisations either proposed or established in these arenas involving to varying degrees European countries during the late 1940s and 1950s.

The North Atlantic Treaty Organisation (NATO) has obviously had a major and enduring impact on the defence and security profile of Western European. But this organisation should not strictly be seen as a European organisation but was, rather, an international or 'Western' alliance established to counter the preceived threat of the Soviet Union and the Communist bloc. By contrast the other bodies in the table, which may be regarded as European

Table 11: *Establishing European Institutions – a Chronology*

1947: the establishment of the Organisation of Economic Co-operation and the European Payments Union to administer and distribute Marshall Plan money.

1948: the Treaty of Brussels, creating the North Atlantic Treaty Organisation (NATO) which brings the original six member states as well as Britain into a military alliance with the United States to meet a perceived Communist threat.

1949: the establishment of the Council of Europe. This body has little power and perhaps is best known as the parent organisation of the European Court of Human Rights. It also serves as a forum for European Parliamentary opinion.

1951: France, Germany, Italy, Belgium, the Netherlands and Luxembourg sign the Treaty of Paris, creating the European Coal and Steel Community (ECSC).

1952: encouraged by the ECSC and faced with the problem of German rearmament the six governments sign the European Defence Community (EDC) Treaty.

1953: in the wake of the EDC came a proposal for a European Political Community (EPC) to embrace both the ECSC and the EDC.

1954: as a result of the French National Assembly refusing to ratify the EDC Treaty both the EDC and EPC proposals collapse. As a salvage operation the much less ambitious West European Union (WEU) is established.

1957: the six ECSC members sign the Treaty of Rome establishing the European Economic Community and the Atomic Energy Community (Euratom).

---

institutions, were nowhere near as successful. Established with only a seasoning of formal powers, these organisations were destined to play a weak and marginal role on the European political scene from the outset.

Although nothing concrete emerged from the proposal, the most significant initiative in the table (apart of course from the creation of NATO) was the move to create a European Defence Community (EDC). This initiative had its origins in a call by René Pleven, the then French Prime Minister, for the formation of a European security and defence structure. Specifically, his proposal, subsequently named the Pleven Plan, was for the creation of a 15,000 strong European Army drawn from the six member states of the ECSC which had been established two years previously.

The main objective, and at the same time the ingenuity, of the Pleven Plan was to bring Germany back into the fold by allowing it to contribute to the defence of Europe while preventing it from rearming unilaterally. To a large extent, the Pleven Plan was less motivated by enlightened Europeanism than by a concern to check new thinking in American foreign policy. At the time, the USA was becoming increasingly involved in the Korean conflict which led people in Washington to question whether an effective counter to Communism could be maintained simultaneously in two different hemispheres. With tensions in Europe easing significantly, American leaders began to propose openly complete German rearmament as a way to guard against Western forces being over-stretched, but to many European governments with fresh memories of the war years this suggestion was completely unacceptable. The Pleven Plan was essentially an attempt to prevent a possible clash between the foreign policy calculations of the USA and the widespread anxiety in many European countries at the prospect of a new German war machine.

The EDC Initiative

Initially the American military leadership cold shouldered the plan, regarding it as unworkable, but the situation completely changed when the French Government persuaded the Adenauer administration in Germany to endorse the initiative. Not only did this decision force the Americans to change their view, but it also brought about a wave of support for stronger pan-European defence arrangements: within a matter of months the Pleven Plan had given way to a proposal for a European Defence Community. Under this new initiative the six member states of the ECSC would integrate the vast bulk of their armed forces so as to create a single supranational European army. As this new defence organisation was considered to be seen as operating outside NATO, an entirely new European structure, closely modelled on the institutional framework of the ECSC, was also proposed.

In early 1951 a diplomatic working conference involving the six ECSC member states was instituted to transform the loose proposals for a European Defence Community into a binding international treaty. At the start it was hoped that Britain might be persuaded to join the project, but the Conservative administration at the time remained steadfastly opposed to involvement in a supranational European defence arrangement. Undeterred by the British reluctance, the six member states spent eighteen months working out the finer points of the draft Teaty. An unusually high degree of consensus among the various national positions allowed the negotiations to be more or less free from controversy. As a result, by the middle of 1952, the Council of Ministers of the ECSC was able to endorse the draft Treaty produced by the working conference and recommend its ratification by the different national parliaments.

The centrepiece of the draft EDC Treaty was the creation of a European military territorial area which would be defended by a new European army. A host of other intermediate objectives and reorganisations was also laid down: for instance, a new European Procurement Office was proposed in order to take over, or at least co-ordinate the defence budgets of the participating countries. The supreme decision-making authority of the EDC would be a Council of Ministers, bringing together the various heads of government of the participating member states. Furthermore, a new Assembly with limited formal powers was envisaged to give members of national parliaments an opportunity to participate in policy formation. To oversee the many organisational and administrative tasks of the new Community and to ensure proper legal implementation of the Treaty a central Commission and Court of Justice were also proposed. In other words, the Draft EDC Treaty intended to produce nothing less than a fully fledged supranational European defence arrangement.

With the ECSC already working successfully and the establishment of a European Defence Community apparently imminent, the question was raised as to whether European integration should consist of a series of independent entities in specific policy sectors or whether they should be tied together under one central institution. No doubt carried along by the tide of Euro-enthusiasm, the leaders of the six member states favoured some arrangement which approximated towards the latter. Hard on the heels of the draft EDC

Treaty came a new proposal for yet another Treaty – this time for the establishment of a European Political Community (EPC).

Opinion differed among the six on whether or not the creation of a political community should constitute a federal Europe in which the participating states would transfer large parts of their policy-making authority to the European level (the Italians were the strongest advocates of the federalist option; the French were the most lukewarm), but the essence was that the EPC would link together the political and economic dimensions of integration. Negotiations on this proposal, however, proved to be drawn out. As a result, consideration of the EDC Treaty by the various national parliaments was delayed. There was, thus, growing impatience with the progress on the issue: the German Bundestag and the assemblies of the Benelux countries had ratified the draft EDC Treaty within a period of weeks.

To some extent the Italians were simply procrastinating on the issue and would have fallen into line if and when the French had adopted the Treaty, but there was a problem with the French. In the intervening two years since the endorsement of the draft EDC Treaty a number of internal and external political developments occurred to make the proposal much less attractive to the French Government. Externally, there was a considerable easing of tensions between East and West. On 5 March 1953 Stalin died and the new Soviet leadership appeared to be actively seeking a rapprochement with the West (signalled by dropping its territorial claim against Turkey in May 1953). Moreover, in July of that year the Korean armistice was signed, bringing to an end another dispute between the two emerging superpowers. With the Cold War thawing many senior French politicans began to question the need for a European Defence Community.

Internally, the new French Fourth Republic was failing to produce a stable political system: a politically fragmented Assembly meant that a number of coalition and minority governments had come and gone in quick succession. In 1954 a vulnerable French Cabinet was in power and was not inclined to risk its existence by making the EDC Treaty a matter of confidence in the French Assembly. Moreover, with the departure of Robert Schuman, a staunch European and architect of the ECSC, from the French Foreign Office, the EDC proposal lost a forceful – some have said, pivotal – advocate. The draft EDC Treaty was left without any fully committed proponents which meant that its fate would be decided by the unpredictable workings of the French Assembly. When the proposal finally reached that body it was defeated by a makeshift alliance of Communist, Gaullist and Socialist deputies. Not only did this decision wreck the draft EDC Treaty but it also sounded the deathknell for the EPC proposal.

As individual decisions rarely have a far-reaching impact it is easy to underestimate the significance of the vote in the French Assembly, but the defeat of the draft EDC Treaty turned out to be of momumental importance. In the first place, it completely shattered the designs of the European federalists – virtually overnight their political project lay in ruins, and it is probably fair to say that this group has never regained the political ground it lost at that time. But perhaps of greater significance, the decision almost certainly embedded European defence and security matters in an Atlanticist framework. If the EDC had been established then it would have probably been only a matter of time before it took major responsibility for the defence of Western Europe. Although this scenario would have entailed an appreciable increase in defence expenditure by European governments, it would also have led to the removal of the American military presence from the region. Two benefical consequences could have flowed from such a situation: Europe would not have been reliant on security provided by the USA and therefore more in control of its own defence destiny; secondly it could have reduced the American financial commitment to defence which contributed largely to US economic decline and the resulting disruption of economic life throughout the world. In other words, the failure of the French Assembly to ratify the draft EDC Treaty fundamentally changed the European political landscape – instead of a 'European Europe', an 'Atlantic Europe' was created.

Along with Britain, the six member states launched a salvage mission in the wake of the EDC and EPC failures, but all that resulted from this effort was the creation of the weak and hollow West European Union. Although the collapse of the EDC initiative had a dispiriting effect on leading pro-European politicians they were determined to press ahead with their objectives. The consensus view, however, was that to avoid another failure, any new integrationist initiative should build on the success of the ECSC and be in the economic field rather than the political arena. As a result of this new thinking the economic aspects of European integration came to the fore, culminating in the creation of the Common Market. Throughout the 1960s, economic issues remained at the centre of the Community agenda, whereas the theme of European political co-operation did arise occasionally but remained mostly on the sidelines.

The Fouchet Plans

The main attempt to revive the flagging notion of a European defence/security arrangement during the 1960s was the Fouchet Plans, and the driving force behind this initiative was the French President, General de Gaulle. Although de Gaulle supported the creation of the Common Market, he was unhappy with the idea that European integration should involve solely economic and technical matters: for him, European integration also required a political component to ensure that the region was not overly influenced by the USA; but his view of a European political/defence arrangement was at odds with the federalist version which had dominated the policy discussions on the issue during the 1950s. In particular, de Gaulle strongly opposed the idea of a supranational European defence arrangement, involving centralised institutions and policy-making. Instead, he preferred a '*Europe des Patries*' in which a gradual convergence would occur between the member states – first on foreign policy matters and then over time on defence and security related issues. In other words, his vision was of an intergovernmental rather than a supranational European political arrangement.

Although de Gaulle and some of his senior aides had been canvassing, even exhorting, the other member states to support this view of European political co-operation since the late 1950s, nothing concrete happened until 1961. Then, at a conference at Bad Godesberg, in that year the member states agreed to establish a special committee under the chairmanship of Christian Fouchet to draft a Treaty establishing some form of arrangement to develop foreign policy co-operation between the six member states of the Common Market.

Since the member states had refrained from setting over-ambitious objectives, it appeared that the Fouchet committee would be able to fulfill its task without excessive difficulty. In fact, however, the member states had never been more divided on the issue: some were content with the division that had emerged between the Common Market in the economic sphere and NATO in the political/defence area; others were reluctant to see European foreign co-operation without British participation; yet another view was that the initiative would only serve to strengthen the emerging French/German alliance inside the Common Market. Because of these differences, Fouchet's assignment was much more formidable than it appeared at first glance.

Despite the obstacles, Fouchet was able to draft a Treaty (the Fouchet Plan Mark 1) which subtly balanced the competing interests of the member states. Apart from a few unresolved issues, agreement appeared to be within reach. Then, in an unexplained and extraordinary eleventh-hour intervention, de Gaulle cancelled all the concessions made by the French negotiators to the other members states by directing Fouchet to reformulate the draft Treaty provisions so that they more or less corresponded to *his* original vision of an intergovernmental European political union. A new draft created was formulated (the Fouchet Plan Mark 2) and put to the other member states. Not surprisingly, the other member states took exception to de Gaulle's behaviour and rejected out of hand the revised Fouchet proposals. This response not only killed the entire initiative, but also meant that, so long as de Gaulle was in the Elysée Palais, France's partners inside the Common Market would not entertain any new proposal on political co-operation. Consequently, the political aspects of European integration remained dormant for the remainder of the 1960s.

The Emergence of the Political Co-operation Arrangement

The Initial Moves

The next step in what was proving to be an elusive quest for a European defence/political arrangement came in 1969. Having completed the first 'negative' phase of Community development by the creation of a customs union the previous year, and now that Pompidou was the French President, the member states were eager to launch a new 'positive' phase of integration. Mostly this new phase would relate to economic and monetary matters, but Community leaders also wanted to include the political dimension in their plans, although given the previous failed initiatives they were uncertain about what form this should take. At the Hague Summit in 1969 the Council instructed the foreign ministers of the member states to investigate the best possible ways of deepening political co-operation between them.

The following year the foreign ministers presented their report – referred to as either the Luxembourg or Davignon Report. The main recommendation was for the establishment of a European Political Co-operation (EPC) arrangement to facilitate foreign policy harmonisation and co-ordination amongst the member states. Specifically, it proposed that the foreign ministers should hold two formal meetings every six months to discuss an agenda prepared by a new intergovernmental Political Committee made up of the political directors of the foreign ministries from each member state. The member states adopted this initiative at the 1970 Luxembourg Council meeting. Within a year numerous ministerial meetings had been held which led to the first joint declaration by way of the new arrangement, on the Middle East.

Clearly the EPC was not a federalist institution obliging the member states to enter into forms of supranational decision-making on foreign policy. Yet neither was it a full intergovernmental organisation for it did not commit the member states to anything more than consulting with each other on all major decisions with foreign policy implications in the hope that common positions could be adopted. If no agreement could be reached then individual member states were free to pursue their own policy line on the issue. Moreover, the Davignon Report failed to address the important issue of how the EPC should relate to EC policies and institutions. Despite this shortcoming and its modest objectives, the creation of the EPC was a significant landmark for it meant that after almost twenty years of trying, the member states of the EC had finally got some type of European arrangement in the political/defence field into operation.

The relationship between EPC and EC institutions was somewhat clarified by the Copenhagen Report adopted by member states in 1973. In particular, the report created a bridge between the two organisations by allowing the Commission to attend EPC meetings. Beyond this linkage the two organisations were to remain formally independent, but as no formal boundary rules or guidelines were established to seperate a EPC matter from a Community matter it has been hard sometimes to work out where the competence of one ends and the other begins. This is particularly the case in distinguishing between the deliberations of the EPC and the foreign minister meetings of the Council of Ministers. For convenience the meetings of these bodies are normally arranged on the same day and frequently the same topics are discussed in each meeting which tends to blur the distinction between the two forums.

A recent example should illustrate the point: on 16 September 1987 the member states agreed to a set of restrictive measures against South Africa. The foreign ministers first adopted the relevant political statement in the EPC meeting and then almost immediately adopted the decision to restrict South African iron and steel imports into the Community at the Council of Ministers meeting. The only discernible feature marking off the discussion in the two bodies was that the political statement was prepared by officials of national foreign ministries and the import ban proposal was drafted by the Commission. The point is not that the two committees work against each other, but that there appears to be a large amount of unnecessary overlap and duplication.

The Progress in the 1980s

An attempt was made to integrate the EC and EPC more closely as part of the Genscher-Colombo Plan in the early 1980s. Along with proposals to introduce a measure of supranational decision-making inside the Community, the plan argued that a single Council of Ministers be made responsible for both EC and EPC matters, that a small EPC secretariat be created and that the role of the President of the Community vis-à-vis that organisation be strengthened. Apart from emphasising the role of the President of the European Council in co-ordinating the views arising from EPC and EC meetings, the member states refused to adopt any of these proposals. From the mid 1970s to the mid 1980s the EPC and the EC therefore remained formally independent but informally closely connected. The Commission, and to an increasing degree from the late 1970s the Presidency of the Council, had the responsibilty of ensuring that the discussions in both bodies ran in parallel and complemented each other.

But did the EPC lead to any significant increase in collaboration between the member states on foreign policy or defence matters? Certainly communication and liasion between national foreign office ministries increased as a result of the formation of the EPC. A direct telex service (COREA) has been created to facilitate the rapid transfer of information between the member states; and a wide range of working parties established under the auspices of the Political Committee of the EPC has allowed national foreign office officials to exchange views and formulate common perceptions of problematic foreign affairs issues. From this diplomatic contact the member states have developed a 'co-ordinated reflex' in which each avoids taking a strong position on international issues without first consulting the others.

Because the EPC is an informal arrangement to promote consultation it has virtually no powers to undertake concrete intiatives or action. It *can* engage in what Hill calls 'declaratory diplomacy' by issuing communiques or statements on world events.[1] EPC has made such pronouncements on a number of occasions – for example, on the Middle East, Portuguese Revolution and the Invasion of Cyprus. In addition, EPC has been used by the member states as a mechanism to prevent non-member countries from exploiting potential differences amongst them. More concretely, decisions taken in the EPC framework can lead the member states to use Community instruments to launch co-ordinated actions. For the most part, these initiatives have involved trade sanctions, some examples of which are outlined below.

Initiatives Taken by EPC

1) Soviet Union/Poland: After martial law was declared in Poland the member states almost immediately issued a joint statement, through the EPC framework, condemning the decision and accusing the Soviet Union of preventing economic and political reform in that country. A few months later, acting within the Community structure, the member states (with the exception of Greece) agreed a measure to reduce imports from the Soviet Union into the Community.

2) The Falklands War: The day after Argentina invaded the Falklands member states issued a strong statement condemning the action. This statement was backed up by a number of trade sanctions. A total ban on exports of arms and military equipment was introduced. In addition, the European Council adopted a regulation which banned all Argentinian imports into the Community initially for one month but which most members states maintained until the end of the conflict (Ireland and Italy were the only countries which failed to renew the regulation).

3) South Africa: The Common Code of Conduct for European Firms in South Africa, agreed in 1977, was the first concrete initiative to emerge from the EPC framework. This action was reinforced by the Community's decision in response to international pressure to ban iron and steel as well as gold coin imports from South Africa. In addition to these import restrictions the Community adopted a decision exhorting member states to introduce measures prohibiting any new investment in South Africa by European enterprises.

None of these actions obliged the member states to participate in any far-reaching or decisive foreign policy initiative over a sustained period of time. Most of them were specific responses to exceptional or dramatic international developments which did not require any long-term commitment from the member states. The only measure which has existed for any reasonable length of time is the code of conduct on South Africa, but this is generally regarded as an ineffective policy instrument.[2] There is little, then, that would lead one to conclude that fully fledged European foreign policy co-ordination is just around the corner as a result of EPC/EC initiatives. Nevertheless, through the EPC, the Community has been able, at least in part, to establish a presence on the international stage – indeed some see the only success of the EPC as the fact that it has given the Community sufficient visibility on world affairs so to convince other states that what it says counts.[3]

The SEA and EPC

When the member states took on the task of revising the Treaty of Rome through the Single European Act (SEA) so that the internal market programme would have a legal base, they also took the opportunity to integrate formally the EPC into the Community structure. During the negotiations there was a difference of view between the British and the French and Germans over what should be the declared aims and objectives of the EPC but these really involved points of emphasis rather than substance. As a result, agreement was reached without much difficulty. Under the clauses of SEA, the EPC was to retain its seperate structure but be linked to the Community by being brought formally under the umbrella of the European Council and by allowing the Commission to attend meetings. This was nothing more than giving legal expression to existing practice. However, something new which the SEA did establish is a small secretariat for political co-operation. The secretariat, to be based in Brussels, is to help increase the administrative and organisational efficiency of EPC and to give it a more visible presence. Apart from some subtly worded clauses which may allow for some creative interpretation in the future, the SEA made no other significant changes to the EPC. No attempt was made, for instance – not even in the form of an inspirational clause – to upgrade the decision-making system of the EPC from its currently strictly intergovernmental character to the more integrationist method of the Community; and Commission President Delors has had to renounce his interpretation of the SEA as giving rise to a Community competence in foreign policy matters. In other words, the SEA did little more than formalise the EPC by linking it to the mainstream Community structure.

The Wider European Defence Debate

Alongside these modest pragmatic steps taken by the member states in foreign policy co-ordination, a major debate erupted about the extent to which Europe should establish its own independent defence arrangements. The main cause of this debate was growing tensions between Europe and the USA on a wide number of economic and foreign policy issues.

The Role of the Peace Movements

By far the most contentious issue was the direction of NATO nuclear strategy. In a new phase of the arms race, NATO in 1979 decided to deploy large numbers of Cruise and Pershing missiles in several West European countries. The novel feature of these missiles was that they were 'theatre' nuclear weapons allowing a nuclear war to be fought between the East and West on European soil without involving the USA. Almost overnight this decision was met with massive opposition: peace and other anti-nuclear organisations mushroomed across Europe or were transformed from pressure groups into mass movements. Demonstrations, regularly involving hundreds of thousands of people and at times reaching the million mark, were held in many European countries throughout the early 1980s. In terms of formal policy these protests did not lead to the reversal of the decision to deploy these new nuclear weapons. (Belgium and the Netherlands postponed the installation of the weapons, but by the mid 1980s all the relevant countries had their full quota, as determined by the 1979 NATO decision, of Cruise and Pershing missiles on their soil.)

Nevertheless, the European peace movement had an immense impact on Atlantic relations. It was a massive physical expression of the fact that large sections of the European public had come to see nuclear weapons and not the Soviet Union as the main threat to their safety. Not only did this dent the central premise on which NATO was formed and functioned, but it also signalled a massive loss of confidence in the way European and American leaders had chosen to defend themselves. Not surprisingly, soon after the deployment of Cruise and Pershing missiles, European security strategist along with senior figure in NATO's military command started to extoll the virtues of conventional forces as opposed to nuclear weapons in the defence of the West. But the damage had been done: NATO strategy was no longer seen as standing above the rough and tumble of normal politics, commanding the automatic support of USA and European Goverments. Within NATO, European governments started to examine proposals more closely to ensure that they would not trigger domestic unrest or controversy, and perhaps even, taking the point from the European peace movement, to see if they best served the interests of the region. In other words, the peace movement changed the political pyschology and the politics of Atlantic relations.

Differing Perceptions over Foreign Policy

Increasing divergence on how European and American governments viewed world developments and events compounded these problems over nuclear strategy. From the early 1970s a wide gap has appeared between the thinking in Washington and the thinking in European capitals on many of the more important foreign policy issues. Europe was less inclined to follow the USA in viewing the third-world liberation movements that emerged particularly in Africa in the 1970s as part of an international Communist conspiracy hatched in Moscow. On the Middle East, the USA's staunch pro-Israeli stance was not reflected in Europe where governments were more inclined to incorporate the Palestinian position. With regard to Latin America, European governments strongly opposed the Reagan administration direct support of the Contras in an effort to destabilise the former Sandinista government in Nicaragua. With the controversial exception of Mrs Thatcher in the UK, few European heads of state were willing to lend their approval to the US bombing of Libya. Taken together these conflicting views could do nothing but place considerable strains on European-American relations. Europeans started to think of America as being prone to 'Rambo-style' diplomacy, while the Americans began to view the Europeans as wimpish and going soft on the need to uphold the American versions of freedom and democracy.

Economic Rivalry

Economic and commercial matters were another source of stress on transatlantic relations. European economic relations were by no means trouble-free during the 1950s and 1960s. But with world growth at an annual rate of six per cent economic frictions were easily resolved. However, with growth slowing and international competition intensifying during the 1970s, commercial and economic disputes quickly became politically sensitive controversies and thus harder to smooth out. European governments were inclined to the view that with the slowdown in economic growth the USA had abandoned its role as leader in the world economy and had begun to pursue policies constructed purely for domestic needs but with harmful international consequences.

One prevalent view in Europe in the mid-1970s was that the USA was only half-heartedly moving against rising world inflation since this process operated to devalue the dollar price of oil, thereby reducing the impact of OPEC's price increases on the US economy. Similarly, in the early 1980s the Europeans complained that the US macroeconomic stance of a tight monetary policy and a loose (some might call it a cavalier) fiscal policy led to interest rates around the globe being artifically high, choking off any possibility of economic recovery in Europe. Reflecting on this situation, one commentator suggested that 'at their worst, America's policy makers are as parochial as Albania's'.[4]

The Americans reciprocated with their fair share of criticism of European economic policy. Singled out for attack has been the Common Agricultural Policy, described by one US official as 'the ultimate in mercantalism'. Agricultural exports are, or at least were, big business for the USA: in 1980 the USA had an agricultural trade surplus of $30 billion. The Reagan administration took the view that part of the Community's interventionist agricultural policies had the effect of subsidising European food products on world markets. The operation of Community steel policy also came in for heavy criticism from Washington. Essentially the US government accused the Community of restricting imports and subsidising exports in the steel sector which meant that, in the context of international surplus capacity, more US steel workers than otherwise would have been the case were loosing their jobs. While these differing perceptions of each other's economic policies have not led to trade wars they have caused heated diplomatic exchanges which are hardly conducive to transatlantic unity.

The Free Rider Problem

Yet another factor fermenting Atlantic strife is what has been called the 'free rider problem'. As the American trade and budget deficits escalated during the 1980s, ways of controlling, if not reducing, federal expenditure became a major issue of concern in Washington, particularly in the Democratic controlled Congress. One defence programme identified as excessively burdensome to the US coffers was the financing of American troops in Europe. Approximately 30 per cent of the US defence budget goes to maintaining US troops in Europe and one estimate suggests that to continue this commitment for the next ten years would set America back about $2.2 trillion; by contrast the financial commitment of European governments to the security of the region is minor.

With the budget deficit looming large, having to foot most of the bill for the defence of Europe began to be regarded as unacceptable by many American politicans. European governments have increasingly come in for criticism for not paying their way and for 'free riding'. The jibe most commonly made has been that Europe could only afford its lavish welfare systems because the US paid for the defence of the region which in turn meant the US Government having to cut its own social programmes. The result of this attitude has been the call for the withdrawal of American troops from Europe. Sam Nunn, one of the most influential US senators on defence and foreign matters has made it plain on a number of occasions that the USA ought to reappraise its commitment to the region if the European governments do not pay more for their own defence. A complete American disengagement from Europe is highly unlikely, at least in the near future, but this issue is another sign of one partner in the Atlantic alliance becoming deeply dissatisfied with the behaviour of the other, aggravating the already high level of distrust and ill-feeling.

Countering this weakly disguised dissatisfaction, even hostility, towards Europe from some leading US politicians is the growth of a negative attitude in Europe towards the USA. During the 1970s European integration had come to a virtual stop: inside the Community, for example, the members states were only able to agree on new initiatives after prolonged and acrimonious discussions. With Europe fragmented no effectve counter existed to growing American unilateralism on world affairs. At times this resulted in the US government riding roughshod over European interests – the dispute over the Siberian gasline is one example. Cumulatively this caused a great deal of frustration, even resentment, on the part of European leaders. Gradual informal pressures have been building up throughout the 1980s to overcome this impotence by a strong independent European voice on the international stage. Mitterrand's EUREKA proposal as a response to Reagan's 'Star Wars' initiative and the almost euphoric reception of the 1992 programme can be interpreted as expressions of these pressures. For the most part, however, such tendencies remain latent in European society, although they could produce an important loosening of the ties between Europe and the USA.

Over the past decade a number of different developments and influences have emerged which have created a major political tension inside NATO. Too may clashes have occurred between Europe and the USA to suggest that the problems facing the alliance are simply a temporary aberration. NATO can no longer operate as it did from its inception in 1948 until the late 1960s – the extent and nature of the current divergences have ruled out that option. One possible way forward may simply be to muddle through, accepting that a difference of view will occur from time to time, but this is unlikely to be the alternative chosen, for it may result in those arguing for a more radical reorganisation of current arrangements gaining support. Reform of some sort appears probable. The real question is what form the changes will take and how extensive will they be.

Reconstructing US–European Relations

Option I: A Dealigned Europe

Realising that it was an inadequate political strategy simply to demonstrate against the presence of nuclear weapons, the European peace movement, under the umbrella of the European disarmament movement, began formulating an alternative defence senario or plan for the region. What it came up with was a programme for dealigning Europe – a Europe 'beyond the blocs'. This option includes a number of different components. In the first place, it would entail a massive if not a total denuclearisation of Europe through both unilateral action and multilateral negotiations. Europe in essence would become a nuclear free zone. All offensive conventional armaments would also be withdrawn so to reduce the perception of an aggressive military posture. In addition, strategies and policies would be pursued to create the conditions for a dealigned Europe. In particular, countries would operate both inside and outside NATO to promote co-operation and rapprochement with the Eastern bloc so to reduce tensions and suspicions.

The development of a variety of multilateral relations, as distinct from the bilateral relations between NATO and the Warsaw Pact, is essential to provide a stable framework for disarmament and détente at a time when the countries of the Eastern bloc are exercising growing economic and political self-determination. Ultimately it is hoped such policies would eliminate East-West confrontations and help the phasing out of the military blocs. It is important to note that this is not a neutralist or pacifist defence option as Europe would still have the military capability to defend itself. But defence arrangements would be organised along the principle of defensive or non-provocative deterrence. In theory, a non-provocative defence policy could be established inside NATO, but it is open to question whether this would actually happen since NATO has consistently followed a strategy of external confrontation. For a defensive deterrence strategy to work means either NATO needs to undergo a metamorphosis or the bloc system is completely eliminated. At present, the bloc system seems to be disintegrating of its own accord, faster than NATO knows how to respond.

The main difficulty with this scenario is that neither a rupture with the USA nor a dissolution of NATO have much prospect of major political support in Western Europe. In spite of all the differences discussed, the notion of an Atlantic community, based on the political, economic and social kinship of North America and Western Europe is still endorsed by most West Europeans; so there is no real basis for a West European community constructed outside, or as an alternative to, the Atlantic community. At the same time, the persistence of East European regimes, although moving towards democracy and market economies, provides a basic political rationale for NATO to most West Europeans, even if they do not share the zeal of US leaderships for a global anti-communist crusade. The recent, dramatic events in Eastern Europe and the USSR have certainly changed the premises of these political calculations, but – so far at least – they have done so more by altering relations between the two major blocs than by creating scope for a third, non-aligned, path for Western Europe.

Option II: A European Superpower

A second strategy is for Europe to transform itself into a 'superpower'. The argument or rationale for this scenario is that Europe has gradually gained its self-esteem and confidence in the postwar period to the point where it no longer needs to remain in an alliance with the USA, which in any event has an essentially different view of world events given its geography, history and politics. As a result, Europe must devise its own independent security arrangements which would entail an internal build-up of conventional forces, and perhaps even establishing its own nuclear capability by pooling together existing French and British stockpiles of these weapons and bringing West Germany in as a nuclear power. Probably the strongest supporters of this arrangement are the French who see it as one component in the construction of a Gaullist Europe. France also has a big economic interest in such a development because of its large armaments industry which is facing severe problems of excess capacity. Some interpreted Mitterrand's resurrection of the West European Union in the early 1980s as laying the first foundations for this arrangement. Some British politicians may also go along with such a project. Significantly perhaps – as Mrs Thatcher's most likely successor – Michael Heseltine has consistently argued over a number of years for a common European arms and aerospace procurement policy so as not only to be able to compete more effectively with the USA but also to ensure the presence of a strong internal capacity to manufacture military equipment. David Owen is a strong advocate of Britain and France developing a close partnership on nuclear weapons as a key aspect of an independent European security arrangement. In the light of continuing budget deficits, there is an increasingly vocal school of thought in the USA which believes that Western Europe should be forced to take greater responsibility for administering and paying for its own defence arrangements. This option then is not without its supporters, although few of them would foresee a complete rupture within NATO.

However, it is unlikely that this option will be adopted by European governments, in any fully fledged or coherent form. Like the dealigned scenario, it would entail a break-up of the Atlantic alliance and although much of the European establishment is disgruntled with USA foreign policy, it is not ready to get involved in an unpleasant and angry divorce. Britain's political class, for example, remains overwhelmingly Atlanticist, while that of Germany may wish to change NATO priorities and strategies but will not support conflict within the alliance. As the attempts at getting some form of foreign policy collaboration within the umbrella of the European Community reveal, it is highly questionable whether there is enough internal common ground to sustain an independent European security system. It is quite conceivable that such an arrangement would be dogged by similar disagreements over policy as those currently plaguing NATO.

Besides the feasibility problem of this project, it is in any case far from a desirable option: constructing a new European military bloc would probably exacerbate rather than extenuate world tensions. For instance, the idea of West Germany having strong influence if not command over a nuclear arsenal could lead the Soviet Union to change its stance radically on disarmament – a point which is well understood in Germany itself. Creating a third superpower bloc would disrupt the fragile and delicate relations between the Soviet Union and the USA. Attempting to negotiate arms control or disarmament agreements in Geneva would become even more diffcult and complex. A superpower Europe, no doubt wishing to flex its muscles, would tend to get drawn into the global contest for power and influence. Although it might be preferable for Bonn, Paris or London to have its finger on the nuclear button rather than Washington, it would be a highly unsatisfactory arrangement in terms of advancing European nuclear disarmament. This option also seems implausible therefore, at least in the absence of very extreme political developments in the USA, which might concurrently produce a government so adventurist or so aggressive that European governments would feel constrained to break with it. At present, however, no major danger of US extremism can be detected – its interventionist ambitions and energies preoccupied with Central America.

Option III: A Decentralised and Reformulated NATO Structure

The third option is for a renewal of NATO through a series of internal changes in its structure and strategy. The main purpose of such revisions would be to create a strong European pillar inside NATO. In concrete terms, two main types of revision would be introduced. First of all, there would be a down-grading of nuclear weapons in the defence of Western Europe and an increased emphasis on conventional military forces. In all likelihood, the numbers of conventional forces would increase substantially if this change were enacted. It is implicitly assumed that Europe would bear the lion's share of the additional cost of installing and maintaining these troops, so to ease the tension between Europe and the USA on the controversial issue of disproportionate US funding of security in the region.

Secondly and in return, the Americans would accept revisions of present NATO structure to allow Europe a greater say and control over NATO strategy as it affects the region. A number of forums already exist inside the NATO structure – most notably the 'Eurogroup' and the European Defence Improvement Programme – for the formulation of European views on security and defence policy. But these bodies do not appear to have the authority or capacity to operate as European defence organs.

Certainly if the Europeans increased their financial commitment to NATO then they would demand a much more decentralised structure than presently exists. It may be that the Americans will allow European governments to use the West European Union, although it is technically outside NATO, as the main organisation for the construction of views relating to the workings of the Atlantic alliance.

There is nothing new about this vision of a 'twin pillar' Atlantic alliance. John F. Kennedy and his defence secretary Robert McNamara were strong advocates of this arrangement back in the early 1960s. Now it is seen as a possible solution to the problems currently besetting NATO. While there is some resistance in Washington to Europeans having a greater say over the direction of NATO strategy in the region, the majority view appears to be that this is the price necessary to save the alliance. Writing in the journal *Foreign Affairs* in 1988 Henry Kissinger suggested that it is imperative that Washington understand the nature of the deep-seated changes occuring in Europe which are fundamentally about Europe regaining control over the region's economic and political destiny. For the conservative-oriented European establishments the proposed reform of NATO would be acceptable because it would balance the increasing demands for a more independent European voice on security matters with the maintenance of existing institutional and political links with the USA and NATO. Of the three different strategies this is the most plausible, but this option is not without its problems. Increasing their defence budgets would be a major financial burden for most West European governments, triggering domestic political discontent; no West European government, not even that of Mrs Thatcher, seems at present ready to do so. Even if NATO became more decentralised and more reliant on conventional methods of defence, it is not at all clear whether this will be enough to reduce current divisions. Not all switches from nuclear to conventional defence necessarily represent genuine moves towards disarmament – NATO strategies have dreamed up some highly confrontationist applications of 'conventional' weapons, some of which approximate to the deployment of tactical nuclear weapons. Once again this kind of development, like the option of a

West European superpower, is a long way from enjoying comprehensive support. Although it would probably be favoured by France, from both political and industrial motives, it would command little support in Germany, where it would be seen both as unnecessarily disturbing NATO and as compromising the process of détente and disarmament, with its long-term prize of reunification.

The Impact of Gorbachev

Most of the perennial assumptions behind Western foreign and military strategies may fail to survive the changes in the USSR associated with the arrival of Mikhail Gorbachev as Soviet leader and with the policies of perestroika and glasnost. Only the impact of these developments on West European co-operation will be discussed here, although their full significance is, of course, much wider. No absolute guarantees exist against the reversal of current Soviet policy, but at present the greater danger would seem to revolve around whether Gorbachev can retain control of the social forces released by glasnost, and whether he can deliver the effective economic reforms promised by perestroika. At least it *is* clear already that ideological and military confrontation between East and West have already lost a great deal of their meaning. Political pluralism, the judicial enforcement of individual rights, the introduction of a market economy, even if they took very different forms in the USSR from those in the USA or other advanced capitalist countries, would necessarily diminish the contrast between the social and economic systems of the superpowers. At the same time, disarmament and demilitarisation of the economy are key political and economic priorities for the new Soviet regime, and have already prompted some startling diplomatic and political concessions in the pursuit of compromise with the West.

Beyond the intermediate nuclear weapons agreement which has already been achieved, there is a new dynamic to the whole peace and disarmament process – resisted of course by military-industrial interests, but mobilising increasing political support in all NATO countries, including the USA. The prospect is starting to emerge, not simply of a reduced level of tension between NATO and Warsaw Pact, but of a comprehensive elimination of the sources of dispute, making possible the reduction of military activity to minimal levels throughout the European continent. It is of enormous symbolic significance that one of the most painful and bitter sources of dispute, the division of Germany, now seems soluble sooner rather than later.

While the changes in Soviet domestic and foreign policy are perhaps most significant for the USA (where the notion of superpower rivalry is so deep-rooted), the developments within the USSR's East European allies are of particular importance to Western Europe, with its close historical and cultural links to these countries. Present developments in a number of East European countries can be attributed in part to the reduction of Soviet constraints on East European society to the simple question of a military pact, leaving the political and economic structures of these countries to be determined internally and autonomously; a reversion to the Brezhnev doctrine already seems out of the question. The symbolic culmination of such a process would again be the reunification of Germany: but concurrently with that prospect, it is possible to anticipate the alignment of some, then perhaps all, of the East European countries with the existing Western model. This entails predominantly market economies, with substantial state intervention and parliamentary democracies, which in the case of Eastern Europe would hardly differ from the West.

This outcome, yesterday a fantasy but today increasingly tangible, would represent an enormous potential extension of West European integration, whether or not Poland, for example, actually adhered to the EC (which is at last conceivable). In this context of a civil reunification of the whole continent, recent projects for a specifically West European military-political unit seem increasingly retrograde and out of place. The emergence of such a unit, with a clearly defined military strategy aimed at the East, would mean an obvious affront to and hindrance of Soviet reform and East European political and economic transformation. The pursuit of military integration would tend to build a serious barrier to political and social unity in Europe as a whole. The construction today of a strong 'European pillar' to NATO, even if Western Europe gained more political autonomy within the alliance, would constitute a modernisation of NATO and its material and political equipment. What is required, on the contrary, is the engagement of the whole alliance in the process of disarmament and the political isolation of those interest groups, in the USA and Europe, which wish to maintain an obsolete level of military preparedness whether for economic or ideological motives.

Although a Community defence structure should be avoided, there is still scope for a constructive European external policy, outside the military sphere – a policy which could go beyond the present pattern of declarations of principle and commit the countries of the Community to a lasting contribution to peaceful transformation in Eastern Europe and economic development throughout the world. The economic weight of the Community today would give enormous force to such initiatives, whose main themes will be outlined here.

An Agenda for a EC External Identity

Given the history of EC foreign policy co-operation initiatives, particularly through the EPC, and the modest clauses in the Single European Act relating to this subject, it is essential that the establishment of a European Community external identity is restricted to a select number of key areas. Three issues demand attention at the top of that agenda.

Improving East-West Economic and Commercial Relations

During the 1970s there was a considerable increase in contact between Eastern and Western Europe on economic and trade matters. A whole host of bilateral agreements were established such as the Franco-Polish and German-Bulgarian economic co-operation pacts. At a European level, communication was opened between the Community and the East European equivalent, the Council for Mutual Economic Assistance (CMEA). In 1976 the two organisations even exchanged drafts on an inter-bloc trading agreement. As a result of these contacts international flows of trade, communication and tourism increased between the two halves of Europe. But the emerging dialogue was ruptured when Soviet troops entered Afghanistan. During the first part of the 1980s, there was virtually no contact between the two organisations. Relations improved, however, in 1985 when Jacques Delors the new President of the Commission went to Moscow to visit CMEA headquarters. Since then extensive talks have taken place between the two organisations leading to the signing of a mutual recognition agreement in 1988.

This agreement could be used as a launching pad to increase economic ties and co-operation between the two Europes. Such a development would have a number of positive by-products. Most of all, it could allow the Community through a number of economic initiatives to help the democratisation process that has gathered speed in Eastern Europe. Already there is talk of the Community devising a 'Marshall Plan' for Poland. Whether initiatives on such a grand scale can get off the ground is open to question, but the principle of the Community working to ease some of the economic difficulties existing in Eastern Europe should be a central theme of any established external identity; current developments in fact make this a high priority.

Relieving Third-World Debt

One recent study puts the volume of outstanding world debt at above $1,200 billion and estimated that annual debt service repayments are running at more than $100 billion. During the 1980s, most debtor nations have experienced an increase in their overall debt service ratio as a result of the decline of export earnings and the rise in the sheer volume of debt. While the situation is not as precarious as in 1982 when Mexico suspended payments on its private debt, it only requires another world recession for the problem to become unmanageable once again. As things stand, it appears that – without assistance – many third-world countries will be caught in a debt trap well into the next century. Evidently outside help from richer countries is required to resolve the problems.

Recently, US Treasury Secretary Nicholas Brady put forward a series of proposals to ease debt burden. But the general response to these was that, although a step in the right direction, the specific proposals were not sufficient to bring genuine relief. In another positive move, the banks have begun to accept their responsibility for creating the enormous mountain of debt by starting to make provisions for writing off some loans. But neither of these initiatives go far enough.

Most of the cost of adjustment still remains with the debtors which will inevitably mean increased impoverishment and low economic growth for these countries. Much more far-reaching action is prerequisite for tackling the structural problem of these countries' debt.

In the middle of 1989, President Mitterrand attempted to persuade the 'G7 group' of leading industrial nations to extend the Baker Plan and launch a much more imaginative and effective strategy. However, the other countries were reluctant to embark on this project, preferring an ad hoc approach to the problem. It is very questionable whether such a pragmatic approach can bring about a long-term solution to the debt crisis. Ideally a comprehensive international solution would be negotiated, but the basis for a common policy at this level seems not to exist at the moment. Because of its own large external deficit, the USA in particular is not in a position to take the lead in devising a financial solution to third-world debt. In the absence of international co-ordination, it may be necessary for the Community to launch its own initiative in this field, in the hope that other leading capitalist nations, particularly Japan, fall into line afterwards. In the short term, the most effective measure would be to speed up the process of the devalorisation of third-world debt; but such action runs the risk of triggering a financial crisis, if no official financial institution acts as 'lender of last resort'. The Community should organise the European central banks to play such a role, so that the informal cancellation already going on would be given official recognition and endorsement. As a result the prospect of speeding up the process would exist, but without the world banking system being plunged into panic.

In the longer term, the only way third-world countries can avoid the debt trap is if a renewed, virtuous circle of economic growth emerges in the world economy which will increase their export opportunities. Once again the Community has a pivotal role to play, for the USA does not have the margins of manoeuvre (given its trade imbalance) to operate as a growth pole and Japan is simply not large enough to take on this role. The Community, with the largest market in terms of population and wealth, has a major responsibility to enact policies and arrangements which will ignite the internal growth dynamics of the poorer nations. Through these dynamics, the Community would be not only benefitting its own citizens but also third-world development. The moral argument against the 1992 programme evolving into a 'Fortress Europe' is that such an arrangement would choke off the possibility of third-world countries obtaining relief from over a decade of poverty and despair. To operate effectively as a growth pole for third-world development will almost certainly require the Community to revise the Lomé Convention which gives preferential trading arrangements to countries and territories historically linked to the member states. A certain amount of devlopment aid is also given to these countries on a similar preferential basis. Many third-world countries not covered by the Lomé Convention, which therefore have to pay (in some instances) the Community's external tariff, view this arrangement with great distrust and resentment. The onus is firmly on the Community to develop a new initiative to make it easier for less developed countries to export to member states.

Resolving Regional Conflicts

These two areas of concern for a Community external identity (outlined above) are largely economic in orientation, but a political component also needs to be developed. A potentially fruitful area for launching an external political initiative is in helping to resolve regional conflicts. Increasingly the Community is seen by many troubled regions of the world as standing between the interests of the Soviet Union and the USA – in a better position to develop peace proposals and mediate between conflicting parties. The Community could, for instance, focus on the Middle East conflict: in particular, the Community might be able to play a constructive part in getting an international peace conference on the Israeli-Palestinian problem off the ground. This issue appears an appropriate starting-point as the member states view the problem in a consensual way, and the Community has over the years been slowly nurturing a Euro-Arab dialogue. A Community-backed peace initiative would probably get a better reception, and have more chance of bringing a solution nearer, than any proposal from either of the two superpowers which both have vested interests in one side and are deeply distrusted by the other. Alongside a Middle East initiative, the Community could follow up its work on measures to combat international terrorism and launch a new proposal in this area for the United Nations.

What has been covered here should not be read as a blueprint for an external identity for the EC. Other issues may be more appropriate for the Community to pursue at the international level (measures to tackle global warming and environmental pollution at a supranational level may prove more urgent and important than any issues covered here, for example). Irrespective of the issue, the key purpose of establishing an external identity must be to project the Community as a civilian rather than military power. In other words, the Community is in a key position to use its influence to *undermine* the security and superpower paradigm which dominates world politics, and to promote a new civilian agenda for international relations – environmental protection, third-world development and so on. In the present climate, the Community has a genuine opportunity to form this new agenda and has the capacity to realise it.

Notes

1 C. Hill, *National Foreign Policies and European Political Co-operation*, Allen & Unwin, London 1983.
2 See M. Holland, 'The EEC Code for South Africa', *World Today*, vol.41 no.1, pp12-15.
3 See P. Tsakaloyannis, 'The EC: From Civilian Power to Military Integration', in J. Lodge (ed), *The European Community and the Challenge of the Future*, Pinter Publishers, London 1989.
4 Cited in S. Williams, 'Unemployment and Economic Structures in the Western Alliance', in A. Pierre (ed), *Unemployment and Growth in the Western Economies*, Council on Foreign Relations, New York 1984, p117.

Further Reading

For a more detailed account of European political co-operation, see P. Ifestos, *European Political Co-operation*, Gower, London 1987, and A. Lipin et al. (eds), *European Political Co-operation in the 1980s*, Nighoff, The Hague 1988. J. Palmer's *Europe Without America?*, OUP, Oxford 1988, is a good account of the tensions between the two regions in the 1980s.

8 Britain and the European Community

In economic terms the influence of the 1992 programme on Britain is unlikely to be dramatic both because the programme will not accelerate integration as much as is usually assumed and because present economic policy in Britain puts very few constraints on external trade and investment. In political terms, however, the effect of the programme has already been dramatic: 1992 is widely perceived as marking a new stage in political integration, which will make future withdrawal virtually impossible and compel all political projects to be formulated increasingly in European terms. The consequence has been to present a serious problem of adaptation to British political parties. For the Conservative government, Europe has become a particularly sensitive issue, a possible weakness in Mrs Thatcher's political defences and the source of several damaging internal disputes. The Labour opposition, however, with a long history of opposition to the EC and often deeply suspicious of its institutions, is only slowly learning to make use of this potential advantage. It is the small parties of the centre, and the Welsh and Scottish nationalists, who have the most impressive record on the development of British relations with the EC and who seem most able to integrate European themes into their own visions, but the polarisation encouraged by our bizarre electoral practices has reduced the influence of their contributions on political debate. This chapter surveys Britain's membership of the EC and the positions of the main parties, it is agreed that the key political question which is to relate membership of the EC to the modernisation of Britain's run-down and uncompetitive economy.

Britain and the Foundation of the Community: a Continent Isolated

At the end of the Second World War, Britain's status as a victor in that conflict and as an imperial power tended to distance it from the newly liberated or defeated countries of the war-torn continent. The Labour government of 1945 was elected on a programme of far-reaching reforms but these had a clear national context – the national health service and the nationalisation of basic industries, for example. There was little enthusiasm for wider European projects. Hugh Dallon, Labour's first Chancellor expressed prevailing views when he said, 'we are determined not to put these gains (that is, policies for a fairer society) in peril through allowing vital decisions on great issues of national economic policy to be transferred from the British Parliament in Westminster to some supranational European assembly... We intend to hold what we have gained in this island'.[1] Leading figures in the Conservative opposition took a similar position: Britain was seen as working in partnership with the USA as architects of economic and political reconstruction in Europe, not as a participant in that process on a par with other European countries. Churchill himself had a far-reaching vision of European construction – in May 1940 he had made a bold offer of complete Franco-British unity to the French government then *in extremis* – but in this, as in many other respects, he was somewhat of an exception to the political rule.

For Britain, European relations were only one aspect of what was still seen as a role of global leadership. Although former colonies soon started to become independent it was thought that the move from Empire to Commonwealth would have a limited effect on external economic relations – no one foresaw that for two decades economic growth in Western Europe would run far ahead of that in the developing countries of the Commonwealth, so that the pattern of Britain's trade would become a serious disadvantage. The 'special relationship' with the USA, although already largely illusory, was much less obviously so than it later became.

The combination of three factors – delusions of grandeur, a preoccupation with domestic reform and the links with the Commonwealth – meant that in the years following the Second World War there was no question of sacrificing national sovereignty. This was reflected in British responses to early attempts to establish Europe-wide political and economic institutions. When the USA put forward the Marshall Plan for European recovery, Britain insisted that the implementing institution, the OEEC, have an intergovernmental character, despite French pressure for a supranational body. Similarly, Britain declined to participate in the European Coal and Steel Community (ECSC) because it was a type of supranational arrangement transferring some control over the two industries from national to European level. The European Defence Community was another example: when French Prime Minister René Pleven proposed the establishment of a European army, Labour foreign secretary Ernest Bevin declared that Britain would not contribute personnel to such a force since the proposal was misconceived; Bevin preferred an Atlantic arrangement to oversee European security. When the EDC proposal finally failed (ironically because of French opposition) and a much weaker and looser body, the Western European Union, was set up instead, Britain did join because national sovereignty was not at stake.

British coolness towards European integration reappeared in the negotiations to establish the Common Market. After the failure of the European Defence Community and the parallel European Political Community proposals, the six member states of the ECSC thought that to prevent another set-back, any future initiative for greater integration and co-operation should be in the economic rather than the political sphere. As a result, these countries established the Spaak Committee to explore the possibilities of deeper economic integration. Britain accepted an invitation from the six to join the committee. However, from an early stage, Britain and the six disagreed over the form of the new initiative, and two issues in particular were the source of disagreement. In the first place, whereas the six wanted a customs union – an economic arrangement in which all barriers to trade are removed between the participating countries and a new common external barrier is erected – the British preference was for a free trade area where trade barriers are removed between countries without any accompanying measures. The basis of British objection to a customs union was that it would undermine the preferential trading arrangements it enjoyed with Commonwealth countries. The second source of difference was that whereas the British wanted the OEEC to co-ordinate any new integration initiative, the six favoured the creation of new institutions. Britain favoured the OEEC because this organisation could only house initiatives which were intergovernmental in character. By contrast, the six wanted new institutions with the capacity to introduce supranational policies if the member states so desired. In the end these differences proved irreconcilable and as a result the six went ahead without Britain and signed the Treaty of Rome establishing the Common Market.

So until the late 1950s Britain took a very narrow view of European integration. Economically, it wanted arrangements which would secure market access but which would not jeopardise its trading links with the Commonwealth. Politically, it was opposed to any arrangements which could threaten the sovereignty of Westminster. Overall it remained immune from the European fervour which had gripped the continental states. On occasions, a touch of arrogance could even be detected in Britain's approach to other European countries. Certainly, the visionary statements made by European leaders were for the most part treated in London as empty and utopian rhetoric. In every round of negotiations Britain's pragmatic style of diplomacy contrasted sharply with the more expansive, enthusiastic approach of other European states. In short, Britain did not consider itself to be part of the European project that emerged in the postwar years and this explains why it remained outside the institutions established at that time.

On the Outside Looking in

Within the space of a few years however, British policy on Europe underwent a *volte face* when Harold Macmillan announced to the House of Commons in 1961 that the

Conservative Government was applying to join the Common Market. A number of factors account for the sudden change in attitude. In the first place, British policy-makers were taken aback by the rapid success of the Common Market. Britain had always underestimated the commitment of the original six member states to European integration. The widespread belief in London had been that the six would be able to achieve a nominal level of economic integration but with little positive impact on economic growth and performance. Now they saw a new economic bloc in formation with enormous potential economic advantages. For Britain to remain outside this arrangement, geographically so close, appeared short-sighted to many politicians.

Other developments were also nudging Britain closer to the Common Market. The relationship with the USA was turning out not to be so 'special'. Whereas the British political class had regarded itself along with Washington as the guardian of the Atlantic Community, the view in Washington was that Western Europe *as a whole* should represent the second pillar of the bloc. The policy of successive US administrations was to encourage Britain to become closer to the rest of Europe. In practice, this policy meant that Britain could not strengthen its economic and political links with the USA to compensate for its exclusion from the Common Market. At the same time the Commonwealth was also showing signs of weakness as a political and economic entity. As decolonisation proceeded, new, independently-minded leaders were emerging in many Commonwealth countries who shared few of British political values or concerns. Economically, there was also an increasing divergence of interest: on the one hand, the Commonwealth countries began to realise that to achieve development meant fostering a wider range of economic relationships than their British connection; on the other hand, the Commonwealth was becoming less and less important as an outlet for Britain's manufactured goods since exports began to be targeted on markets elsewhere. The Commonwealth became a less cohesive organisation, unable alone to advance British economic and political interests.

By the early 1960s Britain was becoming increasingly isolated, caught between the decline of its empire and its exclusion from the new emerging political and economic blocs. Many continued to believe that Britain could stand alone. But a more sober view held sway in Whitehall. There the common view was that for Britain to remain outside wider economic arrangements spelt economic decline and a lack of influence over the direction of world politics. Because of its geographical proximity and the nature of US foreign policy, joining the Common Market was seen as the only viable means of preventing Britain's international isolation. It was this calculation rather than a conversion to the European political project that prompted the Macmillan Government to make its U-turn and apply to join the Common Market. In other words, joining the Common Market was a policy of last resort forced upon the British political establishment by wider political and economic pressures; and this narrow, opportunistic approach has tended to persist.

Although Whitehall was now convinced that it was politically and economically important to join the Common Market, actually negotiating entry proved to be long and acrimonious. The first application made by the Macmillan Government in 1961 was vetoed in 1963 by General de Gaulle after countless rounds of negotiations. De Gaulle believed that Britain would act as a trojan horse for American interests and thus undermine the ability of the existing member states to build firm, cohesive *European* arrangements. A second application was made by Harold Wilson's Labour Government in 1966 in response to worsening domestic economic performance. Again the application was vetoed by de Gaulle in 1967. At the press conference announcing his decision to oppose British membership, de Gaulle emphasised economic rather than political reasons: in his words,

> The Common Market is incompatible with Great Britain's economy as it stands in which the chronic balance of payments deficit is proof of its permanent imbalance .... The Common Market is further incompatible with the restrictions imposed by Great Britain on exports of capital which, on the contrary, circulates freely among the six.[2]

Britain had to wait until de Gaulle resigned in 1969 before entry became possible. Although Georges Pompidou, de Gaulle's successor was also lukewarm about British entry he did not have the stature or the authority of the General, while the other member states wanted new members in order to relaunch the Community after several years of immobilism. So the circumstances were favourable to Britain's renewed application by Edward Heath's Conservative government. After lengthy and at times difficult negotiations Britain, Ireland and Denmark signed a Treaty of Accession in 1972 and became full members at the start of 1973.

The Conservatives and the Community

The ministers of the present Conservative government are often portrayed as reluctant Europeans. Mrs Thatcher's cabinet is usually portrayed as scrambling to board the integration train as it pulls out of the station. But it is misleading to think of the government as simply reacting to initiatives from Brussels. In fact, it has been actively engaged in a struggle to determine the nature and direction of the integration process, to remodel the Community on decentralised and deregulated lines. The emerging difficulties with Mrs Thatcher's European policies are not due to neglect of the Community, but to her ultimate failure to impose her own views upon it and her reluctance to abandon the campaign for 'Euro-Thatcherism' even though it is now a lost cause.

In her 1988 Bruges speech, Mrs Thatcher spelt out her vision of Europe. It was based on five principles: (i) European co-operation and integration should wholeheartedly be encouraged so long as they do not undermine the principle of sovereignty; (ii) the practical resolution of Community policy issues should take precedence over grand European political adventures; (iii) the creation of open markets and the promotion of enterprise should be the aim of the Community and not the establishment of European regulatory frameworks; (iv) the Community should be an open and not a protectionist economic arrangement; (v) the defence of Europe should remain the responsibility of NATO in the context of the Atlantic Community. Her vision was of a Community in which European institutions had little authority over the decisions of the member states and little presence in European markets. It was essentially a project to 'Americanise' European society, and this theme runs through all the Conservative government proposals and initiatives on the Community in the 1980s. It may be worthwhile examining in detail how the British Government attempted to reconstitute the Community along Thatcherite lines. Five policies in particular are examined: Community finances; the Single European Act; technological co-operation; labour market policy; and monetary policy.

Britain and Community Finances

Until recently, Britain's contribution to the European budget was a permanent source of conflict. Every year during the 1970s the Labour government complained in Brussels about the unfair size of Britain's contribution to the budget or about some other aspect of Community finances, particularly the level of spending under the Common Agricultural Policy (CAP). The consistent argument was that it was grossly inequitable for Britain with the third lowest GDP per capita in the Community to be the second largest net contributor to the budget. When the Labour government was defeated, Commission officials probably expected some relief from this constant badgering, but they had not reckoned on Mrs Thatcher. Getting a sizeable rebate on the British contribution, preferably through a reduction in CAP expenditure, became the top priority of the new Conservative government's European policy. At only her second meeting, Mrs Thatcher departed from the traditional *communautaire* method of conducting business and in ill-disguised nationalistic rhetoric demanded 'our money back'.

Initially the other member states attributed this deviant behaviour to inexperience which would resolve itself over time. However, when in 1980 Mrs Thatcher rejected out of hand a number of proposals aimed at giving Britain a rebate on its budget contribution they realised that the behaviour was not a temporary departure from standard practice. After long and patient discussions, a temporary agreement was reached on a formula to calculate a British rebate for 1980 and 1981. But this agreement only brought a short lull: in 1982 Britain blocked an agreement on agricultural prices because it was getting nowhere on a permanent solution to British budget contributions. On this occasion, the Thatcher government was out-manoeuvred by the other member states who took a majority vote on this issue.

Between 1983-84 a hectic round of negotiations took place on the British contribution to the Community budget, reform of the CAP and the budget as a whole. However, no substantial agreement emerged and many of the meetings broke up in discord. Throughout this period, the behaviour of the Conservative government was a constant source of irritation and frustration to the other member states since a number of serious attempts at solving the British problem were undermined by its uncompromising stance on the issue. On several occasions, Mrs Thatcher warned that Britain would withhold its entire budget contribution if a settlement was not made on the basis of her Government's position. Finally an agreement was reached at the Fontainebleau European Council meeting of June 1984. Here Mrs Thatcher accepted a rebate of one billion ECUs for 1986 and a formula which would calculate further rebates at 66 per cent of the difference between Britain's contributions to the budget and its receipts from the budget. What was surprising about this agreement was that it was no more favourable than some previous proposals on the issue. The only reason why Britain settled for the Fontainebleau agreement was that it realised that the patience of the other member states had run out and that the best obtainable offer was on the table. The other members had become tired of Mrs Thatcher's intransigence: for over a year the Council was paralysed by her inability to negotiate a compromise between a French offer of a one billion ECUs rebate and the British demand for 1.36 billion ECUs. At Fontainebleau most member states were prepared to stand firm and even take the Community to the abyss to end Mrs Thatcher's tactics. Britain sensed this determination and compromised on the one billion ECUs offer which had been on the table for sometime. Even from a narrow national viewpoint, British interests were hardly well served by Mrs Thatcher's diplomatic style. From a wider EC standpoint, her willingness to deadlock the Community over a relatively trivial amount of money – about £20 million – raised questions about British commitment to the whole European project.

Although the Fontainebleau Agreement settled the

problem of Britain's budgetary rebate it did not resolve the more general problem of Community finance. In the mid 1980s the Community was in a financial mess, surviving on ad hoc handouts from the member states. Between 1987 and – 1988 a number of meetings were held in an attempt to get a long-term solution. In these negotiations the old dividing line re-emerged: Britain, at times with one or two of the other member states, against the rest. Of course the British readiness for confrontation led to conflict and many of the meetings ended in considerable acrimony. Agreement was finally reached at a special meeting in Brussels in February 1988, when Britain was obliged to compromise on many of its positions. Mrs Thatcher went into the meeting demanding strict ceilings to be placed on EC cereal production and tight controls on the rate of increase in CAP spending. The actual agreement established rather weak disincentives for over-production and the formula to calculate further CAP spending was much more in line with the French and German position than the British view. Greater discipline was introduced into the CAP interventionary system, but this cannot be regarded as a concession to the British since all member states wanted this arrangement.

Mrs Thatcher did, however, gain concessions on the question of overall budgetary discipline. One reason for chronic Community over-expenditure was that the member states agreed to programmes on the basis that their funding would come out of a further budget. As a result of this procedure the Community was unable to develop a transparent budgetary structure by which expenditure could be more closely tied to income. Repeatedly this led to over-expenditure and too many commitments relative to the size of Community coffers. At the Brussels meeting the British government were successful in getting a number of accountancy changes adopted which linked more closely and clearly both sides of the balance sheet. The British thought that these changes would facilitate more budgetary discipline, but overall the 1988 agreement represented a defeat for the British position, basically because of Britain's isolation inside the Council. Ultimately, to get a position approved inside the Community requires the construction of a successful coalition. In the early years Mrs Thatcher had built a coalition of a negative kind: at Fontainebleau member governments, most of them under severe financial pressure, agreed to reject a bigger EC budget. But by the late 1980s Britain was again isolated, as other members were not prepared to starve the EC of cash if this meant a permanent block to the integration process.

Britain and the Single European Act Negotiations

In the early 1980s a group of Euro MPs known as the Crocodile Club headed by Altiero Spinelli succeeded in getting the European Parliament to pass (by a huge majority) a Draft Treaty establishing a European Union. The purpose of this initiative was to relaunch European integration after the Community's poor performance during the 1970s. The Draft Treaty had two basic objectives: firstly, to expand the Community competences in several important respects and to make the relationship between Community institutions and national governments more transparent; secondly, to redress the 'democratic deficit' inside the Community's decision-making process, mainly by increasing the role and powers of the European Parliament. Given the immobilism of the Council at the time, this virtually federalist document appeared to be wildly over-ambitious. The general response to the initiative was dismissive and it was assumed that it would be only a matter of time before the document drifted into obscurity. But when French President Francois Mitterrand addressed the European Parliament in 1984 he threw his weight behind the initiative. The effect of this endorsement was to win a real place for the Draft Treaty on the Community agenda.

At the June 1984 Council meeting the member states established an ad hoc Committee on Institutional Affairs – the Dooge Committee – in response to the European Parliament's Draft Treaty. Britain was opposed to the establishment of this Committee in the fear that it might lead to Community institutions getting greater powers. However, the other member states out-manoeuvred Mrs Thatcher by taking a majority decision on the subject. The Dooge Committee's remit was to make suggestions on how 'a genuine leap forward' could be made in Community affairs.

After deliberating for almost a year, the Committee produced a report recommending a range of actions aimed at revising the Community's decision-making process and increasing the scope of integration, but the Dooge Report was far less federalist in character than the European Parliament's Draft Treaty. For instance, Britain, along with Denmark and Greece, had insisted that a clause be inserted in the final report making it clear that they wanted unanimous voting arrangements to remain inside the Council on issues regarded as nationally important by any member state.

The Milan European Council of June 1985 considered the Report and decided to convene an intergovernmental conference to negotiate amendments to the Treaty of Rome based on its recommendations. With this, the enactment of far-reaching institutional reform looked imminent. Although the Thatcher government was far from enthusiastic about this prospect, the actual negotiations at the intergovernmental conference went very much Britain's way. Thanks primarily to the skill of British negotiators, the Single European Act (SEA) which emerged from this conference did not strengthen, to any great extent, Community institutions. Although the European Parliament was given a more formal role inside the Community's institutional system, it was not given any new rights or powers. In practice, the proposals made by the European Parliament in the Draft Treaty for European Union to increase its own powers had been totally discarded. Qualified majority voting was introduced by Article 100a, but it only covered those tasks and policies required to complete the internal market programme. Other policy areas outside the internal market programme – such as monetary policy and social policy – were not subjected to the qualified majority procedure and so decisions in those spheres would continue to be made on the basis of unanimity. In the area of political co-operation, no revisions of any substance were included in the Treaty.

Overall, the SEA was mainly an 'enabling' document, laying down the legal basis for completing the internal market. Its institutional proposals were minimal. Given that the pressures which had led to the intergovernmental conference were to increase the powers of Community institutions, the actual outcome was fairly remarkable. One major factor determining this outcome was the effectiveness of British diplomacy in exploring reservations among the other member states of a supranational Community. The SEA negotiations should be seen as a notable success for Mrs Thatcher's minimalist position on the Community.

Labour Market Flexibility

During the latter half of the 1970s a body of Community labour legislation was established by the member states. This legislation covers such matters as the protection of workers' rights in the case of mass dismissals, transfer of undertakings and insolvencies, the promotion of equal opportunities policies like equal pay for work of equal value, and the establishment of minimum standards in the area of health and safety at work. A consensus appeared to exist among the member states that some aspects of the Community labour market needed to be regulated by legislation and other public policies and arrangements. But this consensus was disrupted when the Conservative government was elected in 1979. Working from a 'Eurosclerosis' explanation of the Community's poor economic performance, the British government regarded labour market regulations as imposing rigidities and constraints on companies with the effect of undermining competitiveness. From the outset the Thatcher administration was determined to oppose any attempts to increase the Community's presence in labour markets.

For some time the British were highly successful, for by using their veto inside the European Council they ensured that no employment legislation was adopted in the 1980s which might constrain employers; the only exceptions were a number of relatively benign statutes on equal opportunities and health and safety. Draft directives aimed at introducing Community legislation on employee information and consultation rights in complex organisations, parental leave, the protection of part-time and temporary workers all fell foul of the British veto. For example, the proposed Recommendation on the Reduction of Working Time, which had no legally binding force, was strongly opposed on the ground that it would pave the way for bureaucratic interference in British labour market procedures. In an effort to accommodate British objections, amendments were made to the text which emphasised that any reduction in working time must be linked to corresponding cuts in unit labour costs, either directly or through productivity gains. However these changes were still insufficient for the intransigent British government which blocked the revised proposals when they came before the Council.

This uncompromising stance effectively brought Community social policy to a standstill by the mid-1980s. Yet the government recognised that it was bad politics to be seen continually blocking Commission social policy initiatives. As a result, during its 1986 Presidency of the Community, a major initiative called the Action Programme for Employment Growth was launched to re-orient Community social policy around the themes of labour market flexibility and deregulation. In particular, it aimed to abandon any further Community employment legislation. Instead, the Commission would promote new flexible employment patterns and working conditions through the implementation of policies which emphasised enterprise and entrepreneurship.

Recognising that its Action Programme was in direct opposition to the long-standing direction of Community social policy, the British government – after much manoeuvring behind the scenes – secured the Italian and Irish governments as co-signatories. This was a clever move, for it ensured that the initiative could be placed on the Community agenda without experiencing any open opposition from the Commission. The Action Programme was discussed at the December 1986 meeting of the European Council. No fundamental objections were raised against the proposal (which is not that surprising as the governments of the other two most powerful member states, France and Germany, also had right-wing governments at the time). The only reservation voiced on the proposal was that it made no reference to the social dialogue which Delors was attempting to construct between the trade unions and employers at the European level. After minor amendments were made to incorporate this criticism the Action Programme was ratified unanimously. On paper the Conservative government had pulled off a remarkable victory, for it is seldom that a proposal which is not supported by the Commission is adopted by the Council.

Theoretically, this Council resolution obliged the Community to develop a wide range of labour market flexibility measures which would be completely at odds with the previous approach to social policy. But as a result of the Commission's extreme reluctance to develop policy initiatives in this mould, the Action Programme has had nowhere near the impact that was first envisaged. In fact, a subtle counter-strategy by the Commission effectively neutralised the entire programme. Nevertheless, the Thatcher government had been able to block the Commission's project to develop a Community regulatory framework for the European labour market and had almost succeeded in installing a neo-liberal regime in its place.

Monetary Policy

In 1989 the Delors Report recommended that the European Monetary System (EMS), particularly the Exchange Rate Mechanism (ERM), should be strengthened to offset any distorting efforts from creating a completely liberalised financial space in 1992. The chapter on monetary policy examines in detail the Delors Report which outlined a three-stage plan towards greater monetary union inside the Community. Stage I has been accepted by the member states and will see all twelve member states enter the Exchange Rate Mechanism of the European Monetary System. In practice this will mean Britain, Greece and Portugal joining the ERM. Remaining restrictions on capital movements will also be removed. In stage II a European System of Central banks would be created to formulate common EC monetary policies. Finally, in stage III, exchange rates would be locked together, leading to the eventual creation of a single currency. The Council of Ministers would have powers to enforce constraints on national budgets and a federal central banking system would set common monetary policy. The member states, with the exception of Britain, have all accepted the principle of stages II and III, but the Treaty of Rome will have to be amended before either stage can become operational. The Strasbourg European Council of December 1989 agreed on an intergovernmental conference to prepare these amendments.

Creating a European System of Central Banks, irrevocably fixing exchange rates and then adopting a single currency ran diametrically opposed to Mrs Thatcher's view of monetary policy. So hostile was the Thatcher administration to the Report that it hastily produced an alternative proposal – 'An Evolutionary Approach to Economic and Monetary Union' – in an eleventh-hour effort to block the Delors recommendations. The underlying objective of the British proposal for monetary integration was summed up as 'increasing the influence of markets and competition, reflecting the worldwide consensus in favour of working whenever possible with the grain of the market'. The main method suggested for the realisation of this objective was the introduction of currency substitution inside the Community which would have given member state citizens the right to settle transactions in any EC national currency.

This proposal for competing currencies was not a British invention but rather the recycling of an old idea of a neo-liberal guru, Frederick Hayek. The proposal was greeted with widespread scepticism because it would reduce social control over money and finance to an impractical minimum. Private agents could switch very rapidly between currencies, thus provoking considerable instability, while there would be wide scope for divergent monetary policies rather than steady pressure to stabilise the relative values of the different EC moneys. When Mr Lawson tabled the initiative at a meeting of the Community's finance ministers in November 1989, it was unanimously opposed by the rest of the Community. As a result, the proposal quickly faded into obscurity. The short life of the 'evolution' approach to economic and monetary union initiatives highlights how unsympathetic the other member states had become to Mrs Thatcher's purely neo-liberal vision of the Community. While certainly in favour of market liberalisation, the majority of member states accepted that a range of other political, social and institutional arrangements were required to make the 1992 programme succeed.

Britain and the Technological Community

Up to the end of the 1970s European technology programmes were concentrated in the areas of 'big science' that had enjoyed most prestige in the postwar period – aerospace and atomic energy. British governments blew hot and cold on most of these initiatives – reluctant to commit resources but fearful of being left behind. As a result, British participation in the European Space Agency and in Airbus Industrie has been tardy and small-scale, probably to the disadvantage of Britain since both projects have been relatively more successful than Britain's own efforts in these sectors. However, the sectors themselves are no longer central to the kind of technological change which is reshaping modern industry.

In the 1980s, the EC has developed a range of programmes for research collaboration which are closer to the real problems of industrial change – in such areas as information technology and biotechnology. Together with the intergovernmental programme EUREKA, which developed from a French initiative, these make up the 'Technological Community'. This is still a small part of total R&D activity in member countries, but one which is rapidly growing and seen as strategically significant. These developments presented a dilemma to the neo-liberal British government: on the one hand, the programmes used a lot of public money and were an obvious form of intervention, regarded as 'ideologically unsound'; on the other hand, these kinds of investments – in knowledge and highly qualified labour as much as in specific new technologies – may be an important factor in competitive success, so that non-participation could prove costly for British industry. The actual choices of the British government continue the half-hearted and pinch-penny approach of the past. British enterprises and research centres do participate in the European programmes, but on very tight budgets, often with money taken away from other scientific and technological programmes. As a result British industry is less present in the Technological Community than French, for example, in spite of the quality and range of Britain's scientific personnel. No clear signal has been given to researchers in Britain about participation in European initiatives. As the Technological Community develops and claims a growing share of resources this minimalist stance could once again prove very costly.

The Conservatives in Europe: a Summary

Overall, the record of Conservative governments in the 1980s is not one of simple resistance to integration but of an ambitious attempt to take control of the integration process and direct it towards specific goals – a maximum of economic scope for business enterprises but with political sovereignty firmly rooted in nation states. The mid-1980s marked the high point of this endeavour: the free-market 1992 programme became increasingly central to the Community's agenda while other projects were blocked or marginalised, not least by the refusal of national governments, in particular Britain, to provide more budgetary resources. Since that point, however, political and economic forces have tended to reduce British influence. Although the 1992 programme still has very wide support, there is no longer such unquestioning acceptance of neo-liberal doctrines and policy proposals: markets are certainly seen as necessary, but no longer as sufficient, for progress on integration.

The British Conservative government has not adapted to this shift of opinion. It has persisted in its demands for the most narrow, purely market-oriented, views of integration, dragged its feet on new initiatives after failing to block them, and issued rhetorical denunciations of the Brussels bureaucracy (notably Mrs Thatcher's speech in Bruges in 1988). This negative stance has tended to alienate support so that by the time of the Strasbourg Council of December 1989, Britain was in a minority of one on the key questions of monetary integration and the Social Charter, unable to stop these initiatives and without influence over them.

A few years have been enough to dissolve the British effort to control the Community and to isolate the British government. To some extent this outcome reflects general disillusion with the Thatcherite project: in the mid-1980s it was still possible to portray this as a successful strategy for modernisation in Britain; by the end of the decade only a diminishing number of the faithful continued to believe in the transformation of the British economy proclaimed by the government. But there have also been specific weaknesses in the government's approach to EC questions. Like many other political forces, the Conservatives under Mrs Thatcher tried to impose their national priorities on the Community, without making due allowance for the specific nature of EC institutions, for the views and attitudes of other member countries, or for the real dynamics of political and social integration. As a result, policy has been formulated in a very abstract way and Britain's relations with the EC have often been very clumsily managed. It is not purely by chance that European issues have often divided the Conservative cabinet and have occasioned the bitter ministerial disputes which led to the resignations of Michael Heseltine and Nigel Lawson. As with many other aspects of the Thatcher programme, success in European policy has been short-lived. At the beginning of the 1990s Britain still has little influence on Community affairs and is in a poor position to obtain economic advantage from the process of integration.

Labour and Europe

Until recently the Labour Party policy has been hostile to the European Community. But this (formerly) consistent anti-European stance masks the deep political divisions to which the EC has given rise inside the Party. During the 1960s and the 1970s pro-EC forces were the most cohesive and active sections of opinions within the Party. Organised into the Labour Committee for Europe and producing a regular journal called *Europe Left*, they argued the case for British membership of the Community, albeit in a rather uncritical manner. Despite their professionalism, the group had little impact inside the Party, failing repeatedly to get the conference to adopt a pro-Community position. Yet in relation to the wider debate in Britain about Community membership, especially in the 1975 referendum campaign, they played a leading role in convincing the public about the merits of entry. During the 1980s, some of the leading members of this grouping left the Labour Party to form the Social Democratic Party.

Because the anti-EC camp was made up of divergent political groups, no unified body was formed to advocate the case against British membership. Left-wing speeches portrayed the EC as an institution solely designed to promote international capitalism. In fact, a concern for national sovereignty, in particular for the sovereignty of parliament, may have been a more important motive, along with the delusion – not confined to the British right – that Britain was still a world power. Although the anti-marketeer lobby failed dramatically to convince the British public in the 1975 referendum, within the Party opposition remained the dominant view and was consistently able to muster enough trade-union block votes to be adopted as conference policy.

Most of the Party's leadership took a pragmatic view and neither strongly favoured nor vehemently opposed the Common Market. They tended to pay more attention to the economic aspects of British membership than to the political debate. During the 1960s for instance, the pragmatists were prepared to accept that Community membership would be economically advantageous for Britain if the terms and conditions of entry were right. Harold Wilson used this argument as justification for the Labour government applying to join the Community in 1966. But the same people regarded the negotiated conditions which finally brought Britain into the Community in 1973 as inequitable and opposed the decision by the Conservative government to join. Although party policy was in favour of an immediate withdrawal from the Community, the pragmatist consensus in the party leadership enabled it to exclude this commitment from the 1974 election manifesto; instead a promise was made to renegotiate the terms of entry and put these to a referendum.

After winning the election, they kept the promise. James Callaghan and his negotiating team headed for Brussels declaring that the government would substantially revise the terms of British membership of the Community. The reality, however, was that they failed to do so since few major changes were contained in the renegotiated package. Nevertheless, these revised terms and conditions of entry were put to a referendum vote in 1975. During the referendum campaign, most of the pragmatists campaigned for a 'Yes' vote, but they did not take front stage in the debate – that space was occupied by the committed pro- and anti-Europeans. Once the referendum had reaffirmed British membership, the pragmatists dominated the Labour government's approach to the Community for the rest of its period in office. As a result, the focus was more or less on the economic benefits that could be wrung from Brussels.

The concept of *juste retour* – that a balance should exist between the costs and benefits of membership – encapsulated Labour's attitudes to the Community at that time. Although a formula had been developed to calculate potential British budgetary rebates as part of the renegotiated terms of entry, the Labour government continued to try and get its contribution to Community finances reduced during the late 1970s. On a number of occasions these attempts led to acrimonious Council meetings since the other member states refused to make concessions. More successful were efforts to obtain a disproportionate share of the Community regional and social funds as compensation for lack of benefits from the Common Agricultural Policy. But, of course, this success compromised the Funds' main objective of reducing the gap between the rich and poor areas of the Community. Thanks to its 'accountant's' approach, the Labour government helped undermine the ability of the Community to develop solidaristic policies and programmes.

Beyond this budgetary preoccupation, the pragmatist Labour leadership evidently wanted to restrict Britain's involvement in the Community, especially when sovereignty over economic policy appeared to be questioned. It refused to join the European Monetary System when established in 1978, since it was perceived that governmental control over Sterling would be diluted. In a similar vein, Michael Foot, when at the Department of Employment, threatened to use the British veto to stop the Community passing the Mass Dismissals Directive giving legal rights to workers in such situations. Foot simply did not want to be seen introducing such measures on the initiative of the Community. Only when the Employment Protection Act 1976 was on the statute book did Labour agree to the Mass Dismissal Directive. So although the pragmatists in the Labour leadership tolerated membership of the Community, its basic attitude was characterised by a desire to minimise the costs and maximise the monetary benefits of entry.

This absense of a *communautaire* outlook on the part of the Labour government certainly contributed to the *immobilisme* that crept into Community affairs during the 1970s. To some extent, its reluctance to depart with even a morsel of sovereignty and its insistence that the principle of *juste retour* be applied to Community affairs whenever possible established a set of assumptions which Mrs Thatcher subsequently found tailor-made for her approach to Europe.

It was not only the British Labour government which was cool on European integration. Partly because of the economic crisis and partly because of the growth of intergovernmentalism within the Community's decision-making process other member states had also started to assert their national interest more vigorously – for instance, West Germany was decidedly less European and more inward-looking during the 1970s. However, the conclusion must be that the 1974-79 'pragmatic' Labour government's approach to the Community lacked inspiration and vision, and demonstrated how uncomfortable it found membership.

Out of office after the 1979 election, the Labour Party initially retreated into a more or less straight anti-European line. The only consistent argument heard from the Labour leadership tried to berate Mrs Thatcher for failing to secure a reduction in Britain's contribution to the Community budget. No positive programme or policy on Community matters was under consideration in the Labour Party and, in fact, there was a marked tendency to adopt a hostile stance. Probably the factor most responsible for this increase in hostility towards the Community was the rise of the Bennites: in the early 1980s the Labour left, headed by Tony Benn, launched a campaign to capture control of the Party. Being strongly anti-EC was one of its basic positions. Because the pragmatic centre thought there were more important issues on which to challenge the left, this strong anti-EC stance held sway. As a result, the Party adopted a more or less oppositional approach to the Community during the early 1980s.

A number of developments combined to make this line increasingly untenable. In the first place, the departure of many leading moderates, who were also the Party's most vociferous pro-Europeans, to help form the Social Democratic Party and subsequently the Alliance, created pressures to adopt a more constructive approach to Community affairs. To have continued with an oppositional outlook would have given the Alliance the opportunity to expose the shortcomings of this approach, and also to demonstrate how it could offer something different from old-style Labourism. Furthermore, the Party's alternative economic strategy (no matter what version), premised on the belief that national action alone could bring about economic prosperity, was appearing increasingly obsolete. Growing international economic interdependence placed enormous constraints on the operation of such a policy. The failure of the French Socialist government in the early 1980s to enact a national expansionary programme even under relatively favourable domestic conditions highlighted the powerful restrictions imposed by internationalisation. Successive opinion polls in Britain, as well as the 1983 election, indicated that the electorate were simply not convinced that a Labour government could solve the twin problems of poor economic performance and high unemployment through a national reflationary programme. With the economic and political conditions no longer appearing to exist for an alternative economic strategy, the Party faced the dilemma of either having to introduce policy changes or risk its electoral credibility.

So a number of economic and political developments were putting pressure on the Party to revise established policies, including its hardline approach to Europe. Internally, the opportunity to make such changes was made easier by the decline of the Bennite left, which was widely held responsible for the 1983 election debacle in which Labour obtained its lowest ever share of the votes. The concern now was to develop constructive and attractive new policies on a whole range of issues, Europe included. Although there was an eagerness to adopt a more accommodating approach to the Community, there was at the same time a deep reluctance to join the ranks of mainstream European social-democratic opinion and accord full legitimacy to that institution. The Party had been at best lukewarm to the Community for too long to switch immediately to a pro-Community stance.

The leadership's objective then was to formulate a position on the Community which was half way between a pro- and anti-European standpoint or perhaps more accurately a position which was pro-European without necessarily being pro-EC. In other words, the task was to establish a new, updated 'pragmatic' European policy. Attempts to revise the

Party's policy along these lines came from three different quarters. One was a group of Labour MPs led by Stuart Holland and academic economists of a left-Keynesian persuasion. Along with socialist parliamentarians and economists from other West European countries they produced *Out of the Crisis*, which argued the case for a co-ordinated pan-European reflationary programme. This initiative was as much intended to save the Keynesian project as it was to reorient Labour's European policy. In some respects, the book was pioneering as it was the first attempt to get a unified policy standpoint among European socialists with quite diverse outlooks, but it did also have many shortcomings. Two deficiencies in particular stood out. In the first place, the idea of a co-ordinated pan-European reflationary programme was presented in a highly mechanical fashion: little consideration was given to whether such a strategy which was initially devised for the national context could be effectively implemented in a European context given the wide divergences in structure and performance of the various economies. Furthermore, the actual institutional arrangements proposed to enact the programme bordered on the farcical: it was suggested that the United Nations Economic Commission for Europe, essentially a statistics gathering body, should be the main institution to implement the programme. The main reason given for this suggestion was an aversion to the institutional bodies of the Community. Naturally, the idea of the Economic Commission for Europe rivalling the Community as the main pan-European economic authority was dismissed immediately by most experts as ludicrous. Although the *Out of the Crisis* report had these deficiencies, the notion of some form of co-ordinated European reflation still carries considerable weight inside the Party.

In contrast to this support for Euro-Keynesianism, another group argued for a European strategy based on ground-level, agitational forms of action. In particular, it was suggested that Labour should replicate the European peace movement which was successful in mobilising hundreds of thousands of people simultaneously in a number of different countries. With this base it should launch mass campaigns on issues such as welfare, unemployment and so on. According to this group, since strict limits existed to the use of Community institutions as vehicles to implement Labour policies, it would be more worthwhile to build up widespread, public support on such issues in European society. A number of initiatives of this kind were actually launched: for instance, in 1986 a Euro-march on youth unemployment took place. Although this initiative was not a total failure, it was far from an outright success either; such public support as it managed to generate for action on youth unemployment was quickly dissipated.

Clearly, such ground-level campaigns can pay dividends for the left, but as a viable European strategy for the Labour Party the limits of this approach were always evident. In the first place, agitational forms of action tend to have an ephemeral impact, and Labour needed an approach to Europe which would generate more sustainable forms of support. Secondly, campaigns such as the Euro-march against youth unemployment are reactive in character and simply critical in intention; they are therefore not compatible with Labour's requirement to develop a strategic and constructive set of policies towards the Community. Finally, like the Euro-Keynesians, the supporters of the 'agitational' approach wanted the Party to adopt a pro-European approach which accorded only a peripheral role to the Community itself. Given that the socialist parties in the other member states assign full legitimacy to the Community and put it at the centre of their European strategy, purely agitational strategies would only take Labour further away from mainstream European socialism.

Labour's national leadership was also trying to reformulate the Party's European strategy. Although clearly committed to dropping the policy of withdrawal, it found difficulty in developing a coherent strategy towards the Community. Neil Kinnock's proposals for change were indicative of this difficulty: among his suggestions for a new Labour position was a 'new Messina Conference' which would in essence eliminate the supranational character of the Community; a reformed European Council 'which sets its own agenda on issues raised by its own peoples and parliaments' (that is, the Commission would no longer propose policy) and a 'new all-European Assembly' (which obviously had as its unstated rationale an end to direct European elections). These suggestions were simply political shadow-boxing since a Labour government would have no chance of persuading the other member states to take them seriously. In other words, although the national leadership realised it was unable to espouse the act of departure, it still clung to the *logic* of British rejection of the EC.

It was hardly surprising therefore that Labour's new thinking on Europe was incoherent and internally divided. Although each strategy had quite different policy implications for Labour, there was also considerable similarity in all three positions. In the first place, there was a deep reluctance to attach full legitimacy to Community institutions. As a result none of the scenarios made any attempt to align Labour's European policy with the actual political dynamics of the EC. By definition this meant that none of the options envisaged a future Labour government having a close reciprocal engagement with the Community. Furthermore, each strategy projected British preoccupations onto the European plane rather than adapt and co-ordinate Labour's policies to those of fellow socialist parties in other member states. Overall then, the pressures to shift from a purely oppositional position on the Community were not influencing the Party to adopt a pro-EC stance.[3]

There appears to have been no definite outcome to this reappraisal on Europe: the Party did not explicitly reject any of the options, although it can be safely assumed that the national leadership, given its current outlook, would be far from happy with a fully fledged agitational strategy. In the absence of any clearly defined European policy goals, the Party emphasised the nature of its approach rather than the content of its policies programme. Specifically, the emphasis was on using the European plane whenever appropriate to help solve problems such as economic growth, unemployment and so on. The leadership was content with this approach since it projected the Party as being pragmatic and constructive on Europe. But beneath this veneer of consensual pragmatism, marked divisions persisted on which Community instruments could actually help to reach some of the *declared* policy goals. For instance, on the EMS Bryan Gould flatly rejected full British membership on the ground that it would not 'benefit the real economy by enabling us to regenerate industry and tackle unemployment'. Other leading Party members, such as Roy Hattersley, John Smith and Neil Kinnock himself, took the opposite view saying that the EMS may be an indispensable mechanism for a co-ordinated pan-European reflationary programme. There was the image of a reformulated European policy which was widely accepted in the Party, but the reality was that deep divisions continued to exist on the subject.

With the minimum of scrutiny, these divisions should have been detected, but the increasing difficulties the Thatcher government was facing on Europe saved Labour from the spotlight. In fact, Labour set out to capitalise on Thatcher's isolation inside the Community, by declaring itself the Party of Europe. This campaigning slogan has proved highly successful, particularly at the 1989 elections for the European Parliament where Labour made significant gains at the expense of the Tories. The question of Europe has been the first issue for years on which Labour has been able to put the government truly on the defensive. There does appear to be a new willingness to engage in actual political developments inside the Community and an eagerness to develop more meaningful ties with other European socialist parties.

However, actual party policies show that it is not as *communautaire* as sometimes it makes out. Although critical of Thatcher's opposition to Commission efforts to strengthen Community institutions, Labour itself is equivocal about some of the proposals. With regard to the Delors Report, Labour – like the Conservatives – is opposed to stages II and III of the plan. It is true that Labour fully supports the Social Charter, but the impression given is that the full implications of adopting such an arrangement have not been fully grasped. In particular, if the Charter (based on the principles of co-operation and compromise between unions and employers) was adopted by a British government then strong pressures would be created to end Britain's adversarial industrial relations system. Whether Labour or the unions would countenance this is open to debate. In other words, Labour is in danger of simply using Europe as an anti-Thatcher campaigning platform and not facing up to the scale of the changes required before Britain can become an organic part of the Community. The national leadership may bill itself as the Party of Europe, but it has some way to go before it will actually deserve this title.

The Centre

The main centrist political party, the Liberal and Social Democrats, has a much more impressive record on EC issues than either of the two larger parties. This is true of both its components: the Liberals have held a strongly pro-Community position quite consistently over three decades; while the Social Democrats who split from Labour, however opportunist they were on every other issue, at least took a principled position on British membership. Besides, the SDP included Roy Jenkins, a former President of the Commission, among their leaders. At least on the Liberal side, this constructive approach to the Community is part of a general impatience with British institutions, and linked to a radical programme for constitutional change which embraces electoral reform, Scottish and Welsh devolution and the formal enactment of civil liberties.

Although the polarisation of British politics – largely due to the present electoral system – has led to the present eclipse of the Democrats, their arguments for institutional change, including the acceptance of a wider role for EC institutions, command much greater support than is measured by their share of the vote. The failure of successive attempts at economic modernisation in Britain, from Harold Wilson in the mid-1960s to the decay of Thatcherism a quarter of a century later, suggests that there may well be an institutional dimension to Britain's continuing malaise, that the existing political system is unable to generate effective responses to industrial decline or social disorganisation. A renewed attempt at fundamental economic reform may well have to begin with the kind of political changes advocated by the Liberal Democrats, even if they themselves do not hold power. Given their preoccupation with national sovereignty, the two larger parties no longer seem to have a broad enough political reach, nor do existing governmental structures have sufficient mobilising capacity, to promote the deep changes that are needed in economic life.

The EC and British Decline

At the time of Britain's entry into the Community, economists were divided as to the likely effects. The optimistic view was that the removal of tariffs and closer economic relations with Western Europe would provide a salutary competitive shock to the sluggish British economy and compel a more rapid rate of investment and adaptation in British enterprises. Opponents of entry argued that the shock would be debilitating – Britain would be unable to meet the increase in competitive pressure, import penetration would not be balanced by growth in export markets, and external constraints on British economic growth would tighten.

This second view more nearly accords with what has actually happened in the two decades of British membership. After violent fluctuations, Britain is once again compelled to hold back growth by an enormous balance of payments deficit, much of it attributable to a poor trading performance vis-à-vis our partners in the Community. The persistent inadequacy of British economic performance is increasingly measured against the standard set by neighbouring European countries and the use of such a standard itself testifies to the emergence of a European consciousness in Britain. But actual membership of the EC hardly seems to have brought Britain up to the European standard, and may even have intensified problems of industrial competitiveness.

Most commentators, whatever their theoretical framework, place great emphasis on inadequate investment in their diagnosis of British economic ills. The term 'investment' here can be interpreted broadly: there is a lack of modern productive equipment in many industries, but there is also a lack of education and training (that is, investment in human resources), while repeated cost-cutting exercises in the public sector have delayed the renewal of infrastructures and have weakened other activities oriented towards future development, such as technological research. Low rates of investment prevent modernisation and perpetuate today's weaknesses; they also signal a lack of confidence in the country's future and the absence of any convincing and generally accepted strategy for economic renewal.

From this point of view, Britain's relations with the EC are one more example of the general malaise. There has been no investment in these relationships, no long-term commitment to them, either financial or political. The Community has been assessed almost exclusively in terms of short-term costs and benefits, since the prevailing combination of pragmatism and cynicism has not permitted any long-term view of Western Europe's future, nor any long-term strategy to construct Britain's future within it. The wrangle over budget contributions has dominated day-to-day dealings with the EC, probably to Britain's ultimate disadvantage since it has blocked the emergence of a strong well-financed Community, able to intervene in favour of weaker countries. The only longer-term projects have been of a fantastic, or even escapist, character – the Thatcherite aim to 'Americanise' European society and, Labour's dream of a new Messina conference to abolish the European Parliament. Actual engagement with the other countries and political forces involved in European construction, and the slow search for common strategies towards integration have been hard to come by.

Membership of the EC alone has certainly not produced a solution to Britain's longstanding economic difficulties, and a greater commitment to the EC and a more responsible attitude to membership are necessary conditions for a solution. A broad consensus on the need for economic and institutional change, and on the need to mobilise resources on an adequate scale to make those changes possible, have become essential in order to move forward. Given Britain's degree of integration with West European countries, all the main features of a modernisation strategy will be closely affected by European relations: membership of the Community is the only practical way in which those relations can be influenced. So far the approach has been minimalist, reluctant and 'short-termist', as with most other necessary adaptations of Britain's political and economic systems. The move towards a more generous and imaginative view of European construction is part of the reconstruction of Britain itself.

Notes

1 See John Grahl and Paul Teague, 'Labour and the European Community', *Political Quarterly*, January/February 1988.

2 M. Camps, *European Unification in the Sixties: From the Veto to the Crisis*, OUP, Oxford 1969, p213.
3 J. Grahl and P. Teague, *op.cit.*

Further Reading

For economic assessments of Britain's membership of the EC, see A. Winters, *Britain in Europe: a Survey of Quantitative Trade Studies*. For political and policy assessments, see R. Jenkins, *Britain in the European Community*, Macmillan, London 1983; M.A. Al Agraa (ed.), *Britain Within the European Community*, Macmillan, London 1983; and C. Brewster and P. Teague, *EC Social Policy: Its Impact on the UK*, Academic Press in association with IPM.

9 Conclusion

While this book on economic arrangements in Western Europe was being written, a huge political upheaval in Eastern Europe and the Soviet Union was reshaping the geography of the continent. The USSR, struggling with the process of democratic and economic renewal on its own territory, withdrew its military guarantee from the Communist regimes it had installed in Eastern Europe in the late 1940s. Almost immediately their political impotence was dramatically exposed; their economic failures, the inability of centralised command economies to promote modernisation and intensive patterns of development, had been increasingly obvious for many years. Within a few months six former Soviet satellite countries were engaged in rapid transitions towards pluralistic parliamentary democracy on the Western model.

The introduction of functioning market economies requires the dismantling of central planning systems and the creation of new horizontal relations among enterprises which were previously oriented towards the state agencies rather than their customers and suppliers. This is clearly going to be a lengthy process, complicated by the fact that voters can now use the newly democratised political systems to resist the increasing unemployment, widening inequalities and reductions in living standards which seem to be the price of rapid economic liberalisation. Nevertheless there is no longer any doubt that this will be the direction of economic change, and even in the Soviet Union fewer voices can be heard advocating the reform of the central planning apparatus rather than its abolition.

The consequences of this transformation are still difficult to discern, but it is certain that they will dwarf those of the 1992 programme. On the one hand, Europe will be united in a much more fundamental way: in place of rival blocs based on opposed socio-economic systems there will henceforth be just one system, albeit with wide national variations. (Although it is also true that the future evolution of the single European system itself cannot be predicted.) On the other hand, political forces in the West have to absorb the lessons of the collapse of socialist central planning. Very few in the West were actually tempted to advocate the single party political structures of the East, but variants of the Eastern economic model were until recently central to the vision of many labour movements and socialist parties in Western Europe. Socialist economic strategies in the West certainly did not aim at slavish imitation of Soviet planning: a wide role was envisaged for markets and private enterprise; public economic control was to be much more decentralised and diffuse. Nevertheless, the notion of seizing the 'commanding heights', of transferring a large number of the biggest enterprises to state ownership and in this way constructing the core of a planned economy, inspired left programmes in many countries. The unreformability of state ownership and command economies in the East necessarily alters the logic of political debate, and the perception of feasible paths towards more social control over economic life, everywhere in the newly reunited continent.

Despite the intrusion of these major preoccupations, the narrower question of policy direction within the European Community, and hence the subject of this book, has lost none of its immediacy. The reverse is the case: the new international context multiplies the importance of the Community since it is now bound to have enormous influence on the process of social and economic reconstruction in the East and, most probably, within the USSR itself (assuming that most of its member states stay in the union). The debacle of the Soviet model has left a huge economic vacuum and exposed a damaging dependence on outsiders. The new democracies must look to the West for all the factors of renewed development – for credit and finance in hard currencies, for skills and training, for modern producer goods and new technologies, and above all perhaps for economic models, for effective forms of economic organisation.

Economic interactions will develop with all parts of the world, but the size, wealth and proximity of the EC will clearly give it an especially important role in this process of reconstruction. The new economic geography is very favourable to the stronger economies of the EC: rather suddenly they find themselves on the rim of a huge zone with colossal economic potential. Their economic strategies, and that of the Community, will have an even more extensive effect on external patterns of development.

The absence of convincing organisational models in Eastern Europe is reflected in the success of extreme free-market strategies which seem very attractive, at least to the new political leaderships which are now emerging. Partly as a reaction to the failure of state planning, partly as a delayed alignment with intellectual trends in the West, neo-liberal doctrines are winning converts in Eastern Europe at the same time as Western electorates are becoming increasingly suspicious of deregulation, privatisation and liberalisation as solutions to current economic problems. As new proposals for the control and regulation of decentralised economies with big market sectors are being elaborated, the kind of policy strategies adopted within the Community will be critical to economic change well beyond its own frontiers.

Today, it is essentially this question of economic regulation which makes the Community and West European integration such an important issue. In the past, the political movement for European unity could be based on directly political objectives: the essence of the movement was a challenge to the competing nationalisms which had been the source of so much destruction and violence. These political aims are still worthy of respect, but many of them have been substantially achieved – in particular, the reconciliation of France and Germany and the acceptance by both their populations of common political structures. In spite of some rather wild reactions to the prospect of imminent German unification, the close civil, economic and political relations which tie France and Germany and so constitute the core of the Community are not in any danger. Similarly, the European Parliament, even with its present very limited powers, is in itself a worthy political achievement as a democratic body which represents the positive recognition by electorates in member states of a political process transcending national frontiers.

The prospect of a more integrated European identity throws into sharp relief the nature of relations with non-Europe: to internationalists the political claims of the EC must today be secondary to those of wider relationships embracing the people of the developing countries which have the most legitimate claim to international solidarity. The importance of the EC in this context depends on the extent to which it can support economic and social progress in other parts of the world.

The chief significance of the European Community is as an economic unit. For those politically committed to integration, the emergence of the huge EC economy – easily the biggest trading bloc in the world – is a kind of fortunate accident which can be used to promote the original aim of political federation. But what makes the Community a necessary part of any contemporary political thinking about Europe, whether favourable to federalism or not, is the collective economic weight of the member economies and consequently the potential for a collective response to the process of economic internationalisation.

The extension of global trade and investment relationships has gradually weakened national control over economic life, even in countries as large as France or Britain. There are very large constraints on macroeconomic policy when a high proportion of output is traded; finance and credit are difficult to control when international capital mobility has reached present-day levels; the regulation of investment and employment is difficult when multinational companies can move productive activity from one country to another. In all of these spheres the Community, because of its size and wealth, is able to exercise control when other levels of government, national and local, are increasingly unable to do so.

Of course, it is far from inevitable that those possibilities of economic control will be realised. The 1992 programmme, on its own, tends simply to reduce national regulatory power, without constructing new patterns of control at the Community level. Political debate around the 'accompanying measures' to 1992 such as the social charter, monetary union and the expansion of the structural funds, expresses a basic difference in views of European integration: those who regard such measures as essential see integration as a *response* to the globalisation of economic life; those for whom they are superfluous tend rather to see European integration as a *part* of that globalisation. According to the first point of view, the distinctive features of West European socio-economic systems – mixed economies with highly developed social protection, extensive public services and regulated labour markets – can be defended and enhanced by Community-level policies. From the second, neo-liberal standpoint, those specific features are regarded as a disadvantage, and their attenuation as economic internationalisation proceeds is highly desirable, so that European society becomes much more like the US model. What is at stake in such debates is the future degree of social control which will exist over the integrated market economy of Western Europe.

It should be emphasised that these possibilities of social control do not mean either that Community institutions can simply displace those of the member states, or that the Community can deploy the same economic instruments as have typically been used by national governments. The scale of the EC economy, and the complexity and diversity of its economic life, determine that economic regulation at Community level will have to be more abstract and less interventionist than has usually been envisaged in national economic strategies.

Two aspects of this are particularly important. Firstly, the Community is bound to be an essentially open economic system, allowing outside enterprises to operate on equal terms with insiders and not resorting to general trade protectionism as a major instrument of economic policy. The permeability of EC frontiers is inevitable because of its dense and close interactions with a large periphery of neighbouring countries and because each of the member countries has distinct patterns of interdependence with different outside trading partners. The integrated EC economy of the future will not be sufficiently well-defined, in a territorial sense, to privilege internal transactions over external ones. The Community will, on the other hand, be able to enforce strict rules on investment, whether by European or outside firms, and to supervise closely the quality of goods and services whether these are produced internally or imported; but it is unlikely to have the option of severing external economic relations. Sectoral protectionism has, of course, already been used as a bargaining tool and to defend weak industries in a crisis, but the effectiveness of such defence is limited when internal competition continues. It remains a legitimate measure to restrict the growth of imports when this threatens to eliminate domestic producers, but a trade grouping as large and dominant as the EC cannot close off its internal markets without enormous cost to trading partners.

Secondly, the economic control exercised by EC institutions is bound to make more use of general laws and regulations and have less recourse to discretionary interventions than is often the case at member state level. This is both because it is more difficult to meet the information requirements for specific, detailed interventions in an economy of over 300 million people and because direct action in favour of one enterprise or one group of producers is harder to justify when twelve nations are involved. This does not mean that national and, in particular, regional or local authorities cannot make detailed interventions, but it is best if the Community's role in such policies is indirect. It can help to finance detailed programmes at local level where these accord with its regional objectives and it can lay down ground rules for such intervention to avoid beggar-my-neighbour tactics by particular interests. However, it would be administratively inefficient and politically disruptive for the Commission itself, for example, to undertake a very wide range of interventions.

These points are made to emphasise that the EC cannot develop into a powerful and effective authority for the control of economic activity unless the specific nature of EC institutions, and the particular constraints they face, are recognised. In the past, many strategies for Community economic policy have been simple projections of national strategy. When cherished economic projects, such as a major expansion of aggregate demand, or the reduction of dependence on external technologies, or the reconstruction of employment contracts, have seemed to be blocked at national level, then they have been turned into strategies for Western

Europe as a whole without taking into account the difficulties or even logical contradictions involved in the reformulation. The Community, if it develops strong powers, can indeed transform the external environment in which national and local economic policies are implemented: external financial constraints on investment can be eased, while speculation is controlled; educational and health-care systems can be gradually levelled up by experimentation and the imitation of best practice rather than subjected to competitive exercises in cost-cutting; Community regional and industrial policies can reinforce national and local measures against the exclusion of particular areas, groups or individuals from full participation in social life; the EC can become a major force for more rapid development in Africa, Asia and Latin America. But these possibilities can be realised only if strategy takes into account the concrete workings of Community institutions and the scale and complexity of the economy which it supervises.

The constitutional questions raised by a strengthening of the Community's powers are beyond the remit of this book. At present the various projects for closer political union, by federation or otherwise, have not made much headway. For the kind of economic control advocated here important transfers of competence to EC institutions are necessary, particularly by way of increased and stabilised budgetary resources, and through strong monetary institutions. The proposals emerging from the Delors committee for monetary unification are the most ambitious present attempt to move in this direction, although the very conservative nature of these proposals makes it difficult for states with weaker economies to accept them.

The best division of competence between EC and national or local levels of government is often discussed in terms of 'subsidiarity', that is the notion that each governmental function should be assigned to the lowest and and most local governmental institution which is able to carry it out. This is an attractive principle but it does not in itself resolve issues of competence unless the institutional framework is already clear: the term 'subsidiarity' is in fact borrowed from the theory of federal systems where this requirement is met.

Whether monetary functions can be assigned to national or Community level clearly depends on whether a European central bank does or does not exist. The strong central institutions which are advocated here derive from a project for renewed social control over economic life. Although they do not necessarily imply a federal political structure, they do require a major supranational dimension in economic policy and in economic legislation. It should be noted, moreover, that the outcome of a more controlled economic environment would often be to strengthen national governments at present constrained by global market forces.

Whatever constitutional models are advanced for the Community, its development into a strong authority in response to the globalisation of economic life requires a solution for one of the central political problems of the EC – the *democratic deficit*. In institutional terms this is largely a question provoked by the weakness of the European Parliament. As the only directly elected body at EC level, the Parliament would require much more than its present marginal powers to make the Community legitimate as a supernational authority. In the absence of such powers the actual democratic process in the Community remains intergovernmental: the Council of Ministers, the key decision-making body, derives its democratic legitimacy from that of the national governments which are represented in it and this tends both to make it difficult for individual countries to accept decisions which are unwelcome to their own governments, and to restrict the growth of Community-wide political alliances with programmes defined in Community rather than national terms (see Appendix G).

The democratic deficit is not simply an institutional matter; it also concerns the social context of EC political life in the Community. If, in the past, much of the most intense opposition to the EC insisted on the primacy of national governments, this was not always through nationalist motives; there were also democratic issues involved. It was through the institutionalisation of political power in the nation state that modern democratic societies developed. Political processes within nation states depend on dense social interactions, facilitated by shared languages and cultural backgrounds: the political debates which take place at national level are animated by the relatively homogeneous and integrated nature of the population, by the ease with which positions can be communicated, by the existence of many familiar channels through which individuals or groups can participate.

At present, analogous structures at Community level are at an embryonic stage of development: civil society in Europe remains essentially national and the links that tie together political groupings, interest groups and cultural and intellectual associations, across frontiers are much weaker than within each country. In other words, the democratic deficit cannot be eliminated by institutional measures alone: a reinforcement of the Parliament (and of the consultative role of the Economic and Social Committee where EC-wide interest groups are represented) must run in parallel with social integration so that the necessary organisations, channels of information and public interest exist to make the popular control of democratic Community institutions more than an electoral formality. One sign of progress in this direction would be for European elections to be fought around European rather than predominantly national issues, as is still the case today.

Nevertheless, a West European society, embracing all the Community countries and their close neighbours, is already much more than a mere abstraction. Public awareness of European issues, and identification with transnational interests, have been growing – as has knowledge of policies and institutions in other European countries and the use of social, economic and political comparisons within Western Europe as a basis for assessment of practice in one's own country. The European dimension of national social and political life is increasingly recognised, and results not only from economic linkages but from a wider convergence based on shared values and similar aspirations. Clearly this convergence cannot be accelerated by statute, but it can be fostered by particular policies aimed at a sense of European citizenship, at multiplying contact between people from different member states, at increasing labour mobility and at establishing more equal standards of social provision. In this context, the European Social Charter, although it will have few concrete effects on welfare systems or employment practices in the short term, is important in promoting real convergence of provision in the longer term.

These processes are slow and difficult. However, the alternative of relying completely on national parliaments to secure democratic government is increasingly dangerous and unreliable because of the economic internationalisation which threatens to move huge areas of national life beyond democratic control. Even large countries are more and more exposed to unruly global financial forces, to vast processes of restructuring and relocation by multinational companies, and to sudden swings in international competitiveness and patterns of trade. Supranational political authorities are the logical response to these challenges, and the conditions for such a response are nowhere as favourable as they are in Western Europe – rich, homogeneous and with three decades of successful institutional construction behind it. If the opportunity for strengthening democratic control over economic activity is not pursued at Community level, and democratic processes are confined within nation states, then national and local autonomy may even be *weakened* since the stable external environment and solidaristic support which the Community could provide for its member states and regions will not be achieved.

The 1992 programme, both symbolically and in practice, has highlighted the challenge of social control over internationalised economic activity, and thus the challenge of building political institutions to exercise this control and the democratic process on which the institutions will rest. It has been argued throughout this book that such control is possible, that economic strategies exist which can avoid the inequalities and inefficiencies implicit in unconstrained private enrichment, and can subordinate market processes to the imperatives of social justice and civilised development. The means therefore exist, but the question remains as to the will: it is up to the free political activity of Europeans, in overcoming the Community's democratic deficit, to ensure that those means are used.

Appendices

Appendix A: A Dying Industry

In 25 years the agricultural workforce has fallen by 60 per cent and almost fifteen million workers have left the land in EC countries:

Table 12: *Population Active in Agriculture (thousands)*

	1960	1985	Decline
Italy	6,611	2,296	4,315
Spain	4,199	1,766	2,433
France	4,180	1,582	2,598
West Germany	3,581	1,390	2,191
Portugal	2,159	969	1,190
Greece	1,935	1,037	898
UK	1,134	620	514
Netherlands	409	250	159
Ireland	390	182	208
Denmark	362	182	180
Belgium	300	106	194
Luxembourg	24	7	7
EC	25,284	10,387	14,897

As a result the remaining workforce is now very elderly:

Table 13: *Percentage of Active Agriculturalists Over 50 Years Old, 1984*

Italy	45.4
Spain	45.2
France	46.1
West Germany	42.8
Portugal	39.2
Greece	46.2
UK	33.6
Ireland	44.3
Denmark	39.7
Belgium	48.5

Source: INSEE

Huge adjustments have already taken place and future adjustment will have to take account of the age of the farming population.

Appendix B: 'Green' Money and MCAs

In principle, the CAP fixes common farm prices which are applied in all member countries. In practice, currency fluctuations mean that prices diverge. The resulting situation can be difficult to understand.

Consider a simplified example. Assume that to begin with one ECU equals two West German Deutschmarks (DM) or six French Francs (FF) and that the price of a tonne of wheat is fixed at 200ECUs (ie 400DM or 1,200FF).

Now there is a change in exchange rates: the German Mark is revalued while the Franc is devalued so that

$$1\text{ECU} = 1.6\text{DM} = 8\text{FF}$$

But agricultural prices in local currency are *not* immediately changed. We still have a price of 1,200FF in France and 400DM in Germany, but these now correspond to 150ECUs and 250ECUs respectively so that the price is now higher in Germany.

There are good reasons why neither country will be ready,

immediately, to change its price back to 200ECUs. The French, having just devalued, will be preoccupied with fighting inflation and will not want to raise the price of an important consumer good. The Germans having revalued, will be concerned not to deflate domestic demand by cutting the incomes of their farmers. Political considerations reinforce these economic ones. The French population as a whole is suffering a loss of purchasing power while the Germans are enjoying an increase. To change farm prices immediately would mean, in each case, that farmers would be exceptions to the general rule.

What makes the situation even more confusing is that it is often discussed in terms of 'green' exchange rates – that is, notional exchange rates for agricultural trade which are not the actual exchange rates. Thus the green Franc is said to be overvalued and the green Mark undervalued. If the French bring their prices back into line by raising them to 1,600FF (200ECUs at the new exchange rate) this is called 'devaluing the green Franc'; the corresponding correction in Germany (a price cut to 320DM) is called 'revaluing the green Mark'. It is easier here simply to think in terms of price changes rather than notional currencies.

While the price divergence lasts it makes free trade between the countries concerned impossible. In the case considered here all wheat would vanish from the French market to be exported to Germany where it would either be consumed or sold into intervention. Any exports from Germany to France would be blocked.

To permit trade to continue without an adjustment of prices a corrective mechanism had to be introduced, the monetary compensation amounts (or MCAs). France with low prices, had a negative MCA of 50ECUs per tonne. French *exports* pay a *levy* of this amount, French *imports* receive a *subsidy* of the same amount: thus France continues to trade *as though* its internal prices were the ones set by the Community. Germany, similarly, has a *positive* MCA of 50ECUs: exports are subsidised and imports taxed by 50ECUs per tonne so that for German producers as well home and effective foreign trade prices coincide. Therefore the total MCA payable on French exports to Germany would be 100ECUs, the difference between the two domestic prices.

In principle, the price divergence caused by the exchange rate movement should be eliminated by both countries moving back to the Community's agreed price of 200ECUs. The accepted rule is that there can be negotiation about the timing of this correction, but not its direction. This entails that the French are forbidden to lower their prices but can take their time before raising them. However, Germany – where prices tend to be highest because of repeated revaluations of the Deutschmark – has obtained the major concession that from 1984, 'positive MCAs will be immediately converted into negative MCAs'.

What this means is that, after the exchange rate alteration, Germany's positive MCAs of 50ECUs will disappear, while France's negative one will be increased to 100ECUs. This does not change the transitional arrangements – French exports to Germany still pay a tax of 100ECUs, with a corresponding subsidy if goods go in the other direction. But what does change is the eventual price correction: instead of French prices rising and German prices falling back to 200ECUs, there will now be no change in German prices, while French prices rise right up to the existing German level (2,000FF = 400DM per tonne, or 250ECUs per tonne – all at the new exchange rates).

In substance this 'conversion' has eroded price control in the EC, as successive Deutschmark revaluations push up real agricultural prices above their official ECU levels. By these means Germany avoids the implementation of agreed cuts in ECU prices, in a procedure which symbolically expresses German hegemony – the Deutschmark becomes the real denominator of the CAP, and German prices, rather than negotiated ECU prices, are the ones which prevail in the market.

Appendix C: Japan-EC relations – the 'Weak' Side of the Triangle

Recently the Commission has moved away from its noisy condemnations of Japan's trade surplus with the EC. With good reason – if bilateral surpluses are in question the EC's trade surplus with the USA is almost as great as its deficit with Japan (16 billion ECUs as against 21 billion ECUs in 1987).

The Commission now expresses concern at the lack of trade and investment flows between Japan and the Community, relative to both US-Japan and US-EC relations. The suspicion is that Japanese investment (financed by trade surpluses) may be stimulating the US economy and shifting economic growth towards the Pacific while European countries are left behind.

Table 14: *Trade Flows – Exports in 1987, in (US) $ million*

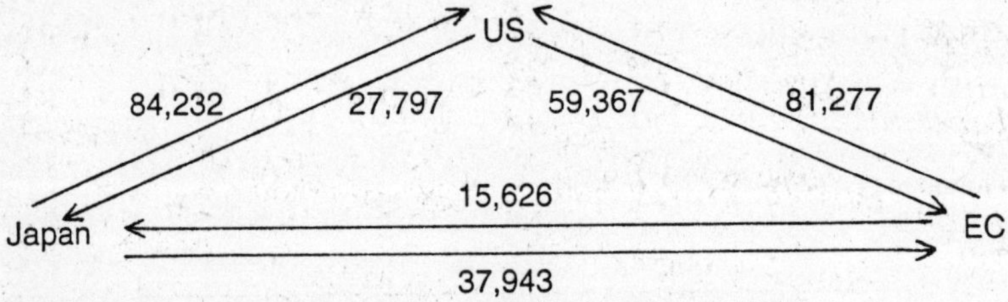

Source: UN, *International Trade Statistics Yearbook*, 1987.

The 'J-curve'

At first, the rise of the Dollar made for an increase in the US trade surplus with the Community. But over time the result was the opposite – an over-valued Dollar and Reagan's boom swung the trade balance decisively in Europe's favour.

Table 15: *EC Trade Deficit (–) or Surplus with USA and Canada (in million ECUs)*

1978	−7,503
	−12,494
	−22,826
1981	−18,367
	−16,951
	− 7,591
1984	6,715
	18,927
	21,154
1987	17,784

Source: Eurostat 6A, *Foreign Trade Yearbook*, 1988.

Appendix D: The Productivity Slowdown

The rapid growth of the Western economies in the 1950s and 1960s centred on historically unprecedented growth rates for productivity. In the 1970s this declined sharply.

Table 16: *Phases of GDP Growth, 1870-1984 (average annual compound growth rates)*

	I 1870-1913	II 1913-50	III 1950-73	IV 1973-84	Acceleration from Phase II to Phase III	Slowdown from Phase III to Phase IV
France	1.7	1.1	5.1	2.2	+4.0	−2.9
Germany	2.8	1.3	5.9	1.7	+4.6	−4.2
Japan	2.5	2.2	9.4	3.8	+7.2	−5.6
Netherlands	2.1	2.4	4.7	1.6	+2.3	−3.1
UK	1.9	1.3	3.0	1.1	+1.7	−1.9
Five country average	2.2	1.7	5.6	2.1	+4.0	−3.5
US	4.2	2.8	3.7	2.3	+0.9	−1.4

Source: Maddison, *Journal of Economic Literature*, June 1987.

Appendix E

Table 17: *The Major Milestones in Community Regional Policy*

17 October 1969
Commission proposal on the organisation of Community instruments for regional development.

October 1972
The Paris Conference recognises the need for a Community regional policy and calls on the Commission to prepare a report analysing regional problems in the enlarged Community and to put forward proposals for creating a European Regional Development Fund before the end of 1973

4 May 1973
Report to the Council on regional imbalances in the Community of Nine.

31 July 1973
Proposal for a Regulation establishing a European Regional Development Fund (ERDF).

December 1974
At the Paris summit meeting of Heads of State or Government, agreement is reached on the financial resources to be allocated to the ERDF.

---

18 March 1975
The Council adopts the Regulation establishing the ERDF and a Decision setting up the Regional Policy Committee (OJ L 73, 21 March 1975).

---

1 June 1977
The Commission presents to the Council:
(i) guidelines for Community regional policy, covering in particular a comprehensive system of analysis and policy formulation for Community regional policy (periodic report), an assessment of the regional impact of Community policies and the co-ordination of national regional policies;
(ii) proposals for amending the ERDF Regulation, in particular the creation of a section for 'specific regional development measures' (non-quota measures).

---

6 February 1979
The Council adopts the above guidelines and proposals.

---

7 October 1980
The Council adopts the first five regulations instituting specific Community regional development measures under the ERDF non-quota section.

---

22 December 1980
In accordance with the Council Resolution of 6 February 1979, the Commission transmits to the Council the first periodic report on the social and economic situation of the regions of the Community.

---

24 July 1981
Commission communication to the Council on the new regional policy guidelines and priorities.

---

29 October 1981
Proposal for amending the ERDF Regulation.

---

28 July 1983
Report on ways of increasing the effectiveness of the Community's structural funds (including the ERDF), requested by the Stuttgart European Council.

---

18 November 1983
New proposal for revising the ERDF Regulation (OJ L 360, 31 December 1983) based on the guidelines set out in the July 1983 report.

---

18 January 1984
The Council adopts the regulations relating to the second series of specific regional development measures under the ERDF non-quota section (OJ L 27, 31 January 1984).

---

7 March 1984
Adoption of the second periodic report on the social and economic situation of the regions of the Community.

---

19 June 1984
The Council adopts the regulation on the reform of the ERDF (OJ L 169, 28 June 1984).

---

1 January 1985
The new ERDF Regulation comes into force.

1988
Programme for Economic and Social Cohesion adopted.

Appendix F

Table 18: *Full List of Measures Proposed by the Commission in its Action Programme*

1. The labour market:
- 'Employment in Europe' report
- 'Observatory' and documentation system on employment
- Action programmes on employment creation for specific target groups
- Revision of Part II of Regulation 1612/68 on the clearance

of vacancies and applications for employment and the related procedural decisions (SEDOC)
- Monitoring and evaluation of the activities of the European Social Fund

2. Employment and remuneration:
- Opinion on the introduction of an equitable wage by the member states
- Directive on contracts and employment relationships other than full-time open-ended contracts

3. Improvement of living and working conditions:
- Directive for the adaptation of working time
- Council Directive on the introduction of a form to serve as proof of an employment contract or relationship
- Revision of the Council Directive of 17 February 1975 (75/129/BBC) on the approximation of the laws of the member states pertaining to collective redundancies
- Memorandum on the social integration of migrants from non-member countries

4. Freedom of movement:
- Revision of Commission Regulation (EEC) 1251/70 of 29 June 1970 on the right of workers to remain on the territory of a member state after having been employed in that state
- Proposal for a Regulation extending Council Regulation (EEC) 1408/71 on the application of social security schemes to employed persons, to self-employed persons and to members of their families moving within the Community and Council Regulation (EEC) 574/72 (laying down the procedure for implementing Regulation 1408/71) to all insured persons
- Proposal for a Community instrument on working conditions applicable to workers from another state performing work in the host country in the framework of the freedom to provide services, especially on behalf of a sub-contracting undertaking
- Proposal for a Community instrument on the introduction of a labour clause into public contracts
- Communication on supplementary social security schemes

- Communication from the Commission to the Council on the living and working conditions of Community citizens residing in frontier regions and of frontier workers in particular

5. Social protection:
- Recommendation on social protection: convergence of objectives
- Recommendation on common criteria concerning sufficient resources and social assistance in the social protection systems

6. Association and collective bargaining:
- Communication on the role of the social partners in collective bargaining

7. Information, consultation and participation:
- Community instrument on the procedures for the information, consultation and participation of the workers of European-scale undertakings
- Commission instrument on equity-sharing and financial participation by workers

8. Equal treatment for men and women:
- Third Community programme on equal opportunities for women
- Directive on the protection of pregnant women at work
- Recommendation concerning child care
- Recommendation concerning a code of good conduct on the protection of pregnancy and maternity

9. Vocational training:
- Proposal for a Community instrument on access to vocational training
- Updating of the 1963 proposal for a Council decision on the general principles for implementing a common vocational training policy
- Communication on the rationalisation and co-ordination of Community action programmes in the field of initial and continuing vocational training
- Proposal concerning the joint programme for the exchange of young workers and youth exchanges

- Comparability of qualifications

10. Health protection and safety at the workplace:

- Proposal for a Council Directive on the minimum health and safety requirements to encourage improved medical assistance on board vessels
- Proposal for a Council Directive on the minimum health and safety requirements for work at temporary or mobile work sites
- Proposal for a Council Directive on the minimum requirements to be applied in improving the safety and health of workers in the drilling industries
- Proposal for a Council Directive on the minimum requirements to be applied in improving the safety and health of workers in the quarrying and open-cast mining industries
- Proposal for a Council Directive on the minimum safety and health requirements for fishing vessels
- Recommendation to the member states on the adoption of a European schedule of industrial diseases
- Proposal for a Council Directive on the minimum requirements for a safety and health signs at the workplace
- Proposal for a Council Directive defining a system of specific information for workers exposed to certain dangerous industrial agents
- Proposal for a Council Directive on the minimum safety and health requirements regarding the exposure of workers to the risks caused by physical agents
- Proposal for a Council Directive amending Directive 83/447/EEC on the protection of workers from the risks related to exposure to asbestos at work
- Proposal for a Council Directive on the minimum safety and health requirements for activities in the transport sector
- Proposal for the establishment of a safety, hygiene and health agency

11. Protection of children and adolescents:

- Council Directive on the approximation of the laws of the member states on the protection of young people

12. The elderly:

- Community initiative for the elderly (Communication and proposal for a Decision)

13. The disabled:

- Proposal for a Council Decision establishing a third Community action programme for disabled people (Helios) for the period 1992–1996
- Proposal for a Council Directive on the introduction of measures aimed at promoting an improvement in the travel conditions of workers with motor disabilities

Appendix G: The Decision-making Framework of the EC

Before July 1987

The Community's decision-making process is outlined in Diagram 1.

European Council and Council of Ministers: The Councils are made up of representatives from the member state governments who safeguard national interests. Their role is to discuss and adopt policy legislation. They work mainly on the basis of consensus and unanimity so that effectively each state has a veto, though the Single European Act has introduced a measure of qualified majority voting.

European Commission: This is the executive arm of the Community, made up of civil servants and experts, divided into Directorates which deal with different subject areas. It has the power to initiate policy and legislation and to carry out decisions. It is intended to represent overall European interests.

European Parliament: The European Parliament has no power to pass legislation; it can only advise and consult. Its influence has grown since 1979, when its members (MEPs) were directly elected.

European Court of Justice: This is the Court of the Community, whose rulings are binding on all member states. It enforces and interprets the Treaty of Rome and all secondary legislation and has the power to hear cases directly and to give opinions on cases referred to it by national courts.

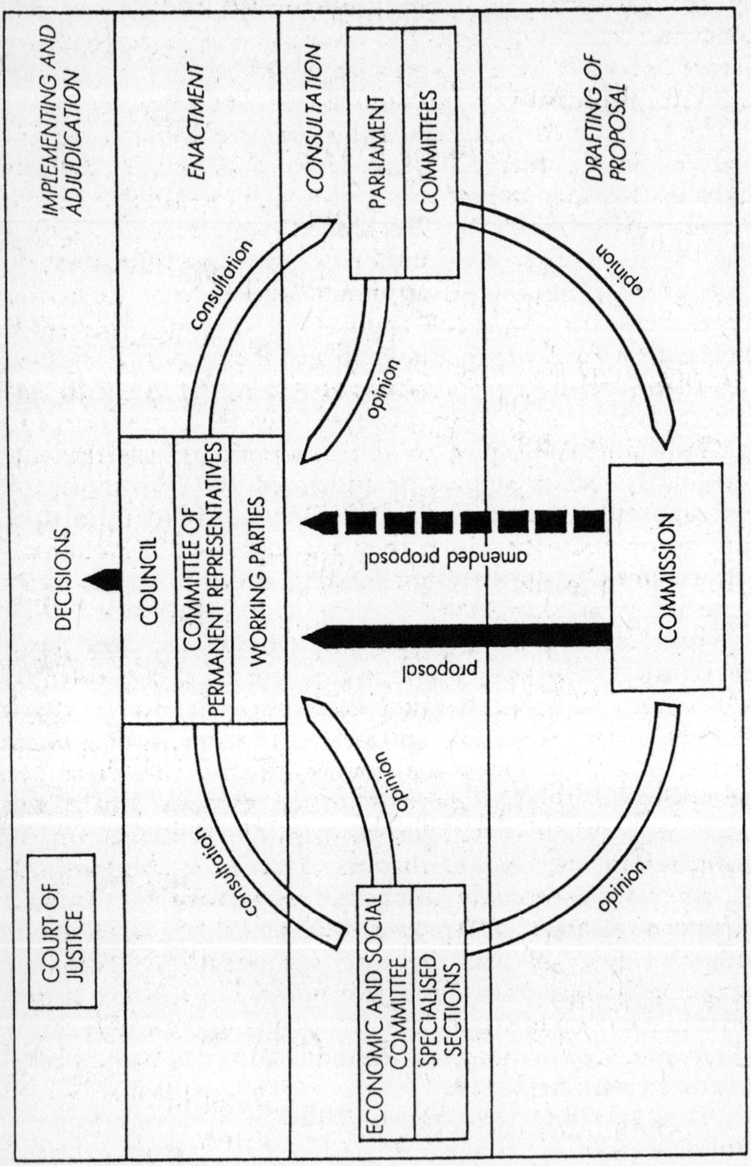

Diagram 1: *The Community's Decision-making Process*

Social and Economic Committee: The Committee is made up of representatives from trade unions, employers and consumer interest groups. The committee must be consulted before decisions are taken on a large number of subjects, and is also free to submit opinions on its own initiatives.

The Council of Ministers is the supreme decision-making body of the Community. Most of the decisions it currently takes are by unanimous voting, although, as detailed below, the Single European Act introduces some majority voting. The Council has the authority to issue Regulations, Directives, Decisions, Recommendations and Opinions. Regulations are of general application: they are binding in their entirety and applicable in all member states. Directives are binding on the member states to which they are addressed as regards the result to be achieved, but leave the form and methods of achieving it to the discretion of the national authorities. Decisions may be addressed to a government, a company, or a private individual: they are binding in their entirety on those to whom they are addressed. Recommendations and Opinions are not binding, though they do carry some 'informal' obligation.

When legally binding policies are made, the main responsibility for ensuring that they are fully implemented falls on the Commission. If the Commission considers that a member state has not properly enacted Community legislation, it can bring the country before the European Court of Justice. The Court of Justice, composed of eleven judges who are appointed for six years by agreement among the governments, ensures that the Treaties establishing the EC, and all subsequently secondary legislation (Regulations, Directives and Decisions), are implemented in accordance with the rule of law. Because secondary legislation is becoming more and more interwoven with the national law of individual member states, the Court has increasingly been called upon to give rulings on the applicability of Community statutes by national courts.

After July 1987

As noted in the text, the Single European Act was introduced to give the 1992 programme a legal base. As the Act changes the institutional framework to some degree, it may be worthwhile explaining its provisions in detail. The Act is a complicated and subtly worded legal document, so it is necessary to break down the contents and place these under different headings: functional provisions; institutional reform; areas subject to the new decision-making structure; and other procedural and lesser changes.

Functional provisions: The central functional provision of the Single European Act is the establishment of a completely liberalised internal market. Article 3a calls for this process to be completed by the end of 1992, and Article 100a (which replaces Article 100 of the Treaty of Rome that urges the approximation of national laws which affect the functioning of the Common Market) is the principal instrument for the accomplishment of this task. The Act outlines in considerable detail the actions that are necessary to establish a true internal market. These are summarised below. One of the central tasks is to achieve the harmonisation of indirect taxes. (Decisions of the Council of Ministers on this issue have to be taken on the basis of unanimity after consulting the European Parliament.)

The Act also allows the Council to adopt measures which 'approximate' national provisions in other areas. In particular, the Act permits the Council to introduce measures which allow for a high level of protection in the fields of health, safety, and environmental and consumer protection. Controls and restrictions are also imposed on member states unilaterally, introducing measures which affect imports. To assist the liberalisation of the internal market, the Council, taking account of the differences between economies, has to determine guidelines and conditions necessary to secure balanced progress. After 1992, the Commission is required to forward proposals for future action in the internal market.

Another key aspect of the Act is the strengthening of economic and social cohesion inside the Community by reducing the regional disparities. To this end, the various sub-parts of Article 130 detail the methods to be used to reduce the backwardness of less-favoured regions, and instruct the Council, within a year, to revise and realign the rules of the various structural funds to meet the objectives.

A further functional area covered by the Act is technology policy and the environment. In the area of technology policy, the Act instructs the Council to establish multi-annual

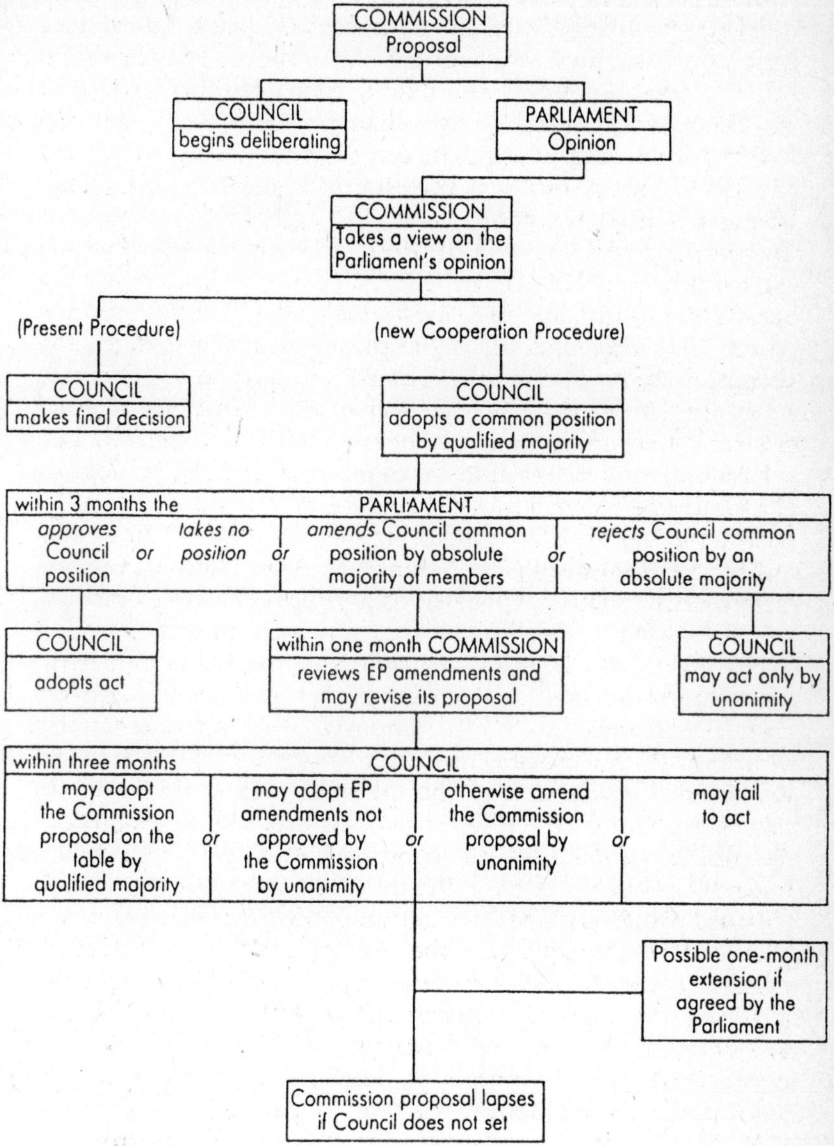

Diagram 2: *The Legislative Process in the EC*

framework programmes, and in relation to the environment, it sets out a series of objectives and defines what action needs to be taken to meet them.

The only other significant part of the Act is that which gives formal recognition to the European Council and provides for European co-operation in the sphere of foreign policy.

Institutional reform: One important aspect of the Single European Act concerns the institutional revisions it introduces into the Community's decision-making process. The objectives of the revisions, known as the co-operation procedure, are to give the European Parliament an enlarged and more formalised role (although it does not give it any further rights or powers) and to introduce qualified majority voting into some areas of Community. The new co-operation procedure will work as follows.

The Council, acting by a qualified majority on a proposal from the Commission and after obtaining the opinion of the European Parliament, adopts a common position. Then the Council communicates that common position to the European Parliament (with a statement of reasons and of the Commission's position). If, within three months, the European Parliament approves the common position or takes no decision, the Council can act on the basis of that policy. Alternatively, the European Parliament may propose amendments to the Council's common position or reject it, in which case, the Council must act unanimously on a second reading. The Commission shall, within a month, re-examine its original proposals and forward to the Council its re-examined proposals (stating its opinion on any unaccepted amendments put forward by the European Parliament: these the Council may adopt unanimously). After this stage the Council shall, by qualified majority, adopt the re-examined proposal (unanimity is required for any amendment). If the Council does not act within three months, the Commission's proposals are deemed to be rejected. Diagram 2 outlines these new decision-making procedures.

It is important to recognise that this new procedure only applies where the Council is operating by the principle of qualified majority voting. The specific articles where this applies are outlined below.

Article 49:	measure to bring about freedom of movement for workers.
Article 54 (2):	directives for abolishing restrictions on freedom of establishment.
Article 56 (2):	(second sentence) directives for co-ordination of national measures providing for special treatment of foreign nationals on the grounds of public policy, security or health.
Article 57:	directives for mutual recognition of formal qualifications; directives for co-ordination of national measures concerning the taking up and pursuit of activities as self-employed persons; (but excluding) directives relating to training for and conditions of access to the professions (where unanimity is required).
Article 100A:	measures for approximation of national provisions as to the internal market.
Article 100B:	proposals for mopping up national measures not harmonised by the end of 1992.
Article 118A:	adoption of minimum requirements for gradual implementation of improvements as regards health and safety of workers.
Article 130E:	implementation of decisions relating to the ERDF.
Article 130Q(2):	adoption of supplementary programmes in the field of regional development.

Other procedural changes are introduced, but these are of a lesser scale. One new provision makes minor changes to the Court of Justice so that it can hear 'certain classes of action brought by national or legal persons'. Under another revision the assent of the European Parliament becomes necessary for the admission of new member states and for the conclusion of certain international agreements.

Considerable confusion exists as to whether the Single European Act is a supranational or intergovernmental document. For instance, Mrs Thatcher has told the House of Commons that the Act does not undermine the Luxembourg Compromise to any great extent. Yet in Ireland the Supreme

Court ruled that a referendum had to be held on the subject because the Act undermined national decision-making in the area of foreign affairs, and thereby jeopardised Irish neutrality. Probably, the Act is best viewed as making a number of statements of intent and objectives in various areas, some of which will involve majority voting. Thus, in the short term, it should not be interpreted as enforcing any significant transfer of political authority from the national to the European sphere. But the changes it introduces will in all probability remove some of the legal and decision-making bottlenecks that have tied up the Community in recent years. As a result, the immediate impact of the Act will be the speeding-up of the Community decision-making process. Beyond that it is too early to make any other predictions.

Index